GLOBAL HISTORY OF THE PRESENT

Series editor | Nicholas Guyatt

In the Global History of the Present series, historians address the upheavals in world history since 1989, as we have lurched from the Cold War to the War on Terror. Each book considers the unique story of an individual country or region, refuting grandiose claims of "the end of history," and linking local narratives to international developments.

Lively and accessible, these books are ideal introductions to the contemporary politics and history of a diverse range of countries. By bringing a historical perspective to recent debates and events, from democracy and terrorism to nationalism and globalization, the series challenges assumptions about the past and the present.

Published

Thabit A. J. Abdullah, *Dictatorship, Imperialism and Chaos: Iraq since 1989*

Timothy Cheek, *Living with Reform: China since 1989*

Alexander Dawson, *First World Dreams: Mexico since 1989*

Padraic Kenney, *The Burdens of Freedom: Eastern Europe since 1989*

Stephen Lovell, *Destination in Doubt: Russia since 1989*

Alejandra Bronfman, *On the Move: The Caribbean since 1989*

Nivedita Menon and Aditya Nigam, *Power and Contestation: India since 1989*

Hyung Gu Lynn, *Bipolar Orders: The Two Koreas since 1989*

Bryan McCann, *The Throes of Democracy: Brazil since 1989*

Forthcoming

Mark LeVine, *Impossible Peace: Israel/Palestine since 1989*

James D. Le Sueur, *Between Terror and Democracy: Algeria since 1989*

Nicholas Guyatt is a lecturer in history at the University of York.

About the author

Bryan McCann teaches Latin American
history at Georgetown University, where he is
Director of the Brazilian Studies Program. He
has written broadly on Brazil's cultural and
social history in the twentieth century. His
first book, *Hello, Hello Brazil: Popular Music
in the Making of Modern Brazil*, was published
in 2004. His current research focuses on
the recent history of urban conflict in Rio de
Janeiro.

The Throes of Democracy:
Brazil since 1989

Bryan McCann

Fernwood Publishing
HALIFAX | WINNIPEG

Zed Books
LONDON | NEW YORK

The Throes of Democracy: Brazil since 1989 was first published in 2008

Published in Canada by Fernwood Publishing Ltd, 32 Oceanvista Lane,
Site 2A, Box 5, Black Point, Nova Scotia BOJ 1BO

<www.fernwoodpublishing.ca>

Published in the rest of the world by Zed Books Ltd, 7 Cynthia Street,
London N1 9JF, UK and Room 400, 175 Fifth Avenue, New York, NY 10010,
USA

<www.zedbooks.co.uk>

Cover designed by Andrew Corbett
Set in OurTypeArnhem and Futura Bold by Ewan Smith, London
Index <ed.emery@the freeuniversity.net>
Printed and bound in Malta by Gutenberg Press Ltd

Distributed in the USA exclusively by Palgrave Macmillan, a division of
St Martin's Press, LLC, 175 Fifth Avenue, New York, NY 10010.

A catalogue record for this book is available from the British Library.
US CIP data are available from the Library of Congress.

Library and Archives Canada Cataloguing in Publication
McCann, Bryan, 1968-
    The throes of democracy : Brazil since 1989 / Bryan McCann.
ISBN 978-1-55266-277-9
    1. Brazil--Politics and government--1985-2002. 2. Brazil--Politics and
government--2003- . 3. Brazil--Social conditions--1985-. 4. Brazil--
Economic conditions--1985-. I. Title.
F2538.3.M39 2008   981.06'4   C2008-903372-8

ISBN 978-1-84277-925-5 hb (Zed Books)
ISBN 978-1-84277-926-2 pb (Zed Books)
ISBN 978-1-55266-277-9 pb (Fernwood Publishing)

Contents

Acknowledgments

I am grateful to the respective publishers for permission to reprint material from two of my previous essays, "The Political Evolution of Rio de Janeiro's Favelas: Recent Works," *Latin American Research Review*, October 2006, 41.3: 149–63 and "Criminal Networks in Urban Brazil," *Georgetown Journal of International Affairs*, Summer/Fall 2007, 8.2: 13–20.

Nicholas Guyatt convinced me to take on the project, and I thank him for that, as well as for his keen critical eye. Ellen McKinlay has ably guided the project to the finish line.

I owe Idelber Avelar a huge debt of gratitude for his generous critical reading and corrections, as well as for the high standard he sets in analysis of Brazilian culture. Jussara Cristina Xavier dos Santos has shared her knowledge of Austin (the one in Rio, not the one in Texas) and much more. Sean McCann gave valuable critical feedback at several stages.

My colleagues at Georgetown University, particularly John Tutino, Erick Langer, Adam Rothman, Amy Leonard and John McNeill, have provided helpful advice and support.

I thank Maria Júlia de Araújo and George Paiva Sieniawski for their research assistance, and Angela Magalhães for continuing to open the doors to new perspectives on Brazil. And my deepest gratitude goes to Mary, Booker and Seamus for making it all worthwhile.

Abbreviations

AI-5	Ato Institucional No 5 (Institutional Act Number 5, the fifth of a series of decrees by Brazil's military dictatorship that effectively shut down Brazil's National Congress, allowed for government media censorship and suspended the right to habeas corpus)
AP	Ação Popular (Popular Action, a militant student group that maintained ties to the Catholic Church)
ARENA	Aliança de Reconstrução Nacional (The National Renewal Alliance)
BNDES	Banco Nacional de Desenvolvimento Econômico e Social (The National Bank for Social and Economic Development)
BRIC	Brazil, Russia, India and China
CEB	Comunidade Ecclesial de Base (Christian Base Community)
CEBRAP	Centro Brasileiro de Análise e Planejamento (The Brazilian Center for Analysis and Research)
CPT	Comissão Pastoral da Terra (Pastoral Land Commission: a Catholic Church office advocating agrarian reform; historically allied with MST)
CUT	Central Única dos Trabalhadores (Unified Workers' Central)
CV	Comando Vermelho (Red Command: prison-based gang of Rio de Janeiro)
DEM	Demócratas (centre-right political party)
EMBRAPA	Empresa Brasileira de Pesquisa Agropecuária (Brazilian Agricultural Research Corporation)
FAFEG	Federação das Associações das Favelas do Estado da Guanabara (*favela*-dwellers' resident association federation)
FARC	Fuerzas Armadas Revolucionarias de Colombia (Revolutionary Armed Forces of Colombia: a Marxist revolutionary faction)
GM	genetically modified
IBASE	Instituto Brasileiro de Análises Sociais e Econômicas (The Brazilian Institute for Social and Economic Analysis)
IBGE	Instituto Brasileiro de Geografia e Estatística (Brazilian Institute of Geography and Statistics)

INCRA   Instituto Nacional de Colonização e Reforma Agrária (The National Institute of Colonization and Agrarian Reform)

IURD   Igreja Universal do Reino de Deus (Universal Kingdom of God Church)

MDB   Movimento Democrático Brasileiro

MIR   Movimiento de Izquierda Revolucionaria (The Revolutionary Left Movement in Chile)

MPB   Música Popular Brasileira

MR-8   Movimento Revolucionário 8 de Outubro (The October 8 Revolutionary Movement)

MST   Movimento dos Trabalhadores Rurais Sem Terra (The Landless Workers' Movement)

NGO   non-governmental organization

OSCIP   Organização da Sociedade Civil de Interesse Público (Organizations of Civil Society in the Public Interest)

PCB   Partido Comunista Brasileiro (The Brazilian Communist Party)

PCC   Primeiro Comando da Capital (The First Command of the Capital)

PDS   Partido Democrático Social (The Democratic Social Party)

PDT   Partido Democrático Trabalhador (The Democratic Workers' Party)

PFL   Partido da Frente Liberal (The Liberal Front Party)

PMDB   Partido do Movimento Democrático Brasileiro (The Brazilian Democratic Movement Party)

PRB   Partido Republicano Brasileiro (The Brazilian Republican Party)

PRP   Partido Republicano Progressista (The Progressive Republican Party)

PSDB   Partido da Social Democracia Brasileira (The Brazilian Social Democracy Party)

PSOL   Partido Socialismo e Liberdade (The Socialism and Freedom Party)

PT   Partido dos Trabalhadores (The Workers' Party)

PTB   Partido Trabalhista Brasileiro (The Brazilian Labor Party)

RITS   Rede de Informações para o Terceiro Setor (Network of Information for the Third Sector)

SEPPIR   Secretaria Especial de Políticas de Promoção da Igualdade Racial (Secretariat for the Promotion of Policies for Racial Equality)

Glossary

açaí   fruit of the açaí palm, high in antioxidants

antenado   literally "[individual] with antennae," slang for "tuned in," savvy

aparelhamento   the stocking of bureaucratic positions with political loyalists

Assembléia de Deus   Assemblies of God, a Pentecostal denomination

Associação dos Moradores   Residents' association; the local *favela* governing council

axé   an umbrella term for several pop musical genres originating in the bloco afro styles of Salvador, Bahia

bancada evangélica   literally "[the] evangelical bench," Brazil's Protestant caucus in Congress

bancada ruralista   literally "[the] rural bench," an interparty coalition of rural politicians

bloco   literally "block," a carnival parade band

bloco afro   a carnival parade band emphasizing pan-African roots and connections, originating in Salvador, Bahia

boca   literally "mouth," a source of narcotics or a major drug-dealing location

Bolsa Escola   literally "School Purse," a federal grant intended to keep children in school

Bolsa Família   literally "Family Purse," an expanded version of Bolsa Escola

caipira   an unsophisticated rustic, a "hillbilly" or "country bumpkin"

Caixa Econômica Federal   Federal Savings Bank

Câmara dos Deputados   literally "Chamber of Deputies," Brazil's lower house of Congress

cargos de confiança   literally "trusty posts," political patronage appointments

carioca   native of Rio de Janeiro

cavaquinho   a small four-string instrument in the guitar family, much like a ukulele cesta básica   basic market basket

ciranda   a ring-dance of Pernambuco

Comissão Pastoral da Terra   Pastoral Land Commission

coronel   powerful rural landowner

Correios   Brazil's postal service

crente   believer (practicing Protestant, predominantly used for
Pentecostal denominations)

cuíca   traditional samba friction drum

descarrego   literally "discharge," the unburdening of spirits

Diretas Já!   literally "Direct [elections], now!" a movement that swept
across the nation in the early 1980s

dízimo   literally "tenth," a tithe

encosto   encroachment by evil spirits

Escândalo das Sanguessugas   literally "Bloodsuckers' Scandal"

Esquadrão da Morte   Death Squad

Estado Novo   the Getúlio Vargas dictatorship of 1937–45

evangélico   evangelical (practicing Protestant, predominantly used
for Pentecostal denominations)

favela   community of largely self-built housing constructed on
irregularly occupied land, outside the formal bureaucratic
structure of the city

forró   popular accordion-based musical genre with roots in rural
Northeastern musical styles

grilagem   claim-jumping and falsification of rural land deeds

Igreja Renascer em Cristo   Reborn in Christ Church

Igreja Universal do Reino de Deus   Universal Kingdom of God Church

indulto   reprieve, commutation of sentence, clemency, pardon

jogo do bicho   literally "the animal game," a popular – albeit illegal
– numbers game

justiceiro   justice-maker

laranja   literally "orange," one who serves as a frontman in a
duplicitous financial transaction

latifúndio   large rural estate

Lei Rouanet   a tax provision that permits firms in Brazil to donate
funds to cultural institutions in lieu of paying a certain portion of
their tax bill

malandro   urban hustler living by his wits

maracatu   parade music of Pernambuco, featuring snare and bass
drums and a syncopated cowbell

marajá   literally "maharaja," civil servants who obtained princely salaries during the dictatorship

mensalão   literally "big monthly [payment]," a political slush fund controlled by the PT

música sertaneja   an umbrella term for pop musical styles emphasizing rural themes and connections

novela   soap opera

pagode   pop samba variant of Salvador da Bahia, based on earlier variations from Rio de Janeiro

pandeiro   tambourine

Pão de Açucar   Sugarloaf

paulistano   native of São Paulo city

pistolão   a letter of reference from a powerful patron, written on behalf of a family member or dependent

Plano Real   literally "Real Plan," Fernando Henrique Cardoso's monetary policy under the presidency of Itamar Franco, intended to steady Brazil's economic growth

proibidão   literally "really prohibited," the banned genre of funk glorifying crime

queima de arquivo   literally "archive burning," evidence suppression or witness suppression

quilombo   runaway slave communities

rock besteirol   easygoing rock and roll, often with blithe or nonsense lyrics

rock cabeça   literally "head rock," variant of rock and roll with intellectual and political pretensions

sertão   Brazil's arid hinterlands

surdo   bass drums

traficante   trafficker

tribo   tribe

Zona Sul   South Zone of Rio de Janeiro

Chronology

1930 Getúlio Vargas seizes power

1945 Vargas's *Estado Novo* overthrown

1950 Vargas elected president

1954 Vargas's suicide in office

1961 Jânio Quadros renounces the presidency

1964 President João Goulart overthrown by a military coup

1968 Institutional Act 5 (AI-5) initiates the full-blown dictatorship

1969 Kidnapping of US Ambassador Charles Burke Elbrick

1977 Igreja Universal do Reino de Deus founded in Rio de Janeiro

1978 Military President Ernesto Geisel initiates slow process of *"abertura"*

1980 Formation of new political parties allowed; PT and PDT founded

1982 First open elections for state governors

1984 MST holds first national gathering at Cascavel

1985 José Sarney enters office as first civilian president since 1964

1988 New Constitution approved

1989 Fernando Collor elected president

1991 *Sertaneja* music reaches national popularity

1992 Collor impeached; massacre at Carandiru prison in São Paulo

1993 Massacre in Vigário Geral, Rio de Janeiro; Chico Science e Nação Zumbi release *Da Lama ao Caos*

1994 Real Plan initiated. Fernando Henrique Cardoso elected president

1995 IURD Bishop Sérgio von Helde kicks statue of Nossa Senhora da Aparecida on live TV

1996 Massacre in Eldorado dos Carajás, Pará

1997 Cardoso privatizes the Companhia Vale do Rio Doce; MST invasions reach their peak

1998 Cardoso re-elected; death of Leandro, of Leandro and Leonardo fame

2001   Widespread power shortages contribute to Cardoso's declining popularity

2002   Luiz Inacio Lula da Silva elected president

2003   Cardoso's Bolsa Escola social program becomes Lula's much-expanded Bolsa Família

2004   Brazil officially approves planting of genetically modified soy; Orkut launched

2005   The mensalão scandal weakens Lula's administration

2006   Bloodsuckers' Scandal; the PCC shuts down São Paulo; Overmundo launched; Lula re-elected; the CV shuts down Rio de Janeiro

2007   São Paulo's murder rate declines sharply; Supreme Court upholds indictment of mensaleiros

Introduction

In 1882, when Brazil was still an empire ruled by the aging Dom Pedro II, the novelist Machado de Assis published a short political allegory in one of Rio de Janeiro's daily newspapers. "The Most Serene Republic" recounted the electoral travails of a colony of spiders blessed with the ability to speak and vote. The spiders, modeling their electoral rules on the Venetian Republic, wove for themselves a bag and filled it with balls bearing the names of candidates for office. All went smoothly until it was discovered that one candidate's name appeared on two balls in the bag. The spiders voted to shrink the bag's opening in order to clamp down on fraud. In the next election, another candidate's ball was left out of the bag – an omission that the electoral officer insisted must have been an inadvertent mistake. The spiders returned the bag to its original size. Subsequent elections were tarnished by an unending series of unforeseen eventualities, and each time the spiders adjusted the process, hoping for a more republican result next time around, confident they would eventually get it right.

Machado satirized both the sterile parliamentary debates of the empire's senate and the hope that matters might improve dramatically under a republican government. A hundred and six years after he published his allegory, a diverse and contentious constitutional assembly stitched together the founding document of a new republic, Brazil's third crack at the form. Its members were entrusted with closing the door on over two decades of military dictatorship and creating formal rules that would sustain the nation's fledgling democracy, giving it room to grow. The constitution they produced in 1988 seems designed with the arachnid republic in mind – it is hundreds of pages long, addressing the minutiae of governance in an apparent attempt to forestall administrative confusion. It has nonetheless been amended some sixty times in its twenty-year history, and calls for emendation of key articles are a recurring motif in Brazilian political debate. Congressional spiders apply themselves with great zeal to these and other legislative tasks, producing a robust and learned body of law with an inconsistent relationship to actual practice.

The anthropologist and political columnist Roberto DaMatta often invokes Machado's allegory in his analysis of these efforts, noting that the Most Serene Republic does not need better electoral bags, it needs better republicans. In Brazil's political arena, the only thing more predictable than renewed calls for constitutional tinkering is fresh political scandal, which burgeons seasonally in impressive variety, providing constant fodder for the vibrant news media.

The young republic stumbles forward nonetheless. Brazil's first republic survived just over forty years, from the end of the Brazilian Empire in 1889 to the Revolution of 1930, which brought to power the Getúlio Vargas dictatorship. Its second, inaugurated with the fall of Getúlio Vargas in 1945, was cut off as a teenager by the military coup of 1964 and the long dictatorship that followed. Its third emerged from the long decline of the military dictatorship in the 1980s, and has by now, in 2008, passed through a troubled childhood and fraught adolescence, entering its third decade with every prospect of attaining vigorous maturity. Brazil has notably not solved the conundrums of constitutional rule, either in crafting laws that will contain its exigencies or in constraining its officials to follow them. But it has created a political arena characterized by vigorous competition, open debate and impressive levels of popular representation.

Electoral rules are only the beginning of this, but they are an important one: from its foundation as an independent nation in 1822 through the ratification of the 1988 Constitution, the voting population was limited by property or literacy requirements and obstructed or distorted in practice by a variety of other customary ruses. Voting is now obligatory for all citizens over sixteen, and elections are transparent. Campaign funding laws are routinely flouted and unscrupulous politicians seek to corral votes with unseemly threats and promises, but these tawdry habits are no more common in Brazil than they are in many democracies, and do not alter the basic reliability of the electoral system: for better or for worse, since the 1980s Brazilians have chosen the officials who represent them.

The more profound expansion of citizenship has been social and economic. Old codes of deference have rapidly become vestigial, old structures of dependence have been weakened. Until relatively recently, living in a *favela* (an informal settlement) was often considered a source of embarrassment, particularly for those seeking jobs in the formal sector. It is now increasingly a source of pride and a valued credential for jobs in municipal government and with NGOs. Before redemocratization, most middle-class families relied on live-in servants, usually paying them a minimum wage that was far short of a living wage. The "maid's quarters" of middle-class apartments are now used mostly for storage space, and "diaristas," or freelance cooks and cleaning women, are more likely to work for several employers and to command salaries significantly better than the still-paltry minimum.

The pervasive nature of these transformations in the post-dictatorship period means that to study Brazil since 1989 makes a great deal of sense, domestically as well as internationally. Brazilians recognize this transition much more deeply as redemocratization in the wake of long dictatorship than as the end of the Cold War. But the international context has also played a decisive role, not only in the recasting of leftwing political strategies in the wake of the Cold War, but in the rise of the pervasive "Washington Consensus" that governed global relations in the late twentieth century, holding that only economic growth can reduce poverty and that growth can be achieved only by reducing trade restrictions. The emergence of digital media, the global spread of informal urban economies, the rise of genetically modified crops – all these international trends of the past two decades have had immense consequences in Brazil, taking on unpredictable local manifestations. From both international and domestic perspectives, Brazil has changed extraordinarily since the close of the 1980s, and this change has now progressed to the point where it can be appreciated and studied historically.

By some lights, Brazil has become more "neoliberal" – requirements of maximum capital flexibility have brought greater economic fluidity without radically altering inequality. It is true that old networks binding patrons and clients have in many cases been superseded by exchanges at a cash nexus of shifting location, where power relations are less personalist but not egalitarian. But the combination of economic growth and the erosion of social hierarchies has yielded not only greater mobility and autonomy, but created a more diverse and representative public life. The anthropologist James Holston describes this transformation as "insurgent citizenship," noting the multiplicity of ways in which poor and working-class Brazilians since the 1980s have achieved greater leverage in the housing market, in employment negotiations and in the use of public space. These achievements remain limited primarily to Brazil's cities, but that is another transformation – over 80 percent of the population is now urban.

"Insurgent citizenship" has by no means eliminated inequality – Brazil remains highly unequal, despite recent progress. Nor is the expansion of political, social and economic citizenship itself a guarantee of successful democracy. Brazil has become more pluralistic, with a greater array of actors entering the public arena, making heretofore marginal demands suddenly central, stretching the fabric that wraps the body politic in ways that were unpredictable a few decades ago. Brazilians cannot be easily bracketed by class, religion, race or region in ways that were until fairly recently not only common but at least relatively enlightening. All these categories have witnessed great internal differentiation and external shifting, overlapping in unexpected ways. This pluralism requires more complex interparty negotiations and renders authoritarian solutions obsolete. But the combination of pluralism and a weak rule of law produces turf battles between interest groups, the consolidation of criminal networks and their increasing stake in the informal economy. Brazil's high rates of urban violence, among the most serious threats to its democracy, are a testament to the dangers of this combination.

In all these ways, developments within Brazil fall into patterns evident across the Global South, particularly in its largest and most dynamic nations. The Washington Consensus has shaped the policies of Brazil's most powerful politicians since the early 1990s. But implementing those policies has required negotiating with regional political machines, whose primary objective was to hold on to bargaining power by cultivating executive alliances and occupying administrative space.

The regional machines – political cartels headed by local bosses – had prospered within the tightly controlled congress of the dictatorship, which used them effectively to carry out local development projects while creating an appearance of popular support. The 1988 Constitution enabled the perpetuation of these machines by granting an outsized representational weight to sparsely populated states: there is one federal deputy for every 26,000 citizens of Roraima, and one for every 366,000 from São Paulo. Disproportionate representation has a cascading effect, allowing congressmen from sparsely populated states to create new municipalities, with each municipality opening numerous opportunities for political appointments and the required transfer of federal funds. These factors have made the regional machines forces that cannot be ignored in the construction of national political alliances.

The discipline of the Washington Consensus and the evolution of the regional machines, in turn, explain why Brazil's macroeconomic complexion and its congressional horse-trading remained relatively consistent despite the rise to power of the once-radical left. The leftwing credentials of its last two presidents notwithstanding, Brazil has never been more capital-friendly. And although these opponents of the military regime have controlled the executive branch since the mid-1990s, the same regional strongmen who once cultivated close ties to the ruling generals continue to survive as Brasília's ineluctable dealmakers.

These same factors explain why the rise of the political left since the 1990s proved either less radical or less disruptive, depending on one's perspective, than it did in neighbors Venezuela and Bolivia and in Ecuador. Brazil was already considerably further along than these nations in its incorporation of popular sectors into the political, social and economic citizenry, making its transition less volatile. The sectors of the left that came to power, moreover, had been grooming themselves for their closeup for decades, leaving little in the way of rough spots that might alarm international observers. In consequence, Brazil led the way in Latin America's "left turn" over the last decade, but did so while balancing the demands of international investors and domestic social movements with surprising success.

The fleeting Washington Consensus that rose to nearly unquestioned dominance with the end of the Cold War and then dissipated with the intensification of new conflicts early in the twenty-first century was kinder to Brazil than to most of its counterparts in the Global South. (It might be argued that the doctrine behind the Washington Consensus has by no means disappeared, but the discipline that went with it no longer holds much sway in Latin America.) Brazil's emergence as one of the world's most powerful producers of commodities, both raw and refined, has given it leverage in global trade, unmatched by its peers. Brazilian ethanol, oil reserves, soy, orange juice, and steel, to name only a few sectors, have enabled the country to keep inflation at bay – beating back the economic dragon of the 1980s – and to dictate the terms of its global economic engagement. Its expansion in high-tech sectors like airplanes and automobiles has given it enviable diversification and domestic market strength.

In contrast to some of its Latin American neighbors, Brazil has buttressed its global trading power without exacerbating domestic inequality or plunging the remnants of an industrial working class into poverty. Inequality rose in Brazil during the hyperinflationary 1980s and then began to decline slowly, with its rate of decline increasing along with the emergence of new social spending programs since 2000. Poverty also increased over the 1980s and into the early 1990s, and since then has fallen faster and farther than inequality. When looked at since the 1970s, Brazil's progress in both these areas has been mediocre. When looked at since the low point of the late 1980s and early 1990s, its progress has been impressive and encouraging.[1]

In consequence, Brazilians tend to be rightfully skeptical of international paradigms that confine the nation to some kind of peripheral role on the world stage. If the concept of a "Third World" still holds relevance anywhere, it certainly does not apply to high-tech, diversified Brazil. Nor can Brazil be squeezed into a "developing world": its regional variations and persistent inequalities within a fluid economy and society are hallmarks of its own kind of development, one that is not permanent but which also cannot be considered simply a transitional phase on the way towards a different kind of international model.

International observers often perceive Brazil as the object of both fascination and sympathy that, when uninformed, borders on condescension. Exotic Brazil, of samba, sex and football prowess, is one side of this coin; impoverished Brazil, of hunger, exploitation and violence, the other. Brazilians are keenly aware of these international perspectives and laugh them off or resent them as the case appears to demand. But whatever the issue, they necessarily tend to see the domestic contingencies much more richly than they do the broad international outlines. If sympathetic international observers often group Brazil into a peripheral category and see it as one of those nations that suffers the consequences of foreign depredations, Brazilians tend to emphasize the nation's difference, and to see the ways local actors have contributed to create current realities, which therefore seem more easily subject to alteration than one might guess from abroad. As a result, the Brazilian perceptions tend to be both more optimistic and more realistic.

Brazil *is* different, after all, and the images of exotic Brazil that attract the longing foreign gaze are part of that difference. Brazil's extraordinary cultural vibrancy can be traced to certain demographic and economic factors, and these are relevant. The forced importation of millions of African slaves up through the mid-nineteenth century left a legacy of deep inequality, but also laid the groundwork for a unique combination of African and European cultural forms and patterns with local inventions. The celebration of this combination in the early twentieth century coincided with the rise of domestic cultural industries, enabling the creation of genres, styles and schools of enduring vitality. Further patterns of international immigration and domestic migration yielded layers of innovation and variation within broad patterns. Yet there is a sense of mystery and compulsion here beyond demography and economy: Brazilians invent and express themselves culturally in part because doing so is understood as part of what it means to be Brazilian, a tautology so enlivening it rarely becomes frustrating.

At the same time, many of Brazil's recent transformations do fit into broader international trends, and it is illuminating to consider these comparatively. Brazil is often compared with Russia, India and China, a grouping of emerging mega-markets now recognized by the shorthand BRIC. Brazil has grown considerably more slowly than its BRIC colleagues, but looks relatively strong in regard to most other indicators. Brazil's combination of natural resources, commodities leverage, high-tech investment and relative lack of population pressures gives it prospects of greater economic stability than its peers. Although Brazil's inequality indices remain worse than those of Russia, India and China, a lower percentage of Brazilians than Indians remains among the very poor. Access to basic infrastructure and sanitation is considerably better for Brazil's urban poor than it is for India's.

Brazil's press is far freer and more robust than that of Russia or China. Its political institutions are more stable than those of Russia and India and more representative than those of China. It lacks the entrenched ethnic and religious conflicts of its colleagues. Brazil's slave-owning past has bequeathed a legacy of enduring racial inequality, and this inequality has become a topic of increasingly vigorous political debate and the target of a range of policies. This is a serious and pressing topic, but is not complicated by a history of recent violence, by passionate territorial feuds, or by a highly volatile international dimension. In all these aspects, it looks relatively benign in comparison with social conflicts in Russia, India and China.

Brazil's greatest deficit in the BRIC context is in the area of education, where its performance is poor. As recently as the 1970s, public education beyond the primary years was effectively limited to the middle class, which enjoyed access to safe, stimulating and high-quality schools. Public education is now nearly universal and has declined drastically in quality. Middle-class families in Brazil's major cities have for the most part put their children in private schools, leaving underfunded and chaotic public schools for those with no power to choose. Brazil's greatest obstacle to both continued economic growth and the deepening of its democracy is the ongoing problem of its educational system.

For over two decades, Brazil has been engaged in what can be termed the throes of democracy – a struggle to incorporate the forces unleashed by the simultaneous collapse of the military regime and the rise of the Washington Consensus, and to restrain them within the boundaries of a democratic republic. As chaotic as it occasionally seems, this struggle has defining tendencies, and tracing these reveals the existence of broader patterns.

Six of these may be considered decisive: these are the patterns that have changed Brazil the most since the 1980s and that are intimately connected to other transformations. They are the rise of the left wing to political power, the growth of urban violence, the conflict in agrarian Brazil between agribusiness and landless workers, the explosion of cultural diversification, particularly in popular music, the growth of Pentecostalism and the emergence of digital media. Considering each of these in turn will clarify Brazil's transformation, making sense of the unfolding of domestic struggles that have given local shape to broad international influences.

The left wing has not only risen to power but has largely set the terms of political debate. No national politician will currently admit to being of the right, and politicians of varying commitments have been able to use the specter of rightwing proclivities to put their opponents on the defensive. Once elected, however, leftwing politicians must engage in expedient negotiations with regional political machines that are deeply invested in maintaining their own position, greatly restraining the impetus for thoroughgoing reform.

The collapse of authoritarian power, the continued existence of venal and truculent police forces, and the growing importance of Brazil in the transshipment of drugs have produced startling violence in the nation's major cities, Rio de Janeiro and São Paulo in particular. Rising urban violence has exacerbated local geopolitical divisions, particularly those between the informal, autoconstructed favelas and the formal neighborhoods and their institutions of power. Local interest groups, including criminal networks, have learned to profit from these divisions, while the residents of both the favelas and the formal neighborhoods suffer. São Paulo has recently made important strides in addressing these issues, while Rio de Janeiro remains locked in a logic of urban conflict.

In the countryside, Brazil has become a first-world agribusiness power without eliminating rural poverty or resolving long-simmering agrarian conflicts. Instead, these conflicts have been incorporated into the mechanisms of the state and have become primarily a competition for federal resources partially obscured by radical rhetoric. These rhetorical battles also overshadow larger concerns about the conditions of rural labor and the defense of unique natural resources, concerns which have yet to inspire coherent policies.

Brazilian culture, in all its manifestations, has also become more pluralistic. Popular music, long a source of national pride and international glory, has blossomed in unpredictable ways. Music scenes in diverse regions have reconfigured genre boundaries and broken the dominance of the Rio–São Paulo axis over musical distribution. In the field of religion, a Pentecostal boom has spread like wildfire over what was once almost universally a Catholic country. Pentecostal denominations compete furiously with one another and across faiths, forcing the Catholic Church, among others, to formulate its own charismatic response. The rapid expansion of digital access has also yielded profound cultural consequences, shaking hierarchies and altering patterns of production. But strong state influence and the continuing prominence of nepotism and family connections give some measure of continuity to cultural production, structuring the unique Brazilian culture market.

Each of these transformations has offered both promise and peril. The chapters that follow explore their consequences in the construction of the fragile spider's web of Brazilian democracy.

1 | The rise of the left

"**They** say politics is the art of swallowing toads. Wouldn't it be fascinating to make the elite swallow Lula, that bearded toad."[2] Such were the sentiments of Leonel Brizola upon running third in the opening round of the 1989 presidential elections, behind Luiz Inácio Lula da Silva and Fernando Collor de Mello. Brizola, an old-school populist and the sitting vice-president of the International Socialist Organization, instructed his loyal followers to support fellow leftist Lula in the run-off election.

Brizola's support made the 1989 election close, but was not enough to overcome the concerted opposition of Brazil's business class, its landed gentry and, most importantly, its media titans. The Globo media empire cast its decisive weight behind Collor de Mello, the inexperienced scion of an oligarchic family from the impoverished northeastern state of Alagoas. Collor de Mello had little to recommend him for the nation's highest office, but most figures of influence found his message of market expansion more palatable than Lula's campaign for aggressive socialist reform. Economist Roberto Campos, Brazil's high priest of free-market discipline, famously quipped that if Lula were to be elected, there were only two possible outcomes (*saídas*), one via Galeão, the other via Cumbica – the international airports of Rio de Janeiro and São Paulo. Campos merely expressed the consensus among most Brazilians of means that a Lula victory would bring economic disaster, at least for them.

Lula kept at it, running again for president in 1994 and 1998, finally winning in 2002 and securing re-election in 2006. But between his narrow loss in 1989 and his decisive victory in 2002, a remarkable transition unfolded. When the bearded toad finally stepped into office, the Brazilian elite, or what was left of it, barely burped and showed no signs of indigestion. The same Globo empire that had savaged Lula in 1989 shone a generously favorable light on his 2002 candidacy and his first year in office. The left's hard-won triumph was apparently categorical and complete.

Three factors enabled this remarkable transition: the decline of the old elite, the increasing willingness of Lula's Partido dos Trabalhadores (PT), the Workers' Party, to work with big business, and the leftward shift of political discourse.

The old elite Brizola referred to in 1989 had largely disappeared by 2002. In 1989, Brazil still had prominent aristocratic figures like Carmen Mayrink Veiga, Jorge Guinle and Filomena Matarazzo Suplicy, privileged offspring of a hereditary oligarchy, born to power and not overly interested in the redistribution of wealth. By 2002, Carmen Mayrink Veiga and Jorge Guinle were both impoverished – by tycoon standards, that is, meaning their family wealth dissolved due to profligacy and bad luck, and they had fallen into the chilly depths of the middle class – and Suplicy's son was a senator for the PT. To be fair, Eduardo Suplicy was active in PT ranks before 1989, but back then he was considered a black sheep of his social milieu, and by 2002 he was recognized as simply ahead of the curve. By 2002 the reigning social figures in Brazil were people like soccer star Ronaldo, model Gisele Bündchen and singer Gilberto Gil. In other words, Brazil no longer had elites, it had celebrities. These celebrities had no inherent or inherited reasons to shrink from leftist politics, and the PT in particular eagerly cultivated their support. Not for nothing did Lula choose Gilberto Gil as his Minister of Culture. The decline of the elite did not turn Brazil into a land of economic equality – distribution of wealth remained extremely uneven. Nor was the importance of family ties lessened, as Chapter 6 will explain. But social and economic mobility increased dramatically, removing any quasi-aristocratic opposition to the left.

Lula and the most powerful faction of his Partido dos Trabalhadores ceased to advocate thoroughgoing socialist reform, at least in polite company, seeking instead to incorporate and appease organized popular movements while hewing largely to the orthodox economic strategy mapped out by Lula's predecessor, Fernando Henrique Cardoso. This enabled the PT to woo business elites as successfully as Cardoso had done during his eight years in office.

Most importantly, the PT, together with a host of like-minded organizations, successfully moved political discourse decisively to the left, and public acceptance of progressive reform – including acceptance on the part of the business sector – moved with it. In 1989, the PT's proposals for broad agrarian reform, for popular participation in municipal budgeting, and for greater political leverage for organized labor federations were all deemed unacceptably subversive by the country's reigning economic powers. By 2002, these and several other reforms initiated by Fernando Henrique Cardoso – race-based affirmative action, direct disbursement of social spending to poor families, greater restrictions on economic development in the Amazon – were deemed inevitable and, with the exception of affirmative action, largely unexceptionable elements of the political landscape by all but a few holdouts.

As these intertwining processes unfolded, the meaning of being leftist in Brazil also changed dramatically. During the military regime, being of the left entailed some kind of struggle against the dictatorship, and in the early stages of redemocratization, it entailed pushing for broader popular participation and the redistribution of wealth. While these latter goals remain rhetorically unifying, they have, in practice, largely been subsumed by the grinding political demands of stitching together governing coalitions and appeasing interest groups. The "rise of the left," then, really means the rise to power of former opponents of the military regime, and the increasing political leverage of the civil-society organizations that have supported them.

Ideology and physiology

A brief glance at the Brazilian political spectrum begins to reveal the nature and extent of the nature of this political transition. Since 1994, the PT's principal opponent has been Fernando Henrique Cardoso's Partido da Social Democracia Brasileira, or PSDB, a party modeled on European social democratic counterparts, advocating a similar "third way" blend of targeted social spending and investment in market expansion. Cardoso himself was widely known as a political theorist and sociologist of the academic left before running for president and, contrary to popular allegations, did not renounce his early beliefs once in office. In early 2007, the Partido da Frente

Liberal, or PFL, perceived in the Brazilian context as the last bastion of conservatives, changed its name to Demócratas (DEM) in explicit homage to the Democratic Party of the United States. Leaders of the renamed party expressed admiration for the US Democrats' historic support of civil liberties and public education, and for Clintonian Democratic administration in particular. The DEM immediately made environmental defense one of its central planks. This shift was rhetorical and not substantive, but demonstrates a central truth in Brazil's political arena: parties and politicians will go to great lengths to run from allegations of rightwing sympathies.

There is no significant party to the right of the DEM. On the other end of the spectrum, a cluster of fragmentary parties continues to uphold more radical views. Most prominent among them is the Socialism and Freedom Party, or PSOL, whose presidential candidate, Heloísa Helena, ran a surprising third in the 2006 election. Helena, a former PT militant, casts the PSOL as the real embodiment of the PT's original vision. (She is also the politician who takes most evident delight in calling Lula a bearded toad.)

New actors in civil society have also come to prominence since the 1980s, such as the Landless Workers' Movement (Movimento dos Trabalhadores Rurais Sem Terra, or MST) and the non-governmental organizations that have pushed for human rights reinforcement. The ability of these organizations to execute effective media strategies in the contentious press of the post-1989 period has made their rhetoric pre-eminent.

The rise of the left has coincided with a period of significant economic and administrative reforms, but many of these – such as the privatization of state enterprises – are not leftist in nature, and the former opponents of the military regime who have come to power have rarely pushed a radical agenda. This moderation has global and local explanations. Globally, the most powerful sectors of the Brazilian left have come to embrace at least part of the Washington Consensus, prizing economic growth and encouragement of foreign investment as the keys to development. Locally, those in power have been constrained by the persistence of regional political machines committed only to their own perpetuation. No governing coalition can function without appeasing these regional machines. All legislation and administration must be filtered through them, putting a substantial damper on potential radicalism.

The regional machines are not ideological, but "physiological," in the apt Brazilian terminology: they occupy administrative bodies and flex bureaucratic muscles. They are characterized by weak party loyalty and strategic adherence to governing coalitions in return for control over specified government resources. The most enduring of these machines have roots in the bipartisan system of the dictatorship, when the only legal parties were the rightwing ARENA (Aliança de Reconstrução Nacional) and the ostensibly opposition party MDB (Movimento Democrático Brasileiro). In reality, both parties became closely intertwined with administration in different parts of the country. Consequently, their surviving powerbrokers are as likely to hail from the PMDB (the Partido do Movimento Democrático Brasileiro, or Brazilian Democratic Movement Party), the successor to the MDB, as they are from the DEM, one of the successors of ARENA. Since redemocratization, new regional powerbrokers have emerged in other parties, but their personalist, interparty networks are far more important than the shifting alphabet soup of their party alliances. None of Brazil's two dozen parties is above the "physiological" temptation, but some are more successful than others at running party machines.

Regional powerbrokers typically extract concessions in ways that substantially alter and sometimes contradict national policies. In order to carry out agrarian reform, for example, Cardoso needed to pump resources into regional machines in sparsely populated states that carried out local policies reinforcing land concentration. As a result, the ability of these powerbrokers to bring first Cardoso and then his rival Lula to the bargaining table has created an uneasy overlap between leftist politics and old-fashioned clientelism – the personalist use of state funds to curry political favor among key interest groups.

The regional machines have been able to rely on curious features of the 1988 Constitution to perpetuate their administrative leverage. Disproportionate congressional representation of sparsely populated states is one of these. The constitutional provision granting "parliamentary immunity" to members of Congress has been another.

Elected officials cannot be prosecuted for "common crimes," covering almost everything not directly electoral, as long as they hold office. A constitutional amendment of 2001 placed some restrictions on these immunities, making it easier for prosecutors to indict congressmen, but a majority vote within Congress can still suspend prosecution, a loophole ably exploited by the regional machines to protect colleagues who have run foul of the law. Congressmen can also effectively time their renunciation of office in order to retain their eligibility in future elections, while requiring the process of indictment and prosecution to begin again.

Open-list elections for congressional representatives, the ability of congressmen to switch parties without losing their seats, and a low standard for the percentage of overall votes necessary for a party to place a representative in Congress all contribute to the proliferation of ideologically indistinguishable micro-parties that exist primarily to trade votes for administrative appointments and project funding.

There are currently over twenty-five parties represented in Congress, several of which have fewer than five seats – an unfortunate consequence of unrestrained pluralism. Much of the work of governing consists of persuading these micro-party representatives to vote with the governing coalition. State governors exercise considerable leverage in this process, because of constitutionally required transfers of federal receipts to state governments. Again, this reinforces the perpetuation of interparty regional machines. These machines have also exploited weaknesses in the judicial branch, such as overlapping jurisdictions and the frequent issuance of staying orders that block imprisonment or seizure of assets until cases reach their conclusion, a process that can take over a decade. Consequently, it has proven almost impossible to serve significant jail time for political corruption, much as some elected representatives have tried. This physiological nature of the political arena, marked by common corrupt practices, places strict limits on the potential consequences of ideological transformation.

Whence the toad? The left's deep background

The current pre-eminence of a broad, multifaceted left springs from the history of opposition to the military dictatorship that governed Brazil between 1964 and 1985. The 1964 coup itself was widely supported, responding to a general sense that the government of President João Goulart was spiraling towards disintegration. By the time the generals finally relinquished their grip, however, they were despised by much of the populace. Having struggled against the dictatorship – particularly if the struggle involved jail, torture or exile – the left subsequently became a valuable political trump card in the period of redemocratization.

This development was completely unpredictable in the early 1960s, when the Cold War was still understood to be a distorted global variation on the local struggle between Getulistas, or supporters of Getúlio Vargas, and anti-Getulistas – as ever, Brazilians necessarily saw domestic political events in the foreground and the international scenery in the distant background. Getúlio Vargas seized power in 1930 in a so-called revolution whose key participants sought only to update an oligarchic republic. But the global context of the crisis of liberal republicanism pushed Vargas into more ambitious experimentation, and he amassed greater power in stages. He inaugurated the Estado Novo dictatorship in 1937, relying on secret police, political prisons and loyal henchman to supplement his popular appeal. His alliance with key industrialists, his patronage of government-organized labor unions, and his astute negotiation of international investment guaranteed the short-term economic growth that underpinned state expansion. Getulismo became both a popular phenomenon and the fuel for a political machine.

Vargas was ousted in the wake of World War II, but his temporary absence from the capital only strengthened his popular appeal, and he returned to power as elected president in 1950. The populist initiatives of this "second regime," like coercing employers into granting generous concessions in order to settle strikes, stoked the ire of the conservative middle class. Over the course of 1954, Vargas's opponents turned the drive to unseat him into a moral crusade. On August 24 of that year, he shot himself in the heart, leaving behind a grandiose letter that pledged his blood for the sake of Brazil's downtrodden, making him an instant martyr.

Vargas's suicide guaranteed the perpetuation of his machine. Juscelino Kubitschek, a regional captain of that machine, won election to the presidency in 1955, and built an administration characterized by massive state projects such as the construction of the new capital at Brasília.

Jânio Quadros, elected in 1960, had built his own populist base in middle-class São Paulo but only secured presidential election by striking a compromise with the Getulistas, making Vargas's protégé, João Goulart, his vice-president. Quadros resigned from office in a failed power play, and Goulart took office in the midst of constitutional crisis. He enlisted the support of his charismatic brother-in-law, Leonel Brizola, governor of Rio Grande do Sul. Brizola, more volatile than Goulart, expropriated multinational corporate holdings and advocated extensive nationalization programs.

Brizola astutely decided that Rio de Janeiro offered a better platform for his political ambitions than did provincial Rio Grande do Sul, and in 1962 won election as a federal representative from Guanabara, the small city-state created when the federal capital was moved to Brasília in 1960, and basically comprising the city of Rio de Janeiro. His ongoing battles with Guanabara governor Carlos Lacerda, a renowned anti-Getulista, helped to bring the national conflict to a crisis.

Goulart dithered, vacillating between attempts to appease radical nationalists and reassure moderate republicans. Wary of radicalism, Brazil's most powerful generals seized power on March 31, 1964. No one expected their intervention to last over twenty years, but the generals who seized power found no suitable candidate capable of defeating Getulismo at the polls. They sought to cleanse the political arena by outlawing existing parties and limiting the political spectrum to two new parties, ARENA and the MDB.

This political narrowing then took on a logic of its own. Increased willingness to use heavyhanded repressive techniques helped bring to power a new cast of officers, more fearful of subversion than their predecessors. The impatient anti-Getulismo of 1964 gave way to aggressive anticommunism. The decisive point of transition came in 1968, when the regime passed the notorious AI-5, the Institutional Act Number 5, which temporarily closed Congress, intervened in the judicial branch, and suspended habeas corpus. With AI-5, the hardline officers seized the full powers of dictatorship.

Exile and underground

Opponents of the regime chose from among a limited range of options. While no one could have known it at the time, the choices made among these options proved enormously influential in determining future political status. As former opponents of the military regime consolidated their political power in the 1990s, their actions in the 1960s and '70s became crucial items on their political resumés, with relative intensity of opposition to the dictatorship helping to determine the new pecking order. A brief glance at the choices made by representatives of the key factions will help clarify this process.

The most aggressive opposition politicians, like Brizola, had no choice but to leave for exile in 1964. Brizola spent the early years of the dictatorship in Uruguay, and then moved to Portugal in 1977, two years after the fall of that nation's Salazarist dictatorship. Portugal became the base for a gathering network of labor-oriented Getulistas and new Brizolistas, who planned their electoral strategy for the long-delayed redemocratization.

More moderate politicians, like the old-line Getulista Tancredo Neves, remained in Brazil, choosing to work for gradual reform within the military regime. The moderates were to give the MDB its limited capacity for contestation and proved a crucial bridge to redemocratization over the course of the 1980s.

Illustrious academics, like Fernando Henrique Cardoso, began to stream steadily out of the country. Some were arrested, tortured and deported, others took flight before they could fall into the wrong hands. Cardoso was among the first to depart, in 1964. He spent the early years of the dictatorship in Chile, at the Economic Commision for Latin America (ECLA), a United Nations-funded think-tank strongly associated with dependency theory. Cardoso did his most influential scholarly work at ECLA, refining the broad strokes of dependency theory into a more nuanced analysis of the possibilities for economic emergence of peripheral nations.

Cardoso returned to Brazil in 1968, and the regime responded by commanding the University of São Paulo to issue his compulsory retirement. Rather than leave for renewed exile, he formed a think-tank with funding from the Ford Foundation. The Brazilian Center for Analysis and Research (CEBRAP) became a nurturing ground for analysis of the regime's flawed development policies.

Student activists formed underground cells affiliated with radical factions. Ação Libertadora Nacional, or ALN, was a splinter faction dissatisfied with the Brazilian Communist Party's reluctance to engage in armed struggle against the dictatorship. Its most energetic participants included José Dirceu, a student radical from São Paulo known for his disdain for anything less than ferocious commitment to the movement. The October 8 Revolutionary Movement, or MR-8, another dissident communist faction, helped pioneer the tactic of robbing banks and supermarkets to fund the revolutionary struggle. It counted among its adherents aspiring journalists like Franklin Martins and Fernando Gabeira.

The MR-8 and the ALN occasionally joined forces, most notably in the kidnapping of US Ambassador Charles Burke Elbrick, in 1969, an episode recalled in the 1997 Bruno Barreto film *O Que é Isso Companheiro?* (marketed abroad as *Four Days in September*). The kidnappers released Elbrick in return for the liberation and safe deportation of a list of political prisoners. A look at the rosters of participants in the episode illuminates the importance of radical opposition to the military regime in laying the groundwork for political influence during redemocratization. Several key organizers of the kidnapping were captured and tortured, some fatally. Other participants fared better. Fernando Gabeira endured arrest and exile, returning to Brazil to write the book that served as the basis for Barreto's film. He later founded Brazil's Green Party, temporarily jumped ship for the PT, and then returned to the Green Party, all while serving as a federal deputy from Rio de Janeiro. Franklin Martins spent years of exile in Cuba, then returned to Brazil to become one of its most prominent journalists, and served as Lula's Minister of Social Communication.

Among the prisoners released in return for Elbrick were José Dirceu, who also spent most of his exile in Cuba, where he underwent plastic surgery, changing his appearance in order to return to Brazil under a false name in 1975. After the regime granted amnesty for political exiles in 1979, Dirceu reassumed his real name, undertook corrective surgery to restore his appearance and became one of the founders of the PT. As one of that party's guiding intellectuals, he played a key role in its gradual rise to power. As Lula's first chief of staff during the first three years of Lula's presidency, Dirceu was the second most powerful man in Brazil.

Other influential factions included Ação Popular, or Popular Action, a socialist network imbued with the spirit of the early liberation theology movement, placing great emphasis on direct action among the poor. Among its founders were José Serra and Herbert José de Souza. The first, an economics student and son of working-class parents in São Paulo, rose to prominence as the president of the National Students' Union. The second, a Catholic activist from the interior state of Minas Gerais, served as coordinator for the AP in the first years of the dictatorship, guiding its growing engagement with Marxist theory. Política Operária, or Polop, was a local faction in Minas Gerais that sought to spread Marxist theory from campus to factory. The economics undergraduate Dilma Rousseff was one of its early teachers. Following the fall of the regime, Serra became Minister of Health under Cardoso, lost the 2002 election to Lula, and then served as Governor of São Paulo. Souza became the most influential social activist of the 1980s and '90s. Rousseff served in PT state administrations in Rio Grande do Sul and then became Lula's second chief of staff and likely PT candidate for Lula's presidential succession.

Conspicuously absent from this brief survey of prominent opponents of the early regime is the bearded toad himself. In 1964, Lula was an entry-level metalworker at a plant in São Paulo's industrial periphery. As such, his working life was structured by the legacy of Getulismo – its guaranteed minimum wage and workplace protections, its worker-training programs, and its vertically organized bread-and-butter-oriented unions. For metalworkers, in any case, the regime's industrialist policies meant steady employment, greatly compensating for reduced political freedoms. It was not until the late 1970s, with the regime's developmentalist policies falling apart at the seams, that Lula would rise to the fore as spokesman for an independent union movement.

When the miracle ends

The military dictatorship bet its reputation on economic growth and lost, for two reasons. Rapid growth in the early 1970s stimulated social habits that eventually conflicted with the regime's strictures, and high inflation in the late 1970s brought growth to a grinding halt, provoking resentment and mobilization by a diverse opposition. The inflationary spike was a global phenomenon, triggered by rising oil prices, and it created complications for authoritarian regimes across Latin America. In Brazil, where the regime had already lost much of its initial support, inflation made the endurance of authoritarianism untenable.

During the so-called economic miracle of the early 1970s, state investments in the steel, petroleum and hydroelectric sectors triggered annual growth rates of over 10 percent. The "miracle" helped generate new appetites and new habits: the dictatorship was politically repressive, but socially tolerant. The 1970s were a decade of rapid loosening of social restrictions in Brazil, in tune with similar transformations in the United States and Western Europe, and ahead of most of its Latin American neighbors. Former political militants expressed their new lifestyle liberation by smoking marijuana in the dunes of Ipanema beach, a habit largely tolerated by the declining dictatorship.

TV Globo led the way in the relaxation of social restrictions. Roberto Marinho, owner of the network, had parlayed his early support of the regime into a host of favorable concessions of regional broadcasting licenses, helping Globo to rise above its competitors. Marinho proved just as astute in his choice of employees, consistently hiring the best writers, directors and producers. One curiosity of this dominance was that the station's most successful writers – particularly those of its prime-time *novelas*, or soap operas – were avowed communist sympathizers. Marinho, well aware of these leanings, voiced no objections as long as ratings were high and political content remained implicit. The writers, for their part, understood – with one or two notable exceptions – that the needs of the melodrama outweighed any political questions.

The result was a peculiar local variation on the populist genre of the soap opera. Like their radio forebears, Globo's novelas often featured orphaned heroes forced to overcome the misdeeds of the rich and powerful in order to claim their true destiny. Globo's novelas of the 1970s added the twist of a pointed disdain for the corrupting influence of capitalism, offset by a brand-specific fascination with consumer goods. This recipe, coupled with plenty of adultery and as much flesh as loosening social norms would allow, gave Globo dominant nightly ratings.

Onscreen, the inflationary spike of the late 1970s only heated up the action, raising the stakes of winner-take-all novela plots. Offscreen, inflation meant a ratings disaster for the regime. Antônio Delfim Netto, Minister of the Interior in the early 1970s, had paid for infrastructural investment by contracting foreign loans at floating interest rates. When oil prices spiked in the mid-1970s, interest rates went with them. Brazil's debt suddenly expanded as foreign investment dropped.

Inflation wreaked havoc on urban middle-class families, many of whom had contracted floating-rate loans in order to purchase the apartments built in the miracle's real-estate boom. Mortgage delinquency spread like dengue fever, and massive foreclosure was not a politically viable option. Instead, the federal bank that backed mortgages swallowed much of the loss. The dictatorship, suddenly in spiraling debt both externally and internally, watched its projects grind to a halt.

Middle-class homeowners founded neighborhood associations to petition for debt relief. Favela residents used their own neighborhood associations to demand infrastructural investment, and the social liberalization of the early decade helped prepare the ground for new movements. The Unified Black Movement united fragmentary race-based organizations into a temporarily cohesive front. The indigenous movement denounced state paternalism. The women's movement organized to convert social liberation into women's autonomy. The gay movement began to expose broad hypocrisies in attitudes towards homosexuality. The regime suddenly found itself besieged by identity-based movements demanding a seat at the table. Participants in these movements began to see redemocratization as the linchpin of political and cultural reinvention.

The reorganization of the left

Having lost the support of the urban middle class, and unable to contract new loans for the kind of development projects that had guaranteed some level of popular support, the regime made the strategic decision to grant these new social movements greater leeway. In neighboring Argentina and Chile, hardline dictatorships cracked down heavily on similar movements, yielding thousands of casualties. In Brazil, the technocratic regime chose a path of gradual opening. Labor strikes and the formation of new political parties, both outlawed since the inception of the regime, were permitted at the close of the 1970s. The former set the stage for Lula's rise, the second for that of Brizola.

The metalworkers' strikes of 1979 on São Paulo's industrial periphery exploited several of the regime's newfound weaknesses. It was no longer politically feasible to lock up strike leaders, but the regime had no history of forcing employers to the bargaining table. The strikers themselves recognized that their political advantage lay not in settling with individual employers but in using a growing wave of strikes to create and cement a new labor federation, the Unified Workers' Central, or CUT.

Lula's humble background – his parents had migrated from the impoverished northeast to São Paulo's growing urban periphery – became an asset in his construction of his political persona. He attracted the enthusiastic attention of academics and Catholic activists infused with the new ideals of liberation theology – the growing conviction within a progressive wing of the Church that a kind of social Catholicism informed by Marxist theory could serve as a basis for radical reform. While the strikes were still underway, representatives from these sectors laid plans for the organization of a socialist party that would make working-class activism the focus of a broader struggle. The PT was in the process of being born.

In the meantime, the new social movements found common cause in a call for amnesty for political prisoners and exiles, a campaign that spread like brushfire across Brazil over the course of 1978 and 1979. Vocalist Elis Regina's 1979 recording of "O Bêbado e a Equilibrista," the Drunk and the Tightrope-Walker, created a popular soundtrack for the movement. The composition, by Aldir

Blanc and João Bosco, offered a political allegory of the abuses of the dictatorship and the tentative steps of a redemocratizing Brazil. One of its most famous lines called for "a volta do irmão do Henfil," the return of Henfil's brother. Henfil, or Henrique de Souza Filho, was a cartoonist for the satirical opposition magazine *O Pasquim*. The tune's success made his brother a celebrity even before most of Brazil knew his name – Herbert José de Souza, soon to be better known throughout Brazil as Betinho.

From without, US President Jimmy Carter also pushed for greater political opening. Unwilling to endure the kind of international opprobrium increasingly focused on the Argentine and Chilean regimes, and unable to crack down domestically, the regime conceded political amnesty. Betinho, Brizola, Serra, Gabeira, Martins and a host of other prominent opponents of the regime flocked back to Brazil. Suddenly Brazil was afire with leftist organizing. The alliances and strategies chosen over the ensuing three years would play critical roles in the rise of the left over the next two decades.

Betinho had spent his long exile cultivating ties in an international network of leftist academics, and upon return to Brazil he put into action his plans to create a leftwing think-tank. Betinho and his colleagues, the engineer Carlos Afonso and the economist Marcos Arruda, established IBASE, the Brazilian Institute for Social and Economic Analysis. Betinho and Arruda had both forged their political commitment as lay activists in the early liberation theology movement. They brought liberation theology's concern for the poor and its denunciations of capitalism to IBASE. Nowhere was this more true than in the institute's attitude towards agrarian reform. IBASE's studies characterized rural poverty as the result of traditional Brazilian tendencies towards land concentration exacerbated by the political reliance of the dictatorship on rural oligarchs. In this analysis, rural inequity was the primary source of the rising urban poverty of the peripheries of Brazil's major cities, because rural land concentration pushed landless farmers to the urban fringe. Agrarian reform thus held out the apparent promise of solving two of Brazil's most pressing problems at once, uplifting its rural poor and slowing the growth of urban poverty.

This made IBASE the key urban voice in the rise of an agrarian reform network. The foundation and growth of the Movimento Sem Terra, or MST, the Landless Workers' Movement, formed the rural basis of that network, and would eventually develop its own highly sophisticated media strategy, as analyzed in Chapter 3. Through the mid-1990s, however, IBASE and Betinho played key roles in giving the message of agrarian reform an academic and urban imprimatur.

Betinho was at the forefront of a trend of lay activists who left Church activities for the independence and mobility of non-governmental organizations. In the early 1980s, activism within the Church was still strong, and many activists in Christian Base Communities, or CEBs, enthusiastically adopted the practice of "occupying spaces" in the broad political struggle, seeing no office as removed from the larger process. Neighborhood associations, literacy programs, rural cooperative boards and municipal social service projects all drew energetic CEB activists. As a result, they were well positioned to make a transition to NGOs in the 1990s, exercising an enormous influence in civil society.

These CEB activists were crucial to the national growth of the PT. The party's organizers deliberately set out to create something that Brazil had not previously seen – a party built from the grass-roots, with dues-paying members, a rigorously structured process of debate and internal elections. The PT of the early 1980s had no wealthy backers; instead, its members, from Lula to the most humble newcomer, were expected to "tithe," paying a small percentage of their salaries to the party's coffers – a practice that endures nearly three decades later.

Brizola was among the first to perceive the PT as a competitive threat. He also founded a new party targeting the working class, the Democratic Workers' Party, or PDT. Brizola soon found himself competing with the PT for the loyalty of old comrades-in-arms, and responded by going directly to the people. While the PT was expanding the base of its party structure by calling upon the energies of CEB veterans, Brizola began drafting community stalwarts who valued practical experience over theory. The PDT, particularly in Rio de Janeiro, became the party of the streets, skeptical of academic as well as political elitism. "Pedetistas," supporters of the PDT, scorned the PT's endless meetings as a façade for the machinations of domineering intellectuals, and "Petistas," supporters of the PT, condemned the PDT as a relic of old-school populism.

The MDB – renamed the PMDB after the legalization of broad party competition – had stronger national representation than either of its new rivals, but it had little popular mobilization. Its state-level office-holders became increasingly known for rent-seeking control over the machinery of local government, and many politicians migrated away from the party over the course of the 1980s. Fernando Henrique Cardoso and several colleagues from São Paulo, for example, left the PMDB in 1988 to found the PSDB, a party that made up for its lack of grassroots support with well-placed administrative allies.

From *Diretas Já* to impeachment

By the early 1980s, the dictatorship had conceded to a process of slow opening, and the opposition had largely accepted that premise, leaving only the details to be hammered out in a constant process of negotiation. In 1982, Brazilians elected state governors from open slates for the first time since 1960. Opposition leaders carried the day in the major southeastern states, with Brizola winning in Rio de Janeiro. The PDT won the plurality of seats in Rio's state assembly: within two years of its invention, it had become dominant in one of the nation's key states.

The opposition victories of 1982 set the stage for a demand for free presidential elections, understood to be the final step in the process of redemocratization. The *Diretas Já* campaign – direct elections, now – that swept across the nation in 1983 and '84 was Brazil's most broadbased grassroots movement. The crumbling shell of the dicta-torship ultimately defeated *Diretas Já* with the only weapon it had left, abstention: the rightwing congressmen simply left the building when the measure was being voted, ensuring it could not be ratified. But the movement's popular enthusiasm forced the dictatorship to negotiate a presidential election the following year.

The 1985 election was neither direct nor open slate – the candi-dates were selected and approved in a Byzantine process controlled by the regime – but it marked an end to the succession of military officers as head of state. The two finalists were Paulo Maluf, a notori-ously corrupt conservative populist from São Paulo, and Tancredo

Neves, the old-line Getulista. Maluf was considered so unsavory that many regime supporters deserted him, throwing their lot behind Neves. They wisely negotiated a compromise, however, asking Neves to name as his vice-presidential candidate José Sarney – like Maluf, a conservative populist head of a regional machine, albeit in this case from the impoverished northeastern state of Maranhão.

Neves won the election and then fell mortally ill with an abdominal infection. Sarney assumed office, temporarily blocking the movement for more radical reform and easing the transition of the regional machines to democracy. The Constitutional Assembly of 1988 gave the left wing another chance. Grassroots organizations proposed hundreds of popular amendments, and the few PT congressmen participating in the deliberations adopted them, building their national reputations in the process. By the end of the year, the body produced a constitution containing thousands of clauses. Some of these were deeply pertinent to a nation emerging from dictatorship – torture, for example, was ruled a crime demanding imprisonment with no possibility of bail. Many, however, were purely aspirational, such as the stated guarantees of rights to education, health and housing. None of these was near to becoming a reality, but the new constitution helped set the terms of future debate and legislation.

The postdictatorship

The ratification of the constitution finally slammed the door shut on the dictatorship, and set the stage for a struggle for power in the increasingly pluralistic political arena of the new democracy, beginning with the 1989 presidential election. Brizola was the frontrunner on the left, Lula the dark horse candidate. The right, showing early evidence of its inability to cope with electoral politics, failed to produce a consensus candidate. Fernando Collor de Mello, representing a tiny startup party, filled the gap by appealing to business interests with free-trade rhetoric. Collor de Mello also campaigned on his project to root out the *maharajas* – civil servants who had hidden their luxurious perquisites in the complex bureaucracy of the dictatorship. Collor's own family holdings, intimately intertwined with the machinery of state government in Alagoas, showed he was not immune to the charms of dubious entitlements. But his rhetoric made for good footage on Globo TV, which gave the dashing Collor extensive screentime.

Globo's coverage helped to polarize the elections. Roberto Marinho's antipathy for Brizola ran deep, and in the opening months of the campaign, Lula came off relatively well in comparison with Brizola in Globo's coverage. Most observers were surprised, nonetheless, when Lula edged Brizola in the first round to earn a second-round confrontation with Collor.

Globo TV, and in particular its nightly news program *Jornal Nacional*, played a key role in the unfolding of the second round. *Jornal Nacional*'s clips from the televised debates highlighted Lula's worst moments and Collor's best. Collor won, and then discovered the difference between campaign support and political alliance. Rather than building a national base, he stocked the highest levels of government with friends. He then attempted an unorthodox anti-inflationary treatment, freezing private savings accounts on the theory that a temporary halt to spending would break the inflationary cycle. The urban middle class that had played a key role in Collor's election was hit hard by the banking freeze and grew suddenly hostile towards the president. Globo television and *Veja* magazine, influential formers of political opinion, echoed and amplified the changing mood.

Then the real scandals started to break. Collor's cronies had organized a scheme of kickbacks and skim-offs on government contracts that was highly similar to the operations of a number of regional political machines. But those regional machines depended on significant leverage over local media – Collor's own family, for example, owned newspapers and television stations in Alagoas. But Collor had no control over national media – on the contrary, national media organs largely controlled his destiny.

Collor deserved to be impeached, but it remains a surprising testament to his political naïveté that he got what he deserved. Over the course of 1992, as scandals broke, a broadbased coalition mobilized to demand Collor's impeachment. The mobilization was similar to the *Diretas Já* campaign in its scope and variety, featuring enormous rallies led by speakers from trade unions, progressive parties and student groups. The difference was that this time Globo was on board, granting ample favorable coverage.

As the storm gathered, Globo broadcast a mini-series called *Anos Rebeldes*, Rebel Years, set in the late 1960s, sympathetically portraying student radicals. The mini-series was a bellwether, sounding a decisive change in the political climate. Globo's writers were coming out of the closet with their political sympathies. The network that had blossomed under the protection of the dictatorship was now portraying the enemies of that regime as heroes, and the regime as the enemy. *Anos Rebeldes* demonstrated that this perspective had now become mainstream, and did so in a way with direct implications for the existing political scenario. Collor's impeachment itself was ultimately less significant than Globo's transition.

Enter FHC

Collor was impeached in 1992, but not convicted of any crime. His primary penalty was the loss of his political rights for eight years, including the right to run for office. His ouster brought to power his vice-president, Itamar Franco, a moderate from Minas Gerais who governed for the next two years. Franco undoubtedly would have gone down in history as one of Brazil's most ineffectual presidents had it not been for his choice of an economic team. He named Cardoso finance minister, and Cardoso brought on board a group of young economists from São Paulo who had seen enough of the failed shocks of the Sarney and Collor years to proceed with caution.

They had little room for error, for Collor's corruption had given a bad name to economic liberalism. In Collor's wake, cutting spending, reducing tariffs and privatizing state enterprises were tarred as neoliberal ruses to enrich insiders and bankers. These denunciations proved compelling to Brazilians stung by Collor's kickbacks, but they were often wrong on the details. The vast majority of the federal government's social spending went to the middle class, in the form of pension payments for civil servants and generous expenditures on higher education. High import tariffs generated reciprocal tariffs that eliminated Brazil's comparative advantage in agricultural sectors. And state monopolies in telecommunications, mining and transportation sheltered inefficient, undercapitalized enterprises incapable of investing in improvements.

Most pressingly, stratospheric inflation penalized the poor and the working class, above all. Salaries and savings accounts indexed to inflation made rising prices a bearable burden for the wealthy. But those working for cash off the books or paid in a monthly wage suffered the effects of devaluation by the day. Shock treatments were politically out of the question, but an orthodox monetary policy backed by strategic liberal reforms was necessary. Only a politician with an air of scholarly competence, a history of struggle against the dictatorship and a broad network of political allies could carry out such reforms. Enter FHC, as he became known in the Brazilian newspapers.

Cardoso and his team instituted the *Real* Plan, named for the new currency they created, replacing the *cruzeiro*. They initially pegged the *real* to the dollar, then allowed it to fluctuate within a predetermined ratio, and eventually allowed it to fluctuate with only limited intervention from the Central Bank. Neither new currencies nor pegging to the dollar were innovative policies – both had been tried and had failed. Other elements of the strategy were more novel. These called for a transitional period: as the old currency was phased out, prices were calculated in "Units of Real Value" indexed to the dollar. Only after complementary policies had slowed inflation was the new currency introduced. In the meantime, the Cardoso team raised emergency funds for short-term social expenditures through new taxes, cut tariffs, aggressively promoted exports and promised privatization. These policies responded to the predilections of the Washington Consensus, yielding massive capital inflows which buoyed the *real* upon its introduction in 1994 and carried it through its first five years with minimal inflation.

While that extended stability was by no means guaranteed in 1994, the initial success of the plan alone was enough to propel Cardoso to victory in that year's presidential elections. Lula, runner-up for a second time, was blindsided by the success of the *Real* Plan, and the Cardoso–Lula rivalry was sealed.

Cardoso's presidency was consistent with his academic career. To begin, there was nothing about President Cardoso's enthusiasm for global trade that contradicted Professor Cardoso's earlier writings. Cardoso's most influential writings had been part of dependency theory, a school of global economic analysis informed by Marxist theory but not rigorously Marxist in its applications. Early dependency theorists replaced class structure with global economic patterns, arguing that international capitalism consigned some nations to peripheral status, necessarily perpetuating that status in order to enrich metropolitan capitalists. Working with Enzo Falleto, Cardoso had responded to this proposition in *Dependency and Development in Latin America*, a dependency-theory text written during Cardoso's ECLA years. Cardoso and Falleto argued that peripheral status was not an inevitable feature of capitalism but the consequence of a contingent array of circumstances. They advocated investment in targeted industrial and technological sectors coupled with broader rural development as a recipe for overcoming the obstacles hindering peripheral development.

Dependency theory, nevertheless, was consistent with a defense of state-owned enterprises and industrial protections in peripheral nations, and implied a challenge to international capital. Those who knew of Cardoso as a dependency theorist were consequently surprised by his presidential policies of privatization and pension reform, and by his pursuit of international investment. His opponents accused him of becoming a toady to international bankers, and alleged that he remarked *"esqueça o que escrevi,"* forget what I wrote, to justify his ostensibly neoliberal policies. Cardoso apparently never said anything of the kind and had no need to – his policies did not contradict his academic work, which represented a reformist position within dependency theory. At the same time, the discipline of the Washington Consensus on one hand and the exigencies imposed by the regional machines on the other certainly dictated to a certain extent the unfolding of Cardoso's policy reform. He needed international investment to shore up the *real*, and he needed to bargain with the regional machines to push through the reforms that would keep investment coming in.

Like contemporary "third-way" political leaders – Bill Clinton in the United States, and Tony Blair in the United Kingdom, most prominently – Cardoso sought to balance market stimulation with social guarantees. He became the first Brazilian president to acknowledge racism in Brazilian society and to institute policies designed to address it. These included a pilot affirmative action program for admission to public universities and recognition of the land claims of *quilombos*, communities founded by runaway slaves and still populated by their descendants. Neither of these initiatives yielded significant results during Cardoso's tenure, but both would be continued and expanded by Lula.

Cardoso had more success with *Bolsa Escola*, or School Grant, which paid poor families a monthly stipend for keeping their children in school. This conditional cash transfer program marked a sea change in Brazilian social spending: for the first time, major federal social spending went directly to the poor, rather than primarily benefiting the middle class. Cardoso also instituted agrarian reform policies, overhauling the federal government's land distribution agency and creating programs to facilitate the purchase, capitalization and market connection of small family farms. As discussed in Chapter 3, these policies met with mixed success, and only spurred the MST and the PT to greater antipathy.

Cardoso's AIDS policy best illustrates the tenuous balancing acts of his administration. In the early 1990s, international AIDS researchers predicted that Brazil would experience a pandemic, with infection spiraling upwards from an existing rate of 1.5 percent. Brazil's profile of existing infection levels and demographic patterns were often compared to those of South Africa. By the end of Cardoso's administration, South Africa had infection rates above 15 percent, while Brazil's stood at approximately 0.6 percent. Brazil owes its relative success in this regard primarily to its provision of free anti-retroviral medicine to everyone with AIDS. Implementing this policy required not only legislative persuasion and effective administration of an enormous program, but a willingness to defy Big Pharma. Brazilian labs reverse-engineered anti-retroviral medicines, enabling the government to live up to its commitment to providing free treatment without bankrupting the health budget. When multinational pharmaceutical companies pressured Brazil to respect their patents and pay high licensing fees, Cardoso's administration steered a cautious course through diplomatic narrows, arguing the fine points of international patent law while defending Brazil's obligation to respond to a public health crisis.[3]

This model leaves much room for debate, beginning with the fact that infection rates declined quickly in the mid-1990s and have not declined since, suggesting other measures are necessary to make further progress. But the policies Cardoso's administration enacted in the mid-1990s demonstrate that he was willing to defy multinational capital on targeted issues.

The Achilles heel of Cardoso's social-democratic strategy was not its appeal to foreign investment, but its articulation with the physiological machines. Cardoso's alliance of convenience with powerbrokers like Antonio Carlos Magalhães of Bahia and Sarney of Maranhão meant that the regional machines continued to prosper within a transforming Brazil.

Privatizations and re-election

Cardoso's support for privatization of state enterprises and for a constitutional amendment allowing re-election of the president outraged his detractors. The privatizations contributed to economic growth and diversification and buoyed the currency, a vital ingredient in staving off inflation. But they also created problems, not the least of these being the provocation of strong popular resentment. Re-election was a disaster, perpetuating the worst aspects of Brazilian politics. Fallout from the compromises necessary to push through re-election contaminated Cardoso's larger project, casting a pallor of assumed scandal on his economic policies.

Cardoso privatized primarily in telecommunications, mining, transportation and energy. The privatization of the state telephone company Telebrás, along with its regional subsidiaries, was the most successful of these ventures. That success can be measured in phones: in 1995, before privatization, there were 600,000 cellphones in Brazil. By 2006 there were 100 million, far more than any other Latin American nation.[4] In the early 1990s, contracting for new phone service in any major Brazilian city required waiting for approximately two years. Most clients instead made third-party arrangements with existing contract-holders, paying large sums for initial service, plus extortionate monthly rent of the line. Telecommunications infrastructure was so antiquated that the networks simply could not support expansion. Residents of major cities regularly responded to telephone calls not by saying "Alô," but by reciting their telephone number – crossed wires were so common that it was necessary to confirm numbers before beginning conversation.

Privatization changed this by facilitating massive growth of the cellphone industry. Cellphones with prepaid plans, allowing users to pay only for the number of minutes they use, have enabled cellphone use across classes. Privatization of telecommunications has also facilitated broad digital inclusion in Brazil, as analyzed further in Chapter 6. Highspeed Internet and wireless connections are common features of urban life in Brazil. Privatization in this sector effectively distributed wealth. State monopolies had facilitated the operation of rent-seeking contract-holders, well-off citizens who literally used their connections to exploit the less fortunate. Market competition yielded improved service and exponentially broader access at a fraction of the price.

The political negotiations accompanying telecommunications privatization were less salutary, leaving a trail of unsavory connections that begins in Cardoso's administration and traverses that of Lula. But the beneficial results of privatization for common Brazilians are evident.

The privatization considered most notorious was that of the Companhia Vale do Rio Doce, a mining and railroad conglomerate. Getúlio Vargas had expropriated the original holdings from international capitalists sixty years earlier. Cardoso's privatization was thus explicitly intended to mark the end of a cycle of state capitalism. As Cardoso said, perhaps prematurely, "the Getúlio Vargas era is over."[5] The Vale do Rio Doce had for years been a marginally profitable but inefficient state monopoly. As international demand for minerals soared, the company languished, incapable of investing in infrastructure. Following privatization, Vale, as it is now known, became the second largest mining corporation in the world, active on five continents. The company exponentially increased its labor force in Brazil, its annual tax payments far exceed the low profits it had made as a state company, and its demand for technological and industrial services has sent ripples of growth through the Brazilian economy.

The downside is primarily environmental: Vale's growth has contributed to environmental problems in parts of the Amazon region, raising questions about whether the Brazilian state has the will to restrain the beast it set free. Vale insists that it has put rigorous environmental controls in place, and that any damage near its operations results from unregulated growth around its projects, but putting the ball back in the state's court has not proven an effective way to protect the environment.[6]

Vale's privatization also entailed high political costs. "*A Vale é nossa*," the Vale is ours, became a nationalist–industrialist rallying cry, consciously echoing Getúlio Vargas's early 1950s mantra, "o petróleo é nosso," the oil is ours. Trade unionists led a popular mobilization against the privatization in the months leading up to the auction in 1997. Cardoso failed to make a convincing political case for privatization, leaving his adversaries to set the terms of the political debate. Mobilization ebbed in the wake of the sale but has flowed again in subsequent years in a campaign for "re-estatização," re-expropriation of the company's holdings.

Critics of privatization often raise the example of Petrobras, the state energy company, founded in the "o petróleo é nosso" days of the 1950s. Petrobras has emerged as a world leader in offshore drilling, refining of low-grade oil, and biofuels, and it has achieved this competitive edge as a state company. If Petrobras can do it as a state company, what prevented Vale from doing the same? Petrobras succeeded partly because of the peculiar economics of oil, which favors cartel politics in a way that bauxite does not, and where globally soaring demand ensures the profitability of virtually any company with a guaranteed supply. And it succeeded partly because of Petrobras's own history of massive investment and sheltered growth under the dictatorship, followed by partial privatization under Cardoso. It bears noting that Petrobras did not enter global oil's first division until Cardoso opened it to foreign investment in the late 1990s.

Eletrobrás is Petrobras's black sheep brother. The military dictatorship invested heavily in hydroelectric power but did not invest in research and development. Eletrobrás lacked both the technical proficiency and political centrality of Petrobras. Cardoso attempted partial privatization of Eletrobrás, following a model similar to his approach with Petrobras, albeit allowing greater foreign control of operations. This privatization was a bitter failure. While California suffered through the notorious Enron-manipulated rolling blackouts of 2000–2001, much of Brazil experienced similar phenomena in the same period. Severe drought interrupting hydroelectric operations played a larger role in Brazil, but the effect was the same – power shortages triggered accusations of political incompetence and profiteering.

Electricity was not a commodity easily exported to globally hungry markets, but a will-o'-the-wisp that needed to be delivered immediately to domestic consumers, many of whom had negligible resources to pay for it. It was not a logical target for privatization, and the multinational companies that bought shares largely avoided the kinds of infrastructural investment that might have allowed Brazil to increase capacity. Consequently, partial privatization in this sector failed, and full-scale privatization undoubtedly would have failed more disastrously. Privatization had several logical and beneficial applications, but not in sectors characterized by a need for close regulation and the subsidization of services that were unprofitable but politically and socially necessary.

More generally, privatization perversely relied on the substantial use of public funds. BNDES, the Brazilian government's development bank, loaned large amounts of taxpayer money to purchasers of stocks in several of the privatized companies. Cardoso's administration justified these loans with the explanation that they were necessary to ensure that Brazilian shareholders held a stake in the privatized companies, and that all would be paid back with interest. The distribution of public loans among small circles within Brazil's financial industry, however, left the administration open to charges of favoritism and collusion.

Privatization also failed to reduce public debt, one of the initial selling points for the policy. The success of the *Real* Plan and subsequent economic growth made public debt less onerous. External debt gradually fell, while internal debt grew, and this has arguably been part of the process of economic diversification that has characterized Brazil since the mid-1990s. But the growth of public debt, in spite of privatization, provided fuel for charges that the policy benefited wealthy investors at the expense of the Brazilian public.

Cardoso's biggest mistake, however, was in pushing for re-election, requiring a constitutional amendment. Amending the constitution had already become common under Cardoso's predecessors, and the issue of presidential terms and succession was already a topic of wide public debate in the Sarney years. But Cardoso had been a delegate in the 1988 convention. He had his opportunity then to speak in favor of re-election, and did not. To turn around a decade later and insist on it, for his own personal advantage, was correctly condemned as sheer hypocrisy. Cardoso's amendment allowed re-election of governors as well as the president, but there was never any doubt that it was written for the immediate benefit of one man, in order to obstruct another.

Again, Cardoso failed to make a persuasive political case for reform. Instead, he wooed parties in the governing coalition through distribution of government offices and promised spending. Governors who had their own interests in re-election also used their powers of the purse to influence legislators in favor of the amendment. Opponents alleged that Cardoso's staff was offering cash payments to congressmen, and Cardoso used his political leverage to quash a proposed investigation of the allegations. The amendment passed, at huge political costs.

Cardoso's second term, typical of second terms, fulfilled few of his expectations, and saw the emergence of a new crop of problems. Cardoso settled for a minor, largely symbolic reform of the pension system, and gave up on other proposed reforms. The international currency crisis devalued the *real*, undermining Cardoso's reputation for economic competence, and the power shortages of 2001 provoked popular resentment. These failures played directly into the hands of Lula and the PT.

The Lula years

Lula the candidate of 2002 had changed dramatically from the fiery strikeleader of 1979 and also from the unpolished debater of 1989. He hired Duda Mendonça, one of Brazil's most successful advertising executives, to run his campaign. Mendonça emphasized Lula's triumph over childhood adversity, his participation in the struggle for redemocratization, and his enduring commitment to an ideal of social justice. He also coached Lula in the presentation of a "Letter to the Brazilian People" that contained a coded but clear message of reassurance to Wall Street. The letter indicted the failures of neoliberalism and blamed them entirely on the Cardoso administration, but it also guaranteed that all existing contracts would be respected, and that Lula would make no rash economic moves – implying clearly that he would not indulge expropriationist fantasies. Mendonça's strategy proved highly successful – Lula came across as the man of the people prepared to balance economic growth and social responsibility, and his opponent, José Serra of the PSDB, came across as a soulless technocrat, compromised by his alliance with Cardoso.

Once elected, Lula fulfilled the economic promises of his letter, largely following Cardoso's economic strategy. He named Antonio Palocci, former mayor of the agroindustrial interior city of Ribeirão Preto, as his finance minister and insulated him from the political demands of the statist wing of the PT, led by his chief of staff, José Dirceu. Palocci and the Central Bank steered an orthodox macroeconomic course, keeping interest rates high to guard against inflation and maintaining a favorable balance of payments.

These policies generated considerable grumbling within the PT, but only a more targeted blow would provoke open dissidence. Like Cardoso, Lula attempted to reform Brazil's pension system. Some 75 percent of Brazil's pension payments go to retired federal workers, who make up only 15 percent of the retired work force. The majority of the recipients are members of the middle class, and many continue to work off the books. This pension load generates an annual deficit of approximately $30 billion dollars, which is covered through regressive taxes, such as high sales and value-added taxes.[7] Both Cardoso and Lula saw pension reform as a necessary step to balancing payments and freeing up funding for directing social spending to those farther down the economic ladder – both central tenets of third-way strategy. Cardoso's attempted pension reform had largely failed. Lula tried in 2003, and found himself facing an uprising from a third of the PT's congressmen.

Dirceu rode hard on the dissidents by kicking four of their leaders out of the party and demanding obedience from the rest. Heloísa Helena, one of the banished four, left in tears, publicly mourning what she charged to be the PT's betrayal of its socialist ideals. She and her co-religionaries founded the upstart PSOL in response. The remaining PT congressmen fell into line, and Lula managed to pass a mild and largely ineffectual reform.

Lula attempted to carve out a presidential identity with a program called Fome Zero, or Zero Hunger, intended to eradicate malnutrition in Brazil. Fome Zero was a continuation of anti-hunger campaigns mobilized by Betinho in the early 1990s. Duda Mendonça envisioned the program as a brilliant marketing strategy but it soon proved misguided. Studies by the Instituto Brasileiro de Geografia e Estatística (IBGE), a government-funded demographic institution, showed that hunger in Brazil was no longer a pervasive problem. The IBGE found that the proportion of the Brazilian population that could be considered clinically underweight, reflecting chronic malnourishment, did not exceed that in many "developed" countries.[8] Obese Brazilians vastly outnumbered hungry Brazilians. The findings were a surprise to most observers, and showed that Brazil's growth in the period of redemocratization, the anti-hunger campaigns of the early 1990s and the improved social spending of more recent years had yielded concrete results. A few impoverished counties in the northeast needed hunger relief, but the majority of Brazilians needed education, health care and employment opportunities – not direct food aid.

Lula beat a hasty retreat from Fome Zero and invested in social programs similar to Cardoso's, increasing their resources. Where Cardoso had experimented with affirmative action, Lula created a Special Secretariat for the Promotion of Policies for Racial Equality (SEPPIR), headed by veterans of Brazil's black movement, to expand and administer these programs. Where Cardoso had increased environmental reserves, Lula named the environmental activist Marina Silva his Minister of the Environment. Where Cardoso had initiated land reform, Lula stepped up the rate of redistribution. In all these cases, Lula's social programs differed from Cardoso's primarily in their connections to the NGOs seeking to represent afro-descendant students, landless farmers and other popular sectors. Lula increased the direct transfer of resources and planning to these NGOs, strengthening their historic alliance with the PT.

Lula's most successful social program has been *Bolsa Família*, the new name for his greatly expanded version of Cardoso's Bolsa Escola. Cardoso's pilot program reached some 2 million families by the end of his administration. By 2006, Bolsa Família reached 11 million families, comprising over 40 million people, or nearly one-quarter of the total population of Brazil. Amazingly, distribution of resources has been well targeted. The rapid expansion of the program in 2003–04 created a variety of anomalies, including distribution of funds to families above the poverty line and failure to require school attendance. But a new administrative team cracked down on the municipal middlemen monitoring local execution, creating a highly efficient program. According to World Bank analysis, by 2006 the program's "leakage" – the amount of funding going to families above the poverty line – had been reduced to 6 percent, a level lower than any comparable global program.[9]

Bolsa Família's monthly stipends – ranging from approximately $20 dollars to $100 dollars a month, depending on level of need – have pulled millions of families above the poverty line, at least temporarily. Opponents have raised four criticisms: they have assailed targeting problems, complained that there is no "exit door" for the program, argued that the program may prevent the poor from looking for work, and alleged that it is primarily an electoral program for Lula. Improved targeting has at least temporarily resolved the first issue, although making sure it does not recur is a different matter. The criticism that there is no "exit door" bears slightly more weight – beyond getting poor children to the schoolhouse door, a policy with only medium-term prospects for improving economic fortunes, the program has no direct impact on their economic opportunities. This is related to the "moral hazard" criticism, suggesting that recipients will relax in the comfort of their $100 monthly stipend and feel no need to find gainful employment. Initial research suggests the opposite may be true: the small monthly stipend, by meeting a basic level of need, may be allowing very poor mothers to leave dangerous informal occupations like tending charcoal kilns or picking through garbage piles in order to search for more remunerative, regular employment. These results suggest that although the program has no "exit door," it may well facilitate the emergence from poverty, or at least from degradation, of many families.[10]

The charge of political use of federal social spending is correct but not damning. Bolsa Família has turned the PT into a political force in the northeast, where it was once weak. But social spending has always been used for electoral purposes, and Bolsa Família has attracted electoral sympathy primarily because it has worked well.

Bolsa Família has flaws. It has brought children to the schoolhouse door, but it has not given them a good education. The Brazilian public educational system is in tatters, with overcrowded classrooms, undertrained teachers and short schooldays – primary school entails about three half-hours of classroom time per day. Education itself urgently needs more funding and better administration. Critics who suggest that Bolsa Família pulls funding away from schools, however, would do better to look for fat in the rest of the federal, state and municipal budgets. Bolsa Família is far from a revolutionary solution to poverty and inequality, but it is a well-executed program, at least in its current manifestation.

Lula's scandals

Bolsa Família's electoral implications proved necessary for Lula, for a wave of scandals within his administration cost him the support of much of the educated southeastern electorate that had voted for him in 2002. The first scandal broke before his election: in January 2002, Celso Daniel, the PT mayor of Santo André, a city on São Paulo's industrial periphery, was kidnapped and murdered. The crime had all the characteristics of a *"queima de arquivo,"* or archive burning, undertaken to eliminate a witness. Daniel's brother revealed that, as mayor, Daniel had initially presided over a kickback scheme extorting payments from local bus companies, and then had attempted to shut the scheme down. According to Daniel's brother, the mayor had kept careful records of the bribes showing that the payments were organized by Dirceu's wing of the PT. Several rounds of police investigation resulted neither in official charges nor in a convincing explanation of the murder.

In 2004, a numbers runner and bingo-parlor operator from Rio de Janeiro covertly recorded Waldomiro Diniz, José Dirceu's assistant, extorting cash in return for political protection. Diniz was fired, and Dirceu and Lula claimed ignorance.

Months later, businessmen bidding on contracts with the Brazilian Post Office secretly videotaped a post office administrator pocketing a cash bribe. The administrator claimed to be representing Roberto Jefferson, a key member of Lula's governing alliance: Jefferson negotiated the loyalty of congressmen from the Partido Trabalhista Brasileiro, a notoriously physiological party, in return for the power to control appointments and expenditures in the post office, among other perquisites.

Jefferson shocked Brazil by admitting the charges and revealing a broader scheme. According to Jefferson, the PT paid members of its allied base a monthly allowance – the *mensalão*, or big monthly – in exchange for votes in favor of PT legislation. Jefferson reported regular payments of $15,000 dollars, with larger sums for particularly sensitive projects. His allegations led to the discovery of extensive corruption. Opposition politicians testified that leaders of the governing base had offered them substantial payments to jump parties, promising the *mensalão* plus an annual bonus of $500,000.

According to Brazil's chief prosecutor – a politically independent position – the PT had moved hundreds of millions of dollars in bribes through fake public relations contracts. After months of investigation, the chief prosecutor presented a detailed description of a criminal network operating in the highest offices of national government. Money came into PT coffers via kickbacks on government contracts, was laundered in the form of bogus contracts for advertising campaigns, and was paid under the table to allied politicians. The indictment did not entirely substantiate Jefferson's claim of regular monthly payments, but did reveal an extensive pattern of payoffs in return for political favors.

Every member in Lula's immediate circle was implicated in the scandal. José Dirceu was indicted as the ringleader of the criminal network. José Delúbio, the PT's treasurer, admitted that the PT's campaign books were systematically fraudulent. Duda Mendonça admitted to receiving millions of dollars in covert payments deposited in foreign bank accounts. José Genoino, president of the PT, was implicated when his brother's assistant was arrested boarding an airplane with $50,000 stuffed in his underpants. Luiz Gushiken, Minister of Communication and one of Lula's closest advisers, was indicted for directing funds from Banco do Brasil contractors into the mensalão.

Over thirty other high-ranking members of the PT and allied parties were indicted for their roles in the scheme. Late in 2007, Brazil's Supreme Federal Court upheld all the indictments, agreeing to hear the cases, in accordance with the schedule allowed by the slow and grinding wheels of Brazilian justice.

The tawdriest case was that of Antonio Palocci. His former assistants from Ribeirão Preto alleged that he had run a similar scheme, using kickbacks from government contractors to grease the wheels of municipal politics and to contribute to Lula's 2002 campaign. Their testimony led to the revelation that Palocci's colleagues from Ribeirão Preto had rented a mansion in Brasília where government contractors wooed elected officials at lavish parties hosted by prostitutes. Palocci denied knowing about the mansion, but Francenildo Santos Costa, the mansion's handyman, testified to seeing Palocci there regularly and described the parties. Palocci's allies illegally acquired Costa's bank records and passed them on to Palocci himself. The records showed an unusual deposit in the weeks preceding Costa's testimony, and Palocci's allies quickly leaked them to the press, implying that the opposition was paying Costa for his testimony. Subsequent investigation showed that Costa's father had made the deposit, for family reasons. It became clear that Palocci, star of the Workers' Party, had pulled the strings at his disposal in order to crush a humble worker whose only offense was his honesty.

The PSDB, the principal opposition party, hardly came off as innocent. Investigation of the mensalão showed that Eduardo Azeredo, president of the PSDB, had operated similar schemes during his failed campaign for re-election as Governor of Minas Gerais in 1998. The PSDB accused Lula of running the most corrupt administration in Brazil's history, but took no steps to sanction Azeredo.

As his ministers fell one after the other, Lula insisted that he was unaware of everything that had gone on around him. This tepid defense served its purpose. Subsequent opinion polls showed that Brazilians tended to chalk up the mensalão scandal to the inevitably dirty nature of politics, and not to hold Lula responsible. Nevertheless, with much of his inner circle driven from office, he needed to shore up relationships with allied parties. He did so in the same way Cardoso had done, by strengthening his alliance with the regional machines, reaching out to the powerbrokers that the PT had once abhorred. Fernando Collor, for example, his political rights restored, was elected senator from Alagoas in 2006. In an irony that demonstrated the strange twists of Brazilian politics in the early twenty-first century, he won the seat vacated by Heloísa Helena for her presidential run. Lula welcomed him into the governing alliance.

Lula also reached out to Paulo Maluf, negotiating ministerial posts with Maluf's party. He was most effusive in his praise of Jader Barbalho, a PMDB congressman from Amazonas. Barbalho had a long history of dubious use of political power, culminating in a scandal in 2001–02 involving millions of dollars skimmed from a federal agency created to promote sustainable development in the Amazon. In one of the scandal's most colorful details, Barbalho and his family collected 5 million dollars to create a frog-breeding farm. At the time, Lula and the PT had condemned Barbalho as the epitome of everything that was wrong with the Cardoso administration. Following the mensalão scandal, Lula welcomed Barbalho into the fold, claiming that he was a progressive congressman who had been unjustly treated.[11]

The new right

Maluf, Collor and Barbalho had once been considered the right wing of Brazilian politics, but they happily allied with the PT when convenient. Cardoso, safely out of office, remarked on the implications of these opportunistic affiliations: "There is no right in Brazil, in the classic sense of the term. Conservative thought allies itself to a Western tradition that establishes as its pillars family, property, customs. Our conservatism has none of that. It is all to do with clientelism [...] the untoward use of the resources of the state. [...] Why has the Brazilian 'right' supported every administration? In recent history, it supported the military regime, it supported Sarney, it supported Collor, it supported me, and it supports Lula. Because its members are not of the right. Those people just want to be close to the state and extract advantages from it."[12]

This helps explain how first Cardoso and then Lula managed

to govern with a fractious Congress and also why their legislative agendas were more modest than many hoped: the regional machines are not necessarily ideologically conservative, but they are highly effective at conserving their own power, blunting proposals for thoroughgoing reform through their own mediation.

Cardoso nonetheless overstated the absence of an ideological right, or at least focused his comments too narrowly. There is a Brazilian right, but not in electoral politics. Instead, the right's greatest expression is in the diverse Brazilian media. Inflammatory allegations to the contrary notwithstanding, the Brazilian media are neither lapdogs of the PT nor tools of retrograde oligarchs. These allegations are themselves evidence of the breadth of perspectives available, if not their depth.

The rise of Lula and PT to executive power has occasioned the corresponding return of a phenomenon not seen in Brazil since the days of Goulart, an oppositional rightwing media. *Veja* magazine is the only organ that has adopted this position as a consistent editorial line, without identifying itself as rightwing, which is the kiss of death in the Brazilian market. But other major organs, including the *Folha de São Paulo*, a paper strongly linked to the push for redemocratization, have also provided space for voices of the new right.

Representatives of the new right cannot be considered an alliance – there are too many disagreements among them. But they share identifying characteristics: they are self-consciously erudite and urbane in their cultural references, they eschew any ties with the "old right" of the regional political machines, and they denounce in particular the overlapping of state power, progressive ideology and patronage. As such, they have become a considerable thorn in Lula's side.

Foremost in that regard is Diogo Mainardi, a sarcastic columnist for *Veja*. Although he identifies himself as a humorist, his political columns have served as a rallying cry for the PT's opponents. Reinaldo Azevedo, a fellow columnist at *Veja* and a blogger at the magazine's website, is the most prolific figure of the new right, blogging thousands of words a day, most of them indicting a leftwing takeover of the machinery of the state. Like several of his colleagues,

Azevedo is a former radical marxist who renounced the affiliations of his youth to become a fiery proponent of the "liberal right."

In this and in other ways, Azevedo follows the example of Olavo de Carvalho, the gray eminence of the new right. Carvalho attributes much of the left's political rise to the São Paulo Forum, a semi-annual congress of Latin American leftist organizations founded by the PT in the early 1980s. The São Paulo Forum has included Lula's PT, Fidel Castro, Hugo Chávez, Evo Morales, Colombia's FARC, Chile's MIR, and a host of other organizations, and Carvalho argues that it has enabled these organizations to extend their power through hemispheric strategies, including the orchestration of apparent disagreements among them. Lula himself has expressed considerable pride over the São Paulo Forum's achievements, but his role as one of its founders undoubtedly influences that appreciation.[13] Carvalho's analysis of the São Paulo Forum has failed to convince many Brazilians, but his denunciations of Brazil's cultural shift have proven more influential.

More moderate figures of the new right include Ali Kamel, executive producer of Globo's *Jornal Nacional* and a frequent contributor to Globo's daily newspaper. Kamel has been an influential critic of expanding racial preference programs in Brazilian universities and elsewhere. Denis Lerrer Rosenfield, a philosophy professor at the Universidade Federal do Rio Grande do Sul, has dedicated much of his recent career to denouncing the MST's revolutionary rhetoric and its strategy of land invasions. Demétrio Magnoli, a geographer at the University of São Paulo and frequent contributor to the *Folha de São Paulo*, has joined Kamel in criticism of compensatory race-based government programs. These figures criticize identity politics and the incorporation of identity-based civil-society organizations into the PT and, by extension, into the workings of the federal government.

This loose network of writers poses an intellectual challenge to the Brazilian left's current pre-eminence, but not an electoral one. The withering sarcasm that typifies the new right is a not a big draw at the voting booth, making it unlikely that any national politician will explicitly seek the alliance of figures like Mainardi and Azevedo in the near future. The rapid growth of the new right's exposure in the wake of the mensalão, however, points to an important counter-trend signaling that the rise of the left may already have hit its high watermark.

On balance

In the late 1990s Luis Carlos Bresser Pereira, Sarney's former finance minister, argued that Cardoso's administration was not really social-democratic, but social-liberal.[14] In his approving analysis, this meant that Cardoso was committed both to liberalization of trade and to redistributive social programs. Bresser Pereira, expressing the consensus of the moment, suggested that there was little alternative to this path, and Lula's continuation of Cardoso's macroeconomic strategy and his major social programs seem to endorse that understanding. But to describe either Cardoso or Lula's administration merely as social-liberal would be to overlook the persistence of the regional machines. In this regard, both recent administrations can be described as social-liberal in their ideology, but operating physiologically, through the regional machines, in their strategy. The internal contradictions of this necessarily inelegant description capture the tensions of redemocratizing Brazil.

The general continuity in policies between the Cardoso and Lula administrations does not mean that they are roughly the same. The mensalão, despite its use of traditional means, constituted something substantially new – the attempt to use bribery to create a fictive representative democracy masking the growing control of a single party over the machinery of the state. Exposure of the mensalão beat back this threat, but only temporarily. A more secure defense against it will require the continued strengthening of institutions that are not subject to the tides of party politics.

The Washington Consensus appears to have entered its decline, and the social liberalism enacted through physiological tactics produced when that consensus was mapped onto longstanding features of the Brazilian political landscape may go with it. But this odd hybrid has a great deal of inertia, and the political panorama has offered little in the way of a real alternative. It bears noting that the PSOL has its origins neither in objection to PT corruption nor in objection to Lula's support of export-oriented agribusiness, for example. Instead, the PSOL originated with its founders' defense of the pension system for government employees created by Vargas and expanded by the dictatorship, an entitlement program accruing to a relatively small but politically powerful segment of the population. The PSOL's rhetoric responds to the decline of the Washington Consensus, but the policies it advocates have been designed to appease entrenched interest groups.

The combination of emphasis on growing global trade, moderate social reforms and negotiation with regional political machines is not what opponents of the dictatorship had in mind as they planned their strategies for redemocratization in the 1970s. But for all its shortcomings, it has made some notable achievements: while inequality remains a defining characteristic of Brazilian life, the combination of economic growth and improved social spending has pulled millions above the poverty line. And Brazilians have, in fits and starts, begun to strengthen their ability to demand accountability from elected officials.

In consequence, the leftward turn that has characterized Latin American politics early in the twenty-first century has been both more profound and less disruptive in Brazil than in neighbors such as Venezuela, Bolivia and Ecuador. The turbulence of gradual redemocratization over the course of the 1980s created an inclusive political arena. Divisions between the factions competing for primacy in this arena are real and deeply felt, but not as extreme as those in neighboring countries, where the steps taken towards full political inclusion have come more recently, and more contentiously.

2 | Urban crisis

In May 2006, a criminal network known as the Primeiro Comando da Capital (PCC), or First Command of the Capital, demonstrated its ability to bring São Paulo to a halt. (The city of São Paulo is capital of the state of the same name, explaining the group's name.) The PCC staged a wave of bus burnings, drive-by shootings and assassinations of police officers and firemen that intimidated residents of the city into hunkering behind barred doors. During the day, few buses circulated and few businesses opened. At night, the streets of what is normally a twenty-four-hour city were deserted. After three days, gang leaders called the proceedings to a halt, the shootings stopped, and *paulistanos* resumed their normal lives. In the meantime, the police had engaged in a spate of retributive violence, killing over thirty alleged gang members in approximately forty-eight hours.

Seven months later, in December 2006, another criminal network, known as the Comando Vermelho (CV), or Red Command, did the same thing in Rio de Janeiro. Typically, the action seemed less organized in Rio, but no less terrifying. Again, after a wave of exemplary violence, the attacks stopped suddenly and *cariocas*, or residents of Rio, returned to the streets.

In São Paulo, the attacks supposedly responded to transfer of the PCC's imprisoned leaders to higher-security facilities, where they would be unable to use their cellphones. Reports also connected the attacks to the PCC's demands for the approval of shipping plasma-screen TVs into the prisons for their World Cup viewing. This concession had initially been granted and then revoked after one TV crate fell open to reveal a cache of rifles. In Rio de Janeiro, the attacks were supposedly meant as a warning to the incoming governor, Sérgio Cabral, to intimidate him into carrying out the same ineffective security policy as his predecessors.

In both cases, however, the attacks served primarily to demonstrate power. This is our city, the networks seemed to say, and we'll shut it down when we wish. A few policy analysts have suggested that the São Paulo attacks were a sign of the success of new security programs in the city, where homicides have dropped precipitously since 2002. In this view, the PCC was waging a last-ditch attempt to retake territory on the city's periphery from which it had been driven by improved policing. Other analysts suggested the attacks had neither a direct cause nor a clear intent, but served primarily to create the atmosphere of urban apprehension in which the networks' economic activities – robbery, kidnapping, drugdealing – best flourished.

The most persuasive explanation, however, looks beyond these questions of PCC and CV strategy to consider the logic of security and violence in Brazil's cities more generally. Factional competition in the electoral arena has its more violent reflection in the urban arena, where interest groups do battle over urban turf. These groups include the police, or sectors within it, collectives and cooperatives of vendors and service providers, and criminal gangs, which themselves are loosely knit into networks. The competition for control of urban space and commercial opportunities between these interest groups generates temporary alliances and shifting loyalties, which in turn provoke moments of crisis. At any given moment, competing interest groups see an advantage in creating crisis, and the 2006 attacks were particularly flagrant examples of these sporadic events.

The result is the proliferation of violence and fortification in Brazilian cities. São Paulo and Rio de Janeiro are cosmopolitan cities offering a full range of urban delights, from world-class theater, art and cuisine to vibrant local culture. They are places where it is possible to live a rewarding daily life of sociability with fellow metropolitans, collectively savoring the democratic opportunities of the urban sphere. But they are also places of fear and distrust, where the police are expected to be violent and the *bandidos* expected to be ruthless. The same could be said of Belo Horizonte, Salvador, Recife and Brazil's other large cities, although concentrating on Rio and São Paulo, the largest and most influential metropolitan regions, will help clarify the nature of Brazil's urban crisis, and the steps being taken to confront it.

Violence and fear have not always been so prevalent in Rio and

São Paulo, and older residents of these cities from all classes fondly reminisce about a period when carjackings, kidnappings, stickups and shakedowns were not a fact of everyday life. Yet as with most historical transitions, the seeds of Brazil's sporadic urban crises were planted and germinated decades, and in some aspects centuries, earlier. They have sprouted and proliferated since the 1970s in part because of urban growth itself. Brazil is now decidedly an urban nation: over 80 percent of Brazilians live in cities, and most live in cities of over a million inhabitants. Rural Brazilians were drawn to the city in the mid-twentieth century and beyond by land concentration in rural Brazil, by low growth in provincial secondary cities, by higher wages in the metropolis, and by the allure of urban culture and mobility. Pell-mell urbanization has strained antiquated urban infrastructure. Insufficient housing, education, and basic services have contributed to the growth of cities characterized by severe inequalities, undermining any sustainable social compact. But growing violence over the past decades also stems from more immediate political causes, and these are more subject to short-term reform. In parts of São Paulo, where broad coalitions have carried out such reforms, there are signs for cautious optimism.

Roots

Colonial Brazilian cities were relatively unplanned in comparison with their Spanish American neighbors. Spanish American capitals had neat grids centered around civic plazas, with Indian quarters clearly defined, and commercial streets defined by sector. Brazilian cities grew relatively organically, expanding geographically, in keeping with the hierarchical arrangements of their leading families. These families directed networks of dependents, some of them intimate enough to live in the family's primary household or at least within its boundaries, others clustered nearby, others stretched farther afield by virtue of their occupations. The overlapping and intermingling of these family networks, plotted onto an expanding urban territory, produced an organic order not easily scrutable to the naked eye. In place of the grids and well-defined functions and sectors, Brazilian cities tended to produce a jumble of mixed functions and intimate proximities across social divides.

This produced a landholding system where boundaries were not clear and where expectations about land use were agreed to informally. While this organic nature produced a wide variety of uses, it also yielded a system where the obstacles to achieving full citizenship – to being a full participant in urban life, sharing in the rights and guarantees of the city – were often all the harder to overcome for being unspoken.

Properties deemed worth passing on – the elite townhouse, the merchant warehouse – were titled and protected in accordance with the written law. Properties deemed contingent – the shack in the backlot built by and for slaves, the basement room let to poor laborers – existed at the pleasure of the property-owner. In cases where there was no clear property-owner – the fisherman's hut on the beach, for example – the most powerful local figure exercised effective jurisdiction.

Brazil's independence from Portugal in 1822 did nothing to alter this coexistence of formal and informal arrangements, where informality implied dependence. The expansion of urban slavery through the nineteenth century increased the complexity of these networks of patronage in Brazil's cities. The abolition of slavery in 1888 turned urban slaves into the free urban poor without fundamentally altering either spatial arrangements or the distribution of rights to the city. The free poor were made to know through a thousand unspoken gestures where they were not welcome, and the police stood ready to remind them if necessary.

The declaration of the republic in 1889 created newly perceived needs for urban codification, at a time when the urban population was growing rapidly due to the influx of freed slaves and the arrival of European immigrants, to be followed shortly by Middle Eastern and Japanese immigrations. Increased codification tended to benefit those who already had a legal stake in property-holding, not those who had been subsisting on the informal concessions of patrons.

The urban growth and reorganization of the young republic did not create urban informality, but led to a growing perception of informality – arrangements once deemed natural were beginning to be recognized as disorderly. The settlement in Rio de Janeiro of hundreds of decommissioned soldiers at the turn of the century increased that perception. The soldiers had fought in the campaign to reduce the millenarian settlement of Canudos, in the northeast. After the campaign and return to Rio de Janeiro, they were released but given no resources to make a stake for themselves in the city. Many built shacks on the Morro da Providência, Providence Hill, overlooking downtown. Local custom counts this as "the first favela." In truth, there were several origins for the informal settlements that later became known as favelas. Some grew directly from former quilombos, others grew next to quarries and farms on the urban fringe. But Providência, because of its prominence, achieved an iconic status.

The republic cemented the distinction between formal and informal, and facilitated the rise of localized networks of power in informal territories. That combination of informality and local strongmen intertwined with the city's economic diversification. Many favelas grew next to factories, for example. The favela of Borel, in Rio de Janeiro, grew on a hill next to cigarette and textile factories, where many of the residents worked. A series of local strongmen claiming predominance over the hill extracted monthly rents in exchange for the right to occupy plots on the hill. Though none of these strongmen had legal title, they bought and sold the land, or the rights to exploit it, from one another. In the late 1950s, a realty company with a stronger but far from watertight legal claim to the land attempted to evict the residents. With the help of a communist lawyer, the residents fought back, winning a series of injunctions. This legal fight, while critical, never yielded a decisive victory – the favelados never won title to their own land – and was always secondary to the fact on the ground of occupied space.

Borel's struggles were typical of those of favelados across Rio, and in Brazil's other large cities, as well. In this fashion, Brazil produced a class of working poor with highly constricted access to the benefits of citizenship. The rights to own property, occupy public space and attend public schools were not conceded in any consistent way to Brazil's urban poor.[15] As a rule, these benefits, where they existed, were granted not as rights but as concessions that might be withdrawn without notice – and often were.

Justiceiros and the CV

During the "Populist Republic" – the period between the fall of the Estado Novo in 1945 and the beginning of the military dictatorship in 1964 – the inherent tensions in this arrangment became more evident. For the first time, the popular press began to expose and disparage habitual police brutality. Rather than clean up their act, police increasingly engaged in extrajudicial violence while ostensibly off duty. Alleged bandidos were found dead by the side of the road, often with their supposed crime scrawled on a note attached to the body: "I robbed." "I raped." Residents of the neighborhoods where these assassinations were carried out learned to attribute them to the *justiceiros*, the justicemakers, or the Esquadrão da Morte – the Death Squad.

The implicit acceptance of these tactics bred police forces known for their investigative inefficiency and corruption. Confessions could usually be beaten out of a suspect, making investigation a luxury, and the habitual use of force cultivated intimidation. Powerful criminals, particularly the *bicheiros*, or numbers-runners, paid off the police rather than risk their retribution.

The inauguration of the dictatorship in 1964 and its increasing severity later in the decade added a new wrinkle. The regime's police arrested not only common criminals, but underground organizers and radicals who practiced bank robbery and kidnapping to further revolutionary goals. The prisons of Rio de Janeiro and São Paulo became academies where members of these factions traded expertise.

The Ilha Grande facility, in particular – an island prison off the southern coast of Rio de Janeiro state – gave rise to a new kind of organization. The political prisoners of Ilha Grande commingled with common thieves in a prison where food was often scarce and the most powerful prisoners determined the pecking order. The political prisoners drew on their experience in the field to organize a faction of the thieves, creating a group powerful enough to defend its own interests and to exert leverage for concessions. The outnumbered authorities, in turn, were interested in keeping the peace within the prison, and made few moves to check the growth of the group. The group charged members lucky enough to win release or to escape with sending funds to improve its fortunes within the prison. The Comando Vermelho (CV) was born.

Bank robbery became the specialty of CV ex-cons and escaped prisoners, who gravitated to the city of Rio de Janeiro in particular. CV operations of the 1970s and early 1980s were characterized by planning, precision and efficiency – involving the simultaneous robbery of two neighboring banks, for example. The leadfooted, stonefisted police could not keep up. The gang modernized and the police did not.[16]

The CV and smaller gangs began to put down roots where police authority was weakest, in neighborhoods that had been most frequently subject to police brutality and where rights to the city had been in shortest supply. As the dictatorship stumbled towards an opening, the criminal networks began mapping themselves onto the geography of the city. The gradual growth of these networks put a premium on order that could not be guaranteed by the police. Shopkeepers and commercial suppliers increasingly turned to private security, provided overwhelmingly by off-duty police, to protect their interests. The inefficiency of the police helped create a demand for their more lucrative off-duty occupation, one less subject to the restraints of the law.

Redemocratization

All these pieces were in place before the close of the dictatorship, but their implications were not fully evident as long as the regime could rely on military intimidation to keep the lid on disorder. Redemocratization allowed suppressed tensions to emerge. In Rio de Janeiro, this created the opportunity both for grassroots mobilization of favelados in pursuit of rights to the city and, perversely, the increasing entrenchment of criminal networks in favela territories.

From the early 1960s through the 1980s, the local Associação dos Moradores, or residents' association – a mainstay of every favela – was the arena of local political power and the proving ground for home-grown activists. Officeholders perceived the associations as a brake against radicalism, and hoped that they would serve as the compliant intermediaries of official will. Their sentiments were embodied in the phrase "we need to go up the hill before the hill comes down to us," a suggestion that only a program of moderate reforms could prevent favelas from growing into hotbeds of communist agitation. The evolution of the associations in the 1960s disappointed these expectations, as they began to concentrate and direct resistance against state measures.

The campaign to wipe out South Zone favelas and relocate their residents in the early 1960s spurred this transformation. A few key squatter settlements were eradicated, but in other targeted favelas, association leaders mobilized followers to resist attempts at removal. In reaction to the eradication campaign, several associations banded together in 1962 to create the Federação das Associações das Favelas do Estado da Guanabara (FAFEG). This umbrella group faced intermittent crackdowns in the mid-1960s, but returned as FAFERJ during the early stages of redemocratization with a slight name change. Following the "fusion" of Guanabara and Rio de Janeiro states, it became known as FAFERJ. Due in part to successful grassroots mobilization by FAFERJ, wholesale eradication of favelas was understood to be off the table as a political option by the early 1980s.

The associations emerged from the removal campaign interested in permanence above all else, and directed all political energy towards this goal. This strategy bore fruit over the 1980s, through the combination of communal work drives in the favelas and savvy vote-bargaining in the electoral arena. In many cases this exclusive focus on permanence left the associations at a loss by the late 1980s, when permanence had been assured and favelas faced urgent new problems that the associations proved unable to address.

Favela activists negotiated the re-emergence of party politics in the 1980s in different ways, with most affiliating with Brizola's PDT (Partido Democrático Trabalhador). The growth of the PDT offered new opportunities for engagement with city and state government, removing the imperative for the grassroots mobilization that had characterized the early 1980s. By the mid-1990s, favelados looked to association presidents to bring in and maintain infrastructure, expecting the association to function as a local branch of city and state government.

In most favelas, the residents' association entered into steep decline in the 1990s, both in its levels of popular mobilization and in its ability to make and enforce decisions. Yet even in favelas where the association was widely regarded as decadent, it maintained its function as gatekeeper and dealmaker. Outsiders wishing to enter a favela for reasons other than purchasing drugs or attending a funk dance were expected to request permission in advance from the association, an unwritten code that applied to local politicians, social scientists, and public health officials. As a result, the association president typically maintained significant leverage over a favela's political connections. While that leverage was often attenuated by the local drug gang's implicit control over the association, it was still through the association that the favela was linked to broader institutions of political power.

The associations increasingly became a conduit for state and city funding. Although association presidents are usually unpaid and have minimal funds in their own treasury, they have the power to direct public resources, choosing the local city-funded trash collectors, nursery-school teachers, public health agents and environmental stewards. By the 1990s, international aid – particularly the celebrated Favela-Bairro program, discussed below – became a lucrative source of this kind of local appointment.

The result was a marked funneling of the political process. Favelas, previously beyond the practical bounds of urban administration, developed closer ties to city and state government, but rather than resulting in widespread democratic participation, this link continued to transfer political leverage to a few individuals.

The drug trade and organized crime

Over the course of the 1980s, the expansion of the CV and the political evolution of the favelas were yoked together by a third phenomenon, the rise of cocaine trafficking. Changing patterns of international policing in the early 1980s made Rio de Janeiro increasingly important as an export node for cocaine produced in Bolivia and Colombia. The availability of cocaine triggered the growth of a local market. Favelas, with their territorial advantages, became favored sites for the packaging and distribution of the product. The CV moved into the cocaine trade, using its profits to strengthen its ability to purchase arms and bribe police. In 1987, a week-long turf battle in the favela of Santa Marta brought these patterns to the attention of most cariocas for the first time. Santa Marta is adjacent to the middle-class neighborhood of Botafogo – conveniently located both for the target population of the cocaine trade and for television coverage of the gangland shootouts. Journalistic coverage of the conflict made it clear that drug trafficking in the favela was no longer a homegrown phenomenon dedicated primarily to the distribution of marijuana within the neighborhood, but now involved heavily armed gangsters violently taking over key territory in order to sell cocaine. Coverage focused in particular on the recruitment and arming of local adolescents by both factions.

The notorious 1993 massacre in the North Zone favela of Vigário Geral subsequently made clear to all observers the position of the police in the rise of the drug trade. Off-duty policemen killed twenty-one residents of the favela in an act of vengeance, apparently after being cut out of their regular payment by the local gang leader. The victims were unconnected to the drug trade. Favelados looking to protect themselves from the violence of the drug trade were clearly not going to get any help from the police.

The emerging drug gangs of the 1980s recognized the residents' associations as the locus of political power and acted to control them. In many favelas, this took the form of an explicit takeover: the leader of the local gang openly nominated a candidate, successfully intimidating prospective opponents or their supporters. The victorious faction in Santa Marta's conflict, for example, nominated candidates in the ensuing election of association officers, and won easily.

The office of favela association president became one of the most dangerous positions in Rio. Presidents who resisted the drug traffic risked assassination, while those who collaborated risked retribution when rivals invaded. Over the course of the 1990s, over a hundred association presidents were killed, and as many fled their homes to avoid a similar fate. In a few favelas, such as Rio das Pedras, residents acted early and violently to keep out the drug traffic, through the creation of homegrown militias. These militias also began to wield power arbitrarily, engaging in their own turf battles.

During the 1980s and '90s, the local cells of the CV and competing

networks recruited their soldiers locally and boasted of their neighborhood ties. The figure of the "Robin Hood of the Hill" became a
notorious stereotype, as successful gang leaders paid for community
centers, sponsored funk dances and subsidized daycare centers in
order to maintain local loyalty. A more recent pattern of takeovers
has seen the rise of gangs with no residential ties to their new territory. Because the new *traficantes* are less likely to have community
ties, they are more likely to use extreme violence to maintain their
authority.

The CV and rival networks have played a less obvious role in
regulating local commerce. Local cells often heavily tax storeowners
and service providers. Suppliers of canisters for the gas-fired cook-
stoves common in favelas, for example, regularly pay a duty on each
canister, a fee that can funnel thousands of dollars a week into the
gang's coffers. Businesses on adjacent streets are equally subject to
extortion. In 2004 Carrefour, the international supermarket chain,
gave up its location on the outskirts of Borel, reportedly after demands from the local gang for subsidies had grown too steep. In
many locations, this chokehold on local commerce may be more
lucrative than the drug traffic itself.

The militias have engaged in similar practices, exercising monopoly control over services like van transportation and pirated cable
television within their turf. Like the traficantes, the militias frequently demand protection fees from anyone wishing to do business
in their area. The results for favelados are higher prices, less accountability and greater insecurity. The associations, either controlled by
or intimidated by these powers, offer no defense.

The militias have prospered primarily in the city's western suburbs. Not coincidentally, these suburbs are also the stronghold of
the city's numbers-running, video poker machine and bingo-parlor
cartels. The *jogo do bicho*, the numbers game or literally the animal
game, is illegal but has cultural and political roots that go back a
century. Bettors wager on specific numbers, represented by animals
– hence the name – making the details of the day's drawings both
easier to remember and more colorful. The city's principal numbers-
running cartels established close relationships with samba schools,
local politicians and police officers beginning in the 1930s, and

greatly strengthened those relationships in subsequent decades. This has given the numbers game functional immunity, punctuated by brief episodes of restriction and prosecution. In recent decades, the gambling titans have diversified into video-poker machines and bingo parlors. The former are illegal, the latter semi-regular – most bingo parlors in the city operate with dubious licenses conceded in far-flung districts. These licenses are then transferred irregularly to Rio and protected through staying orders secured from favorable judges.

It is easy to find a video-poker machine or place a bet on the numbers anywhere in Rio, but the numbers titans are particularly strong in the western suburbs, where their networks of power have overlapped with both police and militias. Rogério Andrade, hereditary chief of one of the most powerful numbers networks, was a fugitive from justice between 2003 and 2006, having been convicted of the 1998 killing of his cousin-in-law and rival outside a suburban bar. But Andrade was hardly running – he regularly traveled with an escort of off-duty policemen. His arrest in September 2006 provoked a split in Rio's state police force. By December of that year, former Police Chief Álvaro Lins was indicted for his ties to the numbers cartel, and several inspectors who had served under him were arrested. Lins himself was able to avoid imprisonment, at least temporarily – his election to state Congress in October 2006 gave him parliamentary immunity.

The turf control of both the drug-trafficking gangs and the militias has led many observers to see them as parallel powers, taking on the functions of the state in the territories they control. In this light, cariocas frequently ascribe criminal control of turf to an "absence of the state." In truth, however, the state invests strongly in many of these areas, through infrastructural projects and local jobs and education programs. Per capita investment in several prominent favelas considered strongholds of the drug traffic far exceeds that in working-class suburbs to the north and west of the city. But state and municipal investment is channeled through corrupt or weak middlemen who accommodate the turf control of the criminal interest groups. This is not an absence of the state, but a distortion of it.[17]

São Paulo

In São Paulo, similar forces produced a geographically distinct variation on these problems, and have led to strikingly different recent trends. Lacking the steep granite slopes that became home to Rio's iconic favelas, São Paulo developed in a "cup and saucer" pattern more typical of Latin America, where the cup was the city's wealthy center and the saucer its impoverished periphery. That periphery has been historically characterized by a dearth of services and by roughly built homes constructed in stages by their occupants. Since the 1980s, the cup and saucer pattern has been altered by the rise of middle-class condominiums in outlying areas, by the emergence of informal housing in neighborhoods closer to the center, and by the gradual extension of infrastructure and services to the working-class periphery. Still, the cup and saucer pattern continues to mark the city's identity.

As in Rio, tensions that accumulated throughout the dictatorship gave rise to increasing violence during the years of redemocratization, characterized by frequent recourse to extrajudicial violence on the part of the police and the rise of territorially based interest groups. The gubernatorial term of Franco Montoro from 1983 to 1986 had many of the same characteristics of that of Leonel Brizola in Rio – a progressive governor granted de facto recognition to informal settlements and sought to preside over broadened access to rights, prompting the expression of popular demands that could not be easily met, and to which future governors responded with renewed repression.

In São Paulo, where public life had never enjoyed the nurturing benefits of Rio's sea and sun, urban fortification rose to prominence earlier. Members of the middle class increasingly came to view once-thriving downtown plazas as no man's land, retreating instead to the sheltered environments of the city's new shopping malls. Instead of bringing democratic mingling into public spaces, redemocratization saw the emergence of new forms of class distinction and implicit division of space. Ibirapuera Park, the thriving green space on the western side of the city, always functioned as a counterweight to this tendency, accommodating use by paulistanos of every class. But Ibirapuera was exceptional in a city of keenly felt class barriers. As in Rio, private security enforced these boundaries, and imposing façades of concrete and barbed wire became São Paulo's new urban style.

Overcrowded prisons generated frequent power struggles among prisoners, followed by police crackdowns. In October 1992, São Paulo's military police invaded Carandiru, an enormous prison on the city's north side, to quell a riot. Before they left they had killed 111 prisoners. The Carandiru massacre, like that in Vigário Geral the following year, became a symbol of the rot and violence at the heart of Brazil's urban security strategy.

As in Rio, São Paulo's prisons gave birth to a gang that responded to dangerous conditions with a will to create discipline through intimidation. Like the CV, the PCC quickly spread beyond prison walls, using extramural crime to subsidize internal control. For the PCC, the favored tool was kidnapping, a crime that became strikingly common in São Paulo in the 1990s. The PCC honed the tactic of "lightning kidnapping," holding a victim just long enough to persuade him to use his ATM card to extract everything from his bank account, or to demand a rapid cash payment from family members. For wealthier victims, the network prepared more elaborate strategies, tracking targets for months before seizing them, secreting them in hideaways and negotiating with their families over the course of weeks.

As political prisoners had proven decisive in the early organization of the CV, an international guerrilla network offered critical strategic support for the PCC's kidnapping operations. The current leader of the PCC, Marcos Herbas Camacho, better known as Marcola, shared a cellblock with Maurício Norambuena, a Chilean revolutionary affiliated with the Frente Patriótico Manuel Rodriguez, a faction of the Chilean Communist Party that took up arms during the Pinochet dictatorship. Rodriguez was convicted of kidnapping and murder in Chile, and escaped and fought in Colombia with the FARC before making his way to Brazil. In 2001, he was arrested and convicted for the kidnapping of Washington Olivetto, one of Brazil's most successful advertising executives. In prison, Norambuena shared his experience in organizing elaborate kidnapping rings with Marcola and the PCC.

Like the CV, the PCC has combined a rhetoric of revolution with a practice of extortion and rule by intimidation. Both the CV and the PCC add the initials PJL, for Paz, Justiça e Liberdade – Peace, Justice and Liberty – to their graffiti. Marcola, in particular, has developed a reputation in some quarters as a rebel intellectual because of his choice of prison reading material, which includes Nietzsche. In the wake of the May 2006 attacks, *Caros Amigos*, a hip monthly magazine, ran an article entitled "The Ideas of Marcola."[18] The "ideas" themselves are a blend of vulgar naturalism and self-serving rationalizations, holding that young men who grow up on the margins of a radically unequal society will inevitably turn to crime, and that the PCC is above all a mutual-aid society for prisoners' defense. As such, they are indistinguishable from an overly simplistic ascription of Brazil's urban security crisis to the social causes of inequality, but their expression by a gang leader gave them a certain cachet.

The PCC can thank, in part, its associated non-governmental organization, Nova Ordem, for favorable publicity. Nova Ordem is ostensibly a prisoners'-rights NGO, but is widely acknowledged to be a legal arm of the PCC. In January 2007, its president and two of its directors were arrested for their role in the August 2006 kidnapping of Globo TV reporter Guilherme Portanova and his cameraman. Portanova was released after Globo agreed to air a five-minute PCC video, in which a hooded gunman denounces Brazil's inhumane prison conditions and threatens retribution against the governor, the police and anyone who supports them.[19]

These tactics have yielded considerable concessions in the past. A PCC-orchestrated wave of prison riots across São Paulo in 2001 resulted in several concessions by penitentiary authorities, including the *indulto*, or indulgence, a day's pass to get out of prison, granted five times a year on special occasions. The indulto is customarily conceded to all prisoners unless judges and prison officials block dispensation on a case-by-case basis. Up to 30 percent of prisoners fail to return from the indulto.

In practice, the PCC now acts to produce miserable prison conditions in order to strengthen its own position. A PCC riot in Araraquara, São Paulo, in 2006 reduced a prison to ruins. Following the riot, hundreds of prisoners grouped in a tiny recreation yard, waited for food dropped by airlift and arranged critically wounded colleagues in a circle in the center of the yard, where they waited days for relief.

Pandora's box

Outside the prisons, the tactic of burning buses seems designed to make life more difficult and terrifying for the working-class residents of the urban periphery, where most burnings have occurred. Bus burnings also help to drive customers to semi-legal van operators, a rapidly expanding sector of public transportation and one in which both major criminal networks are heavily involved. The vans prove no safer, as they are not designed for mass transportation and frequently violate traffic laws. Increasingly, however, there is no alternative, as bus companies abandon money-losing routes in peripheral neighborhoods and limit themselves to central routes.

Van cooperatives in both cities cultivate close ties to powerful parties. In São Paulo, Congressman Jilmar Tatto rose through the ranks of the PT based partly on his ability to mobilize van cooperatives on the eastern rim of the city. Tatto is one of ten brothers, most of whom are active in politics, and who have constructed a powerful branch of the PT in the city's eastern suburbs. He served as municipal secretary of transportation in the mayoral administration of the PT's Marta Suplicy, between 2001 and 2004. Tatto sought to bring the van cooperatives into the formal sector, ending the legal monopoly of the bus companies. He broke the city into eight zones and contracted with separate van cooperatives to provide service in each zone. Several of the van cooperatives were widely believed to be linked to the PCC.

In March 2006, Luiz Carlos Efigênio Pacheco, the president of Cooper Pam, the largest cooperative, was arrested for using cooperative profits to fund the attempted jailbreak of a PCC kidnapper. Pacheco, better known by his nickname Pandora, testified that he had been forced to collaborate by members of his cooperative. According to Pandora, Tatto had granted a concession to Cooper Pam on the condition that it hire drivers and managers from Transmetro, a cooperative that had folded after its president was arrested for his ties to the PCC. Pandora testified that one of Cooper Pam's garages was controlled by the former Transmetro personnel, and funneled profits to the PCC. According to the police, drivers were expected to turn over approximately $500 *reais* a week to the network.[20]

The situation is similar in Rio, where irregular and semiregular van cooperatives control the majority of mass transportation on the periphery. As in São Paulo, since 1995 those cooperatives have shifted from the status of political outsiders to insiders. Anthony Garotinho, governor of Rio from 1999 to 2002, and his wife, Rosinha Matheus, governor from 2003 to 2006, made the van cooperatives a key sector of their political coalition, and intervened on numerous occasions to protect this sector from legal crackdowns.

The van cooperatives make expedient alliances with local powers in the neighborhoods they serve, and these alliances are often considered exclusive: thus, cooperatives that operate in favelas controlled by the CV do not enter favelas controlled by rival networks. When a militia seizes turf from one of the criminal networks, it typically boots out the existing cooperative and replaces it.

Within Rio's favelas, many residents rely on mototaxis, which are more nimble and numerous than the vans. The mototaxis tend to be more closely related to the criminal networks than are the van cooperatives. Some of the same young men who shuttle passengers up Borel's steep main road during the afternoon, for example, can be seen peddling marijuana and cocaine at its *boca*, or drug-dealing location, after midnight. Given the strategic position of the *mototaxistas*, local crimelords have high stakes in making sure they are loyal. Consequently, in both Brazil's largest cities, working-class citizens who wish to get from one place to another often have little choice but to provide funding for informal enterprises with criminal affiliations.

Favela-Bairro

The increasing violence of everyday urban life since redemocratization has provoked a wide array of policy responses, including some notable failures and some encouraging successes. Favela-Bairro is the best known of the failures and illustrates the problems encountered in recent urbanization projects. This program invested over $600 million dollars, most of it in funding from the Inter-American

Development Bank, in slum upgrading in Rio de Janeiro, from 1994 to 2002. The stated goal of the program was integration of favelas into the surrounding city – to turn favelas into *bairros*, or formal urban neighborhoods. Towards that end, the program poured funds into eighty large and midsize favelas in Rio de Janeiro, while a related program, Bairrinho, targeted smaller communities. Favela-Bairro hired teams of architects and social scientists, undertook extensive research projects and crafted sophisticated proposals. Its directors sought to build community support through the incorporation of popular suggestions and the preference for local employment. Many of its projects were successful in the short term – the program's expanded streets and public plazas, in particular, made valuable contributions to local infrastructure. But by the mid-1990s the gulf between favela and bairro was not primarily infrastructural, but social and legal, and Favela-Bairro could not reduce this gulf.

Many of the best-known favelas in Rio, such as Rocinha, Cantagalo and Morro dos Cabritos, had already become areas of great economic diversity by the 1990s, with central commercial strips of multistorey townhouses contrasting with more recently settled zones of poverty. Favela-Bairro alleviated infrastructural needs in some of these poor areas, but tended to concentrate on the central areas within favelas. This concentration resulted both from the program's strategy of investing in central areas as poles of development and from its commitment to working through residents' associations rooted in these central areas. Consequently, Favela-Bairro exacerbated internal inequalities – rents in the central areas of many participating favelas rose rapidly. Poorer residents of these areas moved out to peripheral areas within the favela or to other favelas.[21]

More seriously, as a municipally administered program Favela-Bairro had no power to address issues of security and little power to address issues of land tenure. Security in Brazil is primarily a state issue – municipalities have no police forces, controlling a lightly armed municipal guard at best. The state police are charged with providing urban security, and the federal police with reinforcing and regulating the state police. Rio's city government has been in political conflict with its state government since the late 1980s, and Favela-Bairro did not improve the situation. Consequently, Favela-Bairro could have no positive effect on the control of criminal networks over favela territory.

Similarly, Favela-Bairro had no control over land-titling. Although extension of title to favelados was a stated goal of the program, it was not a goal with any likelihood of success. The political obstacles to a titling project involve actors at community, municipal and state levels. Favela-Bairro did not confront these obstacles, and thus made no improvement in legal land tenure. Indeed, through its inflationary effects on informal rental markets, the program contributed to rising rates of informality. By the program's conclusion, residents of most target communities had rejected it. Favela-Bairro became a perceived success in the international policy world just as local residents increasingly denounced it.

Morro dos Cabritos provides an illustrative case. The Favela-Bairro public plaza in this neighborhood is now deserted and overgrown, its walls and benches already crumbling. Many of the concrete walks and stairways installed by the program are in disrepair. The original program called for funding for maintenance, but political demands and shifting priorities have prevented this. Favela-Bairro built a watertank in Morro dos Cabritos, but for reasons that no one can entirely explain, it was never used. Instead, residents use privately purchased, individual tanks. The Favela-Bairro tank now serves as a lookout for adolescent boys working with the local gang.

In material ways, life in the favela has improved dramatically since the 1980s. All homes are now made of brick and concrete, rather than scrap wood. Electricity is more plentiful and more reliable. Only a decade ago, few residents had telephones, and the favela's one public telephone was a community lifeline. Today, nearly every household in the favela relies on inexpensive prepaid cellphones. As residents point out, none of these improvements stems from Favela-Bairro. The project made improvements to the favela's central street, but local residents do not associate these improvements with the program. Instead, they point to the proliferation of local commerce and to the construction of a huge Catholic church as signs that the community is improving, based on the energy of its residents, not because of Favela-Bairro.

The NGO boom and new security policies

Brazilian non-governmental organizations, which typically carry out smaller, targeted projects, have in some cases achieved greater gains. NGO activity runs a broad gamut from home delivery of tuberculosis vaccines to hip-hop dance classes. But the bulk of NGO presence in the informal neighborhoods of Rio, São Paulo and other cities concentrates on education, broadly conceived.

In most of Rio's mid- to large favelas, NGOs run communal computer rooms, where local residents can sign up for free broadband access, as well as computer classes. Numerous NGOs offer specialized classes aimed specifically at "children at-risk," namely those between ten and sixteen in favelas with strong *tráfico* presence. Among the most effective of these are classes that offer focused preparation for the *vestibular*, Brazil's universal college entrance exam. In the past, the vestibular has functioned to divide classes: middle-class students from private schools not only have better preparation for the vestibular within their schools, but often take a year after high school to take a private course aimed specifically at preparation for the entrance exam. NGOs like Observatório das Favelas, in reproducing this service for free within favelas, have helped begin to transform the population of Rio's free, highly selective public universities.

Some NGOs have been less accountable, and the increasingly close relationship between NGOs and municipal governments has drawbacks as well as benefits. In keeping with global trends, since the 1980s Brazilian municipalities have sought to move personnel and expenses off the books by contracting for services with private providers. Such contracts often go to NGOs, many of which are now licensed as "OSCIPs," or Organizations of Civil Society in the Public Interest. In the best cases, this has produced the "synergy" that boosters of the trend extol, enabling targeted response to immediate needs by drawing on volunteer energy and a mix of public and private funding. In other cases, it has enabled partisan and deliberately obscure use of taxpayer contributions. Such episodes have prompted the inauguration of a Parliamentary Commission on NGOs, intended to investigate allegations of NGO corruption. Brazil's Parliamentary Commissions tend to generate a great deal of dirty laundry and few sanctions. But the threat of bad publicity may lead to greater regulation of the sector, a prospect which can only strengthen the more reliable NGOs.

Only a handful of NGOs have achieved a position of such independence and mutual respect that they are both able to draw attention to police violence and work effectively against criminal turf control. São Paulo's Instituto Fernand Braudel, a think-tank and NGO, stands out in this regard. As a think-tank, the Instituto Braudel has produced valuable research on issues such as education and security in peripheral neighborhoods. As an NGO, it has run model educational programs. Its most successful venture, however, has been its work in Diadema, an industrial suburb of São Paulo and home to several large favelas. In 1997, an amateur videographer secretly videotaped several episodes of police torture and extortion in Diadema's Favela Naval. The videos, subsequently broadcast on TV Globo's *Jornal Nacional*, show officers harassing nonviolent alleged traffic offenders, beating them, taking their money, and in one case fatally shooting a victim. It was hardly a surprise when over the following two years Diadema registered Brazil's highest homicide rates, with more than one person in a hundred murdered annually.

In 2000, the Instituto Braudel initiated a program of research, monitoring and police reform. Crucially, the institute secured the participation of all the key actors, including civil and military police, the city council and community leaders. The policies this alliance put in place were not revolutionary. They incorporated elements of the "compstat" strategy of using crime statistics updated daily to apportion police resources more effectively, methods honed in New York a decade earlier. And following Bogotá, Colombia, they passed a municipal law closing bars at 11 PM. The real achievement lay neither in designing nor enacting these policies, but in stitching together the broad coalition that made them successful. Diadema's homicide rates subsequently dropped 70 percent, and its rates for other violent crimes dropped over 30 percent. [22] The Instituto Braudel deserves only a share of the credit for these improvements, but without its collaboration they would have been unlikely.

Nearby municipalities, including the city of São Paulo itself, also adopted key elements of this model, with the collaboration of state government. Monitoring of police actions, in particular, has been greatly strengthened. The state government also expanded and improved its high-security prisons, and reduced the kind of blanket indultos that have contributed to high rates of escape and recidivism in the past. In the wake of these reforms, violent crime has dropped dramatically in São Paulo since 2003. Homicide rates in São Paulo state have dropped to approximately 11 per 100,000 residents per year, a fraction of former rates.[23]

Violent crime is only part of the problem confronting Brazil's cities. Violence and crime are not coterminous, and reduced violence has not yielded a secure São Paulo, nor one where rights to the city are universally distributed. But the reduction in violent crime is a significant improvement, one felt by the residents of the metropolitan region on a daily basis. That reduction, moreover, makes possible a more rational and professional allocation of police resources towards confrontation with the criminal networks. Among Brazil's major cities, Belo Horizonte has also successfully instituted some of the reforms.

Rio de Janeiro, as well as cities like Salvador, Recife and Fortaleza, are still a long way from reaching this point. The indictment of former Police Chief Lins was an indication that Rio is willing to take police reform seriously. Rates of expulsion of officers connected to drug trafficking have also risen – hundreds of low-ranking officers have been stripped of their badges since 2002. Few, however, have been convicted, and no enduring transformations have been made. Rio has yet to produce the kind of broad coalition that made a difference in São Paulo. Whether São Paulo's improvements or Rio's thrashing in place become the model for urban Brazil depends a great deal on political developments within these cities and on national recognition of interests. As go Rio and São Paulo, so goes Brazil. As yet, no national administration has successfully reckoned with the implications of this truism.

Since the 1950s, Brazilian cities have been ahead of the curve of other cities in the Global South in various transformative trends. Rio and São Paulo witnessed the beginnings of exponential growth on the urban periphery in the 1940s and 1950s. Politicians in those cities attempted massive projects of slum removal and the creation of public housing in the 1960s, gradually lost funding and enthusiasm for those projects, and turned to slum upgrading by the early 1980s. In all these ways, Rio and São Paulo were a decade or two in advance of a similar phenomenon in cities as diverse as Lima and Mumbai. The sharp rise of violent urban conflict in the 1980s and early 1990s also prefigured trends that would spread across the Global South a few years later.

If there is an advantage to this position at the leading edge of urban trends, it is that Brazil has nurtured an extraordinarily sophisticated body of urban self-study. The Instituto Fernand Braudel and the Observatório das Favelas are only two of a plethora of think-tanks and academic departments producing minutely detailed research on urban problems. Since 1990, the tone of that research has changed dramatically from hopes for radical transformation to propositions for practical, cautious reform. Brazil's observers have come to understand urban violence as a condition to be treated and contained, but one virtually impossible to eliminate. As sobering as observation is, it appears necessary for the difficult work of cracking the territorial control of the criminal networks over portions of these vital cities.

3 | Back to the land

On October 21, 2007, a group of approximately 150 activists in the Movimento Sem Terra (MST), the Landless Workers' Movement, invaded an agricultural research farm owned by Syngenta Seeds, a multinational biotech firm, in Santa Teresa de Oeste, Paraná. Syngenta Seeds, the maize and oilseeds division of the Syngenta corporate family, used the farm for experimental production of genetically modified maize and soy seeds tailored to local growing conditions. The farm, only a few kilometers from Iguaçu Falls and the Paraguayan border, lies in the midst of a rich agricultural belt, hotly disputed for years by powerful soy growers and their multinational allies on one side and MST militants on the others. The Olga Benário Settlement, an MST farm named for the communist revolutionary who led a failed uprising in Brazil in 1935, lies only a short distance away, and served as a staging-ground for the invasion.

The MST activists surprised the research farm's security guards early in the morning, confiscated their weapons, evicted them, and occupied the grounds. That afternoon, an armed contingent of approximately forty men, made up primarily of employees of the private security firm hired by Syngenta Seeds, returned to the farm. The guards later claimed that they were attempting to liberate a colleague who had been taken hostage during the morning raid, although no evidence emerged to support that claim. More probably, they were attempting to recover the guns taken from them earlier that morning – guns the MST claimed it had intended to turn over to the police. The MST occupiers resisted. In the ensuing melee, one of their leaders, Valmir de Mota Oliveira, was killed. One of the security guards, Fábio Ferreira, was also shot and killed.

On a superficial level, this grisly but not uncommon episode seemed to crystallize in miniature a larger Brazilian conflict over rural land, development models and the distribution of wealth. A scruffy band of peasant farmers risked life and limb to take on the hired goons of multinational agribusiness, whose absentee land-lords and distant shareholders care only about the bottom line, and disdain concern for environmental sustainability and the plight of the rural poor.

The reality is more complicated. Both the MST and multinational agribusiness firms enjoy a close relationship with actors within Brazilian government. The PT, in particular, has long relied on the MST as a force for rural mobilization and party-building. Encour-aging MST demands was a key strategy for the PT when it was in the political opposition, and accommodating those demands became an obligation for the PT when it rose to executive power in 2002. At the same time, Brazil owes much of its economic growth since the late 1990s to agribusiness and to genetically modified, or GM, soy in par-ticular. Before winning office, Lula and his inner circle made strategic alliances with major soy producers and agribusiness representatives, and have continued to cultivate those alliances in power.

In this case, Roberto Requião of the PMDB, governor of Paraná and a key member of Lula's governing coalition, strongly backed the MST's claim to the land. But Congress ratified laws, subsequently reinforced by presidential decrees, facilitating the expansion of GM cultivation and bolstering Syngenta's position. Overlapping and com-peting regulatory agencies issued conflicting statements, further muddying the waters. The judicial branch, ostensibly entrusted with breaking deadlocks within the state, produced rulings supporting Syngenta's land tenure while criticizing its land use. In the halls of power, the MST and Syngenta sought to bend this bureaucratic deadlock to their own advantage. In the meantime, in the field, MST activists and the private security force hired by Syngenta Seeds took the law into their own hands.

What looks superficially like a conflict over opposed models of development is in fact a conflict within the state and a conflict for the state, where each faction, knowing total victory is out of the question, seeks to maximize its share of the spoils. The MST rank and file and the working-class security guards hired to protect private farms are inevitably the losers in this struggle.

The Syngenta–MST battle can be understood only with background knowledge of the growth of the MST over the 1980s and '90s, the coinciding emergence of agribusiness as Brazil's pre-eminent economic engine, and the relationship of both to transformations in the Brazilian state. Tracing that history, in turn, helps explain not only what happened in Santa Teresa de Oeste, but what has unfolded thousands of kilometers away in the Amazon region. The interplay between multinational capitalist expansion, government development strategies and the political cultivation of organized social movements has produced a rural Brazil marked by episodic violence and unresolved conflicts.

The military regime and the origins of the MST

The distances and diversity of the Brazilian interior are famously mind-boggling. The state of Pará in the Amazon region, at over 1.2 million square km, is about three times the size of Germany, but it is not the biggest state in Brazil (neighboring Amazonas is larger). To travel by bus from Belém, Pará's riverine capital, east to Petrolina in the northeastern state of Pernambuco takes over a day, and leaves behind the lush rainforest, heading into the *sertão*, or dry and dusty backlands of the northeastern interior. To travel south to Rondonópolis, in the neighboring state of Mato Grosso, takes just as long, and plunges you into the heart of Brazil's booming agribusiness; the west is characterized by large estates dedicated to soy production. Traveling much further south to Jaguari, in the agricultural heartland of Rio Grande do Sul, takes four days, crossing the high central plains and the dense industrial southeast; you arrive finally in a region characterized by family-owned farms producing diverse crops primarily for domestic consumption. This size and diversity means that there is and can never be a single agrarian Brazil, and that all policies must be tailored to local needs and subject to local negotiation.

For the military regime in the 1960s and '70s, this meant pursuing policies that differed substantially by region, but that were all char-acterized by a technocratic rationalism imbued with deep concerns over national security. The regime sought to guarantee agricultural self-sufficiency complemented by investment in key export sectors and the subsidized modernization of major producers. At the same time, strategies of agrarian production were designed to complement energy and security objectives perceived as more pressing, including hydroelectric projects, the development of an ethanol industry, and settlement of the Amazon. The regime initiated massive rural public works projects, like the Itaipu Dam, on the Paraná River – not far from Santa Teresa de Oeste – built over the course of the 1970s and early 1980s. The Itaipu, one of the largest dams in the world, supplies a significant portion of Brazil's hydroelectric power, but its creation demanded the eviction of thousands of farming families along the river. The regime offered generous credit lines and sub- sidized imports of technology for major growers, enabling them to expand, consolidate and mechanize, buying up neighboring lands and drastically cutting their work force. And it created EMBRAPA, the Brazilian Agricultural Research Corporation, an agricultural science institution designed to work closely with major growers.

Technocratic rationalism at the level of national policy was often filtered through a high tolerance for corruption at the local level. Rural land titles in Brazil had historically been marked by confusion and competing claims, where the domination of the strong was at least partially offset by common reliance upon *sitiantes*, or informal sharecroppers, living on land claimed by local magnates in return for seasonal labor. While land distribution patterns varied across the country, as a general rule lack of legal title did not prevent the practical existence of smallholders. This began to change rapidly under the military regime, as access to agricultural credit, dependent on legal title, became vital to survival in a changing market. Centrally planned rationalization of titles yielded ample opportunity for brib- ery and kickbacks at the local level. *Grilagem*, the staking of dubious claims to land based on a combination of force and bureaucratic obfuscation, flourished in many areas of the country.

These phenomena bolstered agribusiness and drove small farmers and rural workers off the land. The regime sought to dampen the social consequences of dislocation while accomplishing the goal of territorial consolidation by encouraging colonization schemes in the Amazon. In 1970, the regime created INCRA, the National Institute of Colonization and Agrarian Reform, ostensibly to serve landless farmers. The regime also extended the Transamazónica Highway, connecting remote Amazonian regions to the capital at Brasília and northeastern ports, in order to facilitate the settlement of the interior. *Colonos*, or small farmers, spread out along the highway. Many cleared the land, sold the timber and then went bankrupt. Cattle-ranchers, subsidized by the regime, snapped up cleared lands, and colonos either pushed farther into the Amazon or settled in one of the growing towns along the highway. Strongmen rose to power in these regions, based on their loyalty to the regime and their willingness to enforce local order through intimidation. Indigenous communities and rubber tappers found their lifeways under siege, and environmental destruction spiraled out of control.

Many farmers and rural workers refused either to embark on the Amazonian ventures or to drift towards the burgeoning cities of the southeast, preferring to fight for some opportunity in the rural south and center-west. In the late 1970s, a group of uprooted farmers settled within the indigenous reserve of Nonoaí, in Rio Grande do Sul, an encroachment deliberately overlooked by the authorities, who had no other viable local settlement plan. But in 1978, the Kaingang Indians themselves struck back, driving many of the settlers into impoverished rural encampments on the border of the reserve. Representatives of the Comissão Pastoral da Terra (CPT), the Pastoral Land Commission, a Catholic outreach program for rural Brazilians, began to provide relief to the encampments and to organize meetings.

The CPT was created by young priests imbued with the ideals of liberation theology, a reform movement that swept through the seminaries of southern Brazil in the 1960s and 1970s and was beginning to transform the workings of the Brazilian Church. Liberation theology's blend of Marxist theory and an interpretation of the Gospel oriented towards social activism proved a powerful tonic in a nation in the grips of a rightwing authoritarian regime. Bishops critical of the regime but generally wary of openly denouncing it countenanced the work of the CPT, and in doing so helped to create an enduring movement for agrarian reform.

The CPT activists encouraged the Nonoaí refugees to invade un-productive local land. They were led in this regard by Father Arnildo Fritzen and João Pedro Stédile, an ex-seminarist who worked for the state agricultural department. Late in 1979, over a hundred families led by the CPT occupied a nearby estate. News of their occupation inspired other landless farmers to occupy a neighboring farm, and the encampments grew quickly. They drew the attention of advocates for redemocratization, winning popular support and making a vigorous crackdown unviable. The constant threat of removal ultimately convinced the settlers to depart, but not before they had won access to a nearby farm with the aid of the Church. The land invasion had proven a success, making the tactic an important resource in agrarian conflicts and convincing growing numbers of landless farmers to enlist the aid of the CPT.[24]

Families displaced by the Itaipu Dam went through a similar process of early organization and activism, with the aid of both the CPT and the locally powerful Lutheran Church. By 1984, these two wings of a growing agrarian movement had joined together, and began to reach out to compatriots across the country. Their meeting in Cascavel in January of that year is generally considered the official inauguration of the MST. By the close of the conclave, the defining elements of the MST were in place. The CPT and the nascent MST would work together and would be in many instances indistinguishable. Their defining goal would be distribution of land to the landless, to the exclusion of nearly all other considerations regarding rural labor. The MST would share the CPT's liberation theological principles, but it would wed these to the structural discipline of the Central Única dos Trabalhadores (CUT), the militant labor federation that had emerged from the São Paulo metalworkers' strikes of the late 1970s, and that also participated in the Cascavel meeting. Through the CUT, the movement would maintain close ties to the growing PT, and its leaders would become the founders of local PT offices in much of rural Brazil. The movement would be deliberately national in scope, seeking to maximize its political leverage through coordination of land invasions in varying regions, from the modernizing agrarian south, to the impoverished northeast, to the volatile Amazon.

The MST would place great value on grassroots participation, but its insistence on declaring consensus for all strategic decisions would reinforce the power of an unchanging hierarchy: the leaders emerging from the Cascavel meeting, Stédile, in particular, would dominate the organization for decades. Stédile and his closest allies on the central committee instituted training programs for young militants in the field, charging them with organizing local encampments. These centrally trained militants effectively set the agenda for local decisions, often turning the demand for consensus into an intolerance of dissent.

By the mid-1980s, urban Brazil was well along the road to redemocratization, but the same could not be said of rural Brazil, where political control by powerful landowners – both the modernizers of the south and the inefficient *coronéis*, or colonels, of the north – was still considered an essential feature of national order. This helps explain the unwillingness of the MST to play by the rules. In the 1980s, filing for redistribution of unproductive land through INCRA was, aside from being laborious and time-consuming, unlikely to produce favorable results. Large landowners successfully used INCRA to trade rural properties, selling holdings to the government for more than they were worth. Recipients of small plots often ended up with unviable tracts and exorbitant loans.

MST invasions also entailed considerable labor and risk, but it was hands-on, communal labor rather than isolating bureaucratic struggle. And above all invasion made possible and enforced a collective undertaking, a goal idealized by the CPT.

The 1988 Constitution held out the possibility of changing this dynamic. Even the military regime's 1967 Constitution had ostensibly required that all land fulfill a "social function," but the requirement was so vague that it held out no promise of significant agrarian reform. The 1988 document went several steps further, linking the social function of property to a "dignified existence for all," and to "the well-being of the property owners and the workers" – passages written with the advice and strong advocacy of the CPT. The constitution further charged the federal government with expropriating land that was not fulfilling its social function and redistributing the property. Former owners of expropriated lands were to be indemnified in "títulos de dívida agrária," or rural debt titles, a federal bond of inconsistent value.[25]

In practice, the new constitution did not lead to rapid agrarian reform. Bureaucratic procedures continued to be an inefficient method of pursuing redistribution. Land expropriations did increase, but did so in direct proportion to MST invasions. MST leaders perceived invasion as the only method likely to cut the Gordian knot of bureaucratic reform. They successfully used constitutional language about the social function of land to justify invasions that were nonetheless illegal: the rule of law made no allowance for invasion as a method of speeding along wheels of bureaucracy, but the practical circumstances seemed to demand it. Over time, the tactic that had once been a strategic necessity became the organization's identifying modus operandi. Land invasions went from being a response to the unconsolidated rule of law in the countryside to an obstacle to its consolidation.

Cardoso and rural Brazil

The inauguration of Fernando Henrique Cardoso in 1995 brought to power a president who believed that agrarian modernization required both fomenting agribusiness and carrying out broad agrarian reform. During Cardoso's years in office, both agribusiness and the MST would increase their leverage within the government.

While the dynamics of agrarian reform had changed little since redemocratization, the agricultural sector had changed dramatically. Sarney and Collor cut subsidies and tariffs that had protected domestic growers, and by the time Cardoso came to office these cuts had produced striking consequences. Many large growers had gone under, leading to consolidation of land by diversified corporations. Ethanol accounted for an ever-larger share of domestic fuel consumption, leading to expanding sugar cultivation, particularly in western São Paulo and Paraná. Cattle ranching, long subsidized by the federal government, emerged as a surprisingly competitive sector, with drastic consequences for the Amazon. In the midst of these changes, the old rural oligarchy was declining, replaced by a thriving agribusiness sector.

Cardoso continued free market policies, partially offsetting their consequences by renewing investment in EMBRAPA and renegotiating debts with farmers. Brazil's agricultural sector began to look more like that of the United States, where large growers carried substantial debt, confident of their ability to use it as leverage for favorable policies, while working closely with major multinational corporations and relying on poorly paid migrant workers.

Brazilian agriculture, in contrast to that of the United States, thrived without the benefits of high subsidies. Brazilian soy, orange juice, corn, cellulose, rice, beef and chicken became staples on the world market, in many cases leading their sectors in total production and export value. Brazil remained the world's largest coffee exporter, although the importance of coffee in the nation's export portfolio declined dramatically. Through renegotiation of loans and the balancing of export and domestic demand, Cardoso's administration achieved unprecedented stability in agricultural prices. The relative cost of the *cesta básica*, or market basket of basic staples, declined steadily – a key achievement both in the struggle to beat back inflation and to defeat hunger. The market price of chicken for one *real* per kilogram figured prominently in Cardoso's re-election campaign in 1998. Prices subsequently rose during the international financial crisis a year later, but remained historically low in relation to per capita income.

Patterns of political representation lagged behind the agricultural economy. The old rural oligarchy was disappearing, but the *bancada ruralista* – the interparty coalition of rural politicians that had long defended that oligarchy's interests – remained strong. Cardoso negotiated with this bloc, many of whose most prominent members were part of the PFL, the PSDB's partner in the governing coalition. The vestigial *bancada ruralista* became a strong defender of the landowners and local strongmen of the Amazon. A growing environmental movement, with its own congressional allies, confronted them.

That movement had first come to broad attention with the murder of Chico Mendes in 1988. Mendes was the leader of a rubber tappers' union who made a crucial alliance with Catholic lay activists in the Amazon in early 1980s. Through them, he connected with international environmentalists who valued rubber tapping as a sustainable form of Amazonian development. Mendes, in turn, latched on to environmental advocacy as the best way to advance his union's cause, dramatically changing political dynamics in the region.[26] His execution by the hired thugs of local strongmen became an international celebrity cause, forcing greater national attention towards environmental devastation. By the time Cardoso took power, the environmental network was highly sophisticated in its presentation of scientific evidence and in its pursuit of political leverage.

Responding to its demands, Cardoso increased protected territories through the creation and expansion of indigenous reserves and national parks. These protections suffered from several obvious shortcomings: federal staff to oversee them was ludicrously overstretched, enforcement of their boundaries depended on state police often allied with loggers, and landless farmers continued to push into the region, burning and clearing. Expansion of protected areas did reduce the trade value of such land – because it could not legally be bought and sold, it was less likely to be the target of development. Cardoso reinforced this legal protection through bureaucratic reorganization. He cracked down on corruption within INCRA and created a new Ministry of Agricultural Development, less subject to local clientelist demands. These changes notwithstanding, many local actors – smalltime loggers and miners, charcoal-harvesters, and desperate colonos – still stood to reap short-term gain from deforestation in protected areas, and relatively few were in a position to defend the goal of preservation.

The environmental movement worked closely but uneasily with the MST – the same congressmen, predominantly from the PT, became strong representatives for the interests of both environmentalists and the MST. In practice, MST invasions did not always sit well with goals of environmental protection, adding a further element of volatility to land struggles in the north.

In August 1995, military police attempted to carry out a judicial order of eviction of an MST occupation in Corumbiara, in the western Amazon. Heavily armed police supplemented by private security forces hired by the farm's owner met with resistance from the settlers and opened fire. Nine settlers were killed, many more injured. Two members of the military police also died. In March 2006, MST activists blocked a highway near Eldorado dos Carajás, in the northern state of Pará, demanding immediate settlement on nearby land. Negotiations failed, and the roadblock persisted into

April. On the 19th of that month, state military police converged on the activists and began firing teargas. The activists resisted, and one of their members fired on the police. The police then opened fire, killing nineteen, many at close range, and at least one after he had been taken into custody.[27]

The Corumbiara and Carajás massacres riveted national attention, shaming the state police of Rondônia and Pará and the federal government. A TV crew from a Globo affiliate had captured the Carajás massacres, and the footage was shown widely and repeatedly. Popular sentiment, particularly in the metropolitan southeast, swung in favor of the MST. Sebastião Salgado, a Brazilian photographer in the midst of a major documentary project on migrant workers, had been for many years a sharp-eyed observer of conflict over rural land in Brazil and a supporter of the MST. After the Carajás incident, Salgado compiled his photographs of rural Brazil and MST settlements into a stunning exhibition. A year after the massacre, Salgado published the work in the book *Terra*, accompanied by a CD featuring music by famed popular composer Chico Buarque, including the stirring "Assentamento," or "Settlement," the first-person narrative of a farmer who has fled the urban periphery in search of land and dignity in rural Brazil. This narrative conformed perfectly to the analysis of agrarian reform published by Betinho and IBASE and to the burgeoning metropolitan enthusiasm for the MST.

In that same year, filmmaker Tetê Moraes made a documentary entitled *O Sonho de Rose*, or Rose's Dream, a followup to a shorter film she had made ten years earlier about an MST settlement in Rio Grande do Sul. Moraes's first film had been largely ignored. *O Sonho de Rose*, in contrast – again featuring Buarque's "Assentamento" – was celebrated by national and international audiences.

Those audiences were influential but minimal in comparison to the millions that saw *O Rei do Gado*, a Globo telenovela of 1996–97. The "Cattle King" of the novela's title falls in love with a migrant worker living in a landless workers' encampment, where much of the drama unfolds. The organization's leaders are portrayed as shrewd political manipulators, but its rank and file members are depicted as heroic and humbly noble. The works of Salgado, Buarque and Moraes helped to shift academic opinion in favor of the MST. *O Rei do Gado* served perhaps the more influential role of persuading a popular audience that agrarian reform was just and necessary.

Agrarian reform under Cardoso

This shift could not have been more timely for the MST. Over the preceding years, the MST had concentrated its energy on invasions in the Pontal de Paranapanema, a fertile peninsula between two rivers in western São Paulo. The Pontal de Paranapanema had been the target of massive grilagem under the military regime, and the MST chose it as an arena for testing the dubious titles of the *grileiros* and pushing for settlement on productive land. This required a decisive change in strategy: until the mid-1990s the MST had justified invasions by claiming that occupied land had been unproductive, and therefore was not fulfilling a social function. In the Pontal, the organization began invading productive farms, based on the premise that their titles were bogus. In earlier political contexts, this tactic would not have proven viable. In the wake of Corumbiara and Carajás, it proved successful.

São Paulo's state government, still reeling from the Carandiru prison massacre of 1993, could not risk a heavyhanded crackdown on MST invasions. The federal Ministry of Justice, tarnished by the recent episodes in the north, exercised further leverage in favor of restraint. As a result, the Pontal invasions played out primarily in the tortuous Brazilian courts, and activists faced relatively low threat of immediate eviction or violence. Taking advantage of this opportunity, over ten thousand families occupied land in the Pontal between 1995 and 2000, peaking precisely in 1997 and 1998. Most of these invasions were initiated by the MST, but the land rush quickly led to schisms within the movement, with several splinter groups competing for turf.[28]

Cardoso and Raul Jungmann, his Minister of Agrarian Development, found themselves negotiating with a hydra whose heads made demands in unison but could only be placated individually. The MST's organizational structure accentuated this tendency. Rather than registering formally as a political party or even an NGO, a step that would have required greater fiscal transparency, its leaders continued to identify it as a social movement without a central hierarchal structure – a notion much belied by the prominence of Stédile and a small cast of militants. MST leaders insisted that negotiation take place at the local level, but concessions made to individual encampments served only to foment greater demands in other locations. This diversity of fronts yielded a broad spectrum of conditions. Some states, Paraná in particular, continued to rely on military police to forcibly evict MST invaders. Others, like Rio Grande do Sul, used state resources to support MST encampments and to push the federal government towards further concessions.

Cardoso and Jungmann sought to skirt these problems by undertaking agrarian reform that elided direct negotiations with the MST. In keeping with the outsized faith in the beneficent tendencies of the market that imbued international lending practices in the 1990s, they attempted a reform through market mechanisms. Fulfilling the letter of the constitution, they expropriated land, indemnified former owners with agrarian debt titles, distributed plots to farming families, ensured them access to credit, and required them to pay off the value of the land at low interest rates. The program successfully distributed land – over 500,000 families received plots between 1995 and 2002. Many of these did not thrive – even relatively low-interest loans still burdened incipient farmers with debt before they could develop connections to markets. Unlike large farmers, who could use debt as leverage, small farmers were generally required to pay up or sell off.[29] The program nonetheless gave new impetus to family farming in Brazil, as many recipients, particularly those in the south, successfully integrated with expanding agribusiness.

MST pressure undoubtedly pushed Cardoso to deepen agrarian reform, but the reform he instituted failed to relieve that pressure. MST leaders rejected it for three reasons: it did not leave any role for the MST itself, it created individual plots instead of collectives or cooperatives, and it was created by Fernando Henrique Cardoso. The MST, alllied since its inception with the PT, had positioned itself squarely in opposition to Cardoso before his inauguration. It maintained this stance for the eight years of his presidency, underlining it with invasions of the Cardoso family's rural estate on more than one occasion. Stédile blasted the Cardoso and Jungmann program as a neoliberal sop and stepped up land invasions.

At the same time, the MST became increasingly dependent on federal subsidies. The federal government, through INCRA and the Banco do Brasil, invested in infrastructure and basic services, including roads, electricity, water and sewage, in MST settlements. Through the 1990s, INCRA disbursed funding for these expenses to settlement organizers, who turned over a percentage directly to the MST's national leadership. As the number and size of MST settlements increased, the organization became a client of the same federal government it vociferously denounced.

In the final years of Cardoso's term, popular opinion shifted once again. The MST leadership had overplayed its hand: its continued invasions and rejection of Cardoso's agrarian reform began to alienate moderate supporters. Jungmann seized the opportunity to clamp down on MST funding. He cut back on bulk disbursements to settlements, directing resources to individual families in their place, and he threatened to cut off INCRA loans to MST-affiliated cooperatives that passed on a percentage of the money to the MST itself.

By the close of the Cardoso years, agribusiness reigned supreme. Market-based agrarian reform had settled hundreds of thousands of families without fundamentally altering the nature of the agrarian economy. The condition of rural workers continued to be characterized by grinding labor, poor pay, uncertain tenure and limited access to education. The MST, focused heavily on land redistribution, did little to address these conditions.

Lula and the Amazon

Those who expected that Lula's inauguration in 2003 would bring a radical transformation in the countryside were soon dissuaded by his choice of ministers. Lula named Roberto Rodrigues, a landowner with strong ties to agribusiness, his Minister of Agriculture. Rodrigues had a long history of advocacy on the part of rural cooperatives, but primarily for those linked to export production. He represented the latest stage of agricommercial diversification in Brazil, showing the increasing interdependence of multinational firms like Monsanto, Syngenta, Cargill and Archer Daniels Midland with rural cooperatives of family-owned farms. Lula named Luiz Fernando Furlan his Minister of Development. Furlan was the chief administrative officer of

Sadia, Brazil's largest chicken-processor, and scion of the family that had founded the corporation. Benefiting from the price stabilization and export-orientation of the Cardoso years, Furlan had made Sadia a major international player, exporting frozen chicken across the globe and aggressively pursuing opportunities in meatpacking and processed foods. Neither Rodrigues nor Furlan had historic ties to the PT, much less the MST. Their selection indicated that the federal government would continue to develop its agrarian policies with an eye towards export-oriented agribusiness.

Lula reaffirmed this commitment through a subsequent alliance with Blairo Maggi, Brazil's Soy King. As governor of Mato Grosso, Maggi had led the trend of soy expansion, pushing Amazonian de-forestation, and as CEO of the Maggi corporation he had led Brazil's transition into GM agricultural production.

Lula attempted to balance these alliances with nominations on the left, naming Luis Marinho of the CUT as his Minister of Labor and the Trotskyist Miguel Rossetto, another CUT veteran, as his Minister of Agrarian Development. Lula also named José Graziano, an agricultural economist and longtime member of his inner circle, the Secretary of Food Security, responsible for the much-publicized Zero Hunger. But Zero Hunger soon fell off the political map, and neither Marinho nor Rossetto was in a position to meet MST demands. The organization signaled its displeasure by invading and occupying INCRA offices in Mato Grosso. Lula made amends, continuing to negotiate with the MST and appearing at rallies wearing its trademark red cap. He also continued resettlement, granting land to 380,000 families by the end of his first term – slightly surpassing Cardoso's rate without altering the dynamic of agrarian reform.

Lula's nomination of Marina Silva as Minister of the Environment was more consequential. Silva had been a close colleague of Chico Mendes and was a key figure in the transition of Amazonian rubber tappers from isolated syndicalism to broadbased environmentalism via collaboration with Catholic activists and an international green network. Silva became one of the most independent voices in the administration, advocating the reinforcement of environmental protections. She became the lone voice in the cabinet to question seriously the idea that growth overrode all other concerns. Without overstepping the bounds of her ministry, she defended sustainable development over short-term exploitation. In doing so, she ably linked domestic movements for environmental protection to international concerns over global warming. In May of 2008, Lula replaced Marina Silva with the more development-friendly Carlos Minc.

By the end of Lula's first term, rates of deforestation had slowed along the arc of destruction – the long curving front encroaching on the rainforest from the northeast and the center-west – but then picked up in the first years of his second term. New roads connecting Mato Grosso with Amazonian river shipping brought Brazilian soy to international markets more cheaply. Mining and hydroelectric investments in Pará brought jobs and revenue, and held out the promise of increasing Brazil's insufficient supply of electricity. But these investments exacted a high environmental price: major projects in the region led to unplanned growth, resulting in expanding nodes and arteries of deforestation.

Development practices in the region have improved, partly through Silva's advocacy. Legal logging in the region is now ostensibly sustainable. Even sustainable logging, however, may increase the risk of uncontrollable fires, the single greatest danger in the Amazon. Logging in any form leaves behind dead trees and creates clearings open to sun and wind – conditions ripe for a blaze. Illegal logging is still prevalent, and poses a much greater risk.

Some corporations have vowed to make environmental protection an ostensible priority. Vale, the behemoth mining company, refuses to sell its iron ore to companies that do not conform to Brazil's environmental and labor laws.[30] In this case, international pressure by environmental advocates on a high-profile company has yielded some trickle-down benefits at the local level. But Vale's projects in the region inevitably raise the value of adjacent lands, triggering legal and illegal economic activities with high environmental costs.

The rubber-tapping model of sustainable extractive enterprise has now been duplicated in numerous areas, like harvesting of the *açaí* fruit and fishing for the enormous *pirarucu*. This approach to regional development holds out great promise of complementarity with the growing importance of the rainforest as a global carbon sink, likely to a play a decisive role in future carbon-trading markets. But these vulnerable extractive enterprises employ only a fraction of the region's residents, and the propensity of carbon trading to facilitate enduring environmental protection is as yet unproven.

The most encouraging developments in the region's recent history have been the simultaneous expansion of minimal labor protections and educational opportunities. Ranchers in the region have traditionally had the power to enforce labor control at the point of a gun, defying state and federal laws with impunity. This problem is far from solved, as attested by the 2005 murder of Sister Dorothy Stang, a liberation theology advocate for the Amazonian poor and for environmental defense. Like Mendes, Stang was murdered by the hired guns of a local landowner, demonstrating that the fundamental dynamics of land conflict in the region have not yet changed. But a stronger network of NGO advocates, greater federal oversight, and increasing media attention have led to some improvements. Literacy rates and school attendance have climbed. Education remains precarious and underfunded, but the first step, that of expanding accessibility, has largely been accomplished.

The MST and biotech

Bolsa Família, Lula's targeted social-spending program, has played a significant role in this latest transformation, and has helped fuel a pattern of growing migration from the peripheries of southeastern cities – São Paulo in particular – to the northeast, partially reversing what has been the dominant trend for decades. Because the cost of living is substantially lower in the northeastern interior than it is in São Paulo, the Bolsa Família stipend goes much further in the northeast. Many of these towns now count on direct government funding, in the form of Bolsa Família checks and a new guaranteed pension for aging rural workers, as their primary source of revenue. This is hardly a recipe for growth, but it does have some favorable consequences. The poverty, sparsity and insufficient infrastructure of towns in the northeastern and northern interior is itself a major obstacle to sustainable development. In restoring a prospect of viability to some of these towns, new social spending patterns may yield unexpected dividends.

Although many of its members depend on Bolsa Família, the MST disdains the program. Just as Bolsa Família has given some rural families the resources to pass over work tending illegal charcoal ovens, it has also allowed them to move out of MST encampments. At its peak in the late 1990s, the MST attracted not only landless farmers and migrant workers but a wide range of other participants, including refugees from the impoverished neighborhoods of the urban periphery. Many of its members had no agrarian experience. Although the MST is often described as a peasant organization, its members do not fit any traditional definition of peasants – they are not local farmers defending a traditional way of life, but highly mobile workers instilled with a sense of collective mission and willing to take risks in search of economic opportunity. By providing a monthly stipend, Bolsa Família has subsidized the search for opportunity and undermined the sense of collective mission.

PSOL politician and MST advocate Plínio de Arruda Sampaio condemns precisely this aspect of the program: "There is a strong indication that Bolsa Família decreases the combativity of people to fight for agrarian reform. It is the most perverse effect of the program." Dom Tomás Balduíno of the CPT agrees: "it is a fact that Bolsa Família undermined the struggle of the landless. Only where there is political consciousness will the occupations continue."[31] The MST's leaders echo this opinion, strangely concurring in this regard with figures like Reinaldo Azevedo of Brazil's new right, who argue that Bolsa Família encourages dependency. In contrast to Azevedo, who condemns the creation of open-ended welfare commitments, the MST, long dependent on the federal budget, objects primarily to the individualization of funding under Bolsa Família.

Between 2003 and 2006, as Bolsa Família grew, the MST shrank. There were 60,000 residents in MST camps in 2003, and only 10,000 in 2006. Some of these residents have been successfully settled, but Bolsa Família has peeled off others. For the first time in twenty years, their numbers have not been renewed. This does not necessarily translate into the decline of the MST: a change in presidential administrations could easily lead to a resurgence in numbers. In the meantime, the MST has changed its tactics, campaigning against agribusiness and biotech. Although the number of MST participants fell dramatically in Lula's first term, the number of land invasions remained consistent between 350 and 400 annualy.[32] Their targets changed, however, focusing increasingly on land owned by multinational corporations like Syngenta Seeds, and the cellulose exporters Aracruz and Votorantim.

The MST and allied NGOs simultaneously organized a campaign to press legislators to ban genetic modification in Brazil. This campaign attracted international and national support, but soon ran into three obstacles. First, EMBRAPA has long been at the forefront of GM technology, distributing its seeds for nominal fees to Brazilian farmers. Its research has proven critical to expanding production in Brazil's central savannahs and its northeastern arid lands. A strict law against genetic modification would thus undermine EMBRAPA and the farmers who depended on it. Second, major growers in the south had been acquiring Monsanto's seeds for years through informal networks in Argentina, where genetic modification was legal. By 2004, approximately 30 percent of Brazil's soy crop was genetically modified, and the political leverage of its soy growers made it unlikely that they would be forced to make drastic changes. Monsanto, meanwhile, pressed for full legalization and licensing.[33] Third, the PT was itself split on the question, with some PT legislators advocating blockage and others advocating greater permission and licensing. This conflict led to a flurry of provisional measures and conflicting standards among several regulatory agencies.

This was the context for the MST invasion of the Syngenta Seeds research farm in Santa Teresa de Oeste. In 2005, Congress passed a biosecurity law allowing GM cultivation under stringent restrictions, including a buffer zone within ten kilometers of protected areas. The Syngenta farm lay six kilometers from a protected area, and in March of 2006 was fined one million *reais* by IBAMA, the Brazilian environmental protection agency. The MST used the fine to justify its first invasion a few days later. Syngenta Seeds won judicial rulings requiring the state government of Paraná to evict the occupiers, but Governor Requião refused to comply. Instead, he attempted to expropriate the farm, declaring Syngenta Seeds unwelcome in Paraná. The judiciary overruled Requião, and the MST temporarily decamped to a location outside the farm. In March 2007, Congress ratified the expansion of GM, and regulatory agencies reduced the buffer zones to under one kilometer, bolstering Syngenta's position. These events set the stage for the renewed invasion in October and its violent outcome.[34]

It was not an outcome likely to affect the larger politics of agrarian use. Syngenta Seeds will survive the interruption of its activities in Paraná. Requião will reap short-term electoral advantages from his apparent defiance of a multinational corporation. GM cultivation will continue to spread, agribusiness will remain one of Brazil's economic engines, and the remaining core of the MST will continue invasions, fighting for its political life.

Brazil's combination of surging agribusiness, unresolved agrarian conflicts, endangered rainforest and diversity of agro-political zones is unique. It is a first-world producer of commodities, with greater room to grow in that regard than any of its immediate competitors. Given the strength of Brazil's domestic producers and the success of EMBRAPA, Brazilian growers are not as vulnerable to exploitation by Monsanto and Syngenta as their peers in some other Latin American nations. EMBRAPA and other domestic research institutions meet many of the biotech needs of Brazilian growers, making it less likely that local producers will be strongarmed into exploitative contracts with multinational corporations. Given the diversity of local agrarian arrangements and the strong political interest in continued agrarian reform of some kind, it is also unlikely that homegrown corporations like Maggi and Sadia will consolidate sufficiently to exercise pre-eminent control over the agrarian economy.

Until now, government agencies like EMBRAPA, IBAMA and CTNbio – the government commission on biosecurity – have as often worked at cross purposes as in harmony. To a limited extent, this disagreement is salutary, allowing for representation of diverse political positions within government. EMBRAPA is capable of tailoring genetic modification to local conditions, ensuring that Brazil does not become beholden to Monsanto and Syngenta. CTNbio has the expertise to evaluate specific uses of genetic modification and the authority to halt those that do not meet rigorous standards. Strengthening CTNbio and insulating it from partisan pressures will be the best way to make sure that Brazil's biotech future is safe and sustainable. IBAMA has the authority, at least on paper, to investigate and prosecute environmental damage associated with boom-ing agribusiness. If these three agencies can reach a consensus on agricultural development, their chances of upholding the interests of the Brazilian population in affordable food, international exchange and environmental protection will rise significantly. Even at their current inconsistent strength they check corporate manipulation of Brazil's agricultural market. As a result, food security and the protection of culturally vital staples is not an immediate issue in Brazil in the way it has been in Mexico or Japan.

Brazil's increasing dependence on agribusiness since the 1980s makes it vulnerable to a commodities bust. Rising international de-mand, the diversity of Brazilian production, and stabilization funds designed to offset price fluctuations for key crops provide some protection against this risk. But if the price of soy drops substantially or consistently, the Brazilian economy will suffer the consequences. Such a downturn would necessarily cut into funding for agrarian reform and likely exacerbate agrarian conflict. The agrarian reform and social spending carried out by Cardoso and Lula have reduced the MST's influence and brought growth and some redistribution to the countryside. Deeper reform, improving the conditions of agrarian labor and investing in the economic life of provincial towns, has received less political attention, but will be even more vital.

The agribusiness boom that began in 1990, more than any other single factor, has propelled Brazil's economic emergence, putting the down payment on its membership in the trendy BRIC club. But in joining this club, Brazil has depended on factors that make it unlike any other country – its massive expanses of undeveloped arable land and its combination of sophisticated biotech and cheap labor. Meanwhile, one of Brazil's other unique qualities, its dominion over the world's largest carbon sink in the Amazonian region, has received much rhetorical attention and some legislation, but little in the way of true protection.

Brazil's major rural zones have grown interdependently, but in markedly different ways. The south is characterized primarily by cooperatives of family-owned farms heavily engaged in diverse agribusiness for domestic and international markets. The west and center-west are characterized by large landholdings, often corporate-owned, also oriented towards agribusiness, with less diversity. The northeast remains impoverished and inefficient, but the expansion of EMBRAPA's interests in the region has already begun to change this pattern, and northeastern farms contribute heavily to biofuels and to domestic food crops. The north, principally in the Amazonian areas, is the region of greatest volatility and risk. It is likely to be the most crucial region in the future. All parties involved recognize that importance, but few agree on how to insure against disaster.

4 | Different drummers

Brazilian popular music appears to be an inexhaustible natural resource. It comes burgeoning forth in prodigious quantity and variety, year after year. Brief seasons of apparent drought are subsequently revealed to be periods of underground growth, resulting in bumper crops the following spring. And the more that is harvested and brought to market, the more that sprouts up to replenish the fields, for the harvest itself seeds the next growth.

Luiz de Camões, one of the great poets of the Portuguese language, once referred to what might be termed the unforgiving debt burdens of literary production by writing to his muse, "The more I pay you, the more I owe you." In considering the collective production of Brazilian popular music, the terms are reversed: the more that gets paid out, the richer Brazil is.

The period since the 1970s has not produced an iconic genre in the way of the *samba de morro* of the 1930s or the *bossa nova* of the late 1950s, both of which distilled and expressed a cultural sensibility of the moment. But they have given rise to other important developments, primarily the breaking of the Rio–São Paulo dominance over distribution, and the proliferation of new genres and subcultures. Rio de Janeiro and São Paulo were the centers of the recording and broadcast industries from the 1920s through the 1980s – figuratively speaking, all transmission waves emanated from these towering poles. Many talents from other parts of Brazil, particularly the northeast, made it big in the music industry, reshaping it in the process, but they did so by coming to Rio or São Paulo first, launching into stardom from there.

In Brazil since 1989, this has changed dramatically. These cities are still the capitals of the industry, but their role is no longer decisive nor indispensable. It is now possible to rise to regional and even national stardom in Salvador, Brasília or Belém de Pará without ever relocating to Rio or São Paulo. The once-provincial cities have now become capitals in a new network of transmission and distribution. This national realignment is mirrored by developments within cities, as the urban peripheries themselves have become centers of production and distribution of popular music. Much of this activity now takes place in the informal sector, independent of the formal market, still structured by major multinational recording companies and domestic television networks.

A profusion of genres and styles accompanies this transition. *Sertaneja, caipira, forró, samba-reggae, axé, samba de coco*, and *maracatu* are all forms that have emerged or have been revived and transformed in the past three decades outside of Rio and São Paulo, relatively independent of the whims of the old capitals. Musicians and audiences in Rio and São Paulo have not been idle: they have produced their own new sounds in funk, hip-hop, techno-bossa and other styles, as well as leading revivals of more traditional genres like samba de morro and *choro*. The result is a rich and fragmented musical market. Niche audiences, sampling and scratching, viral marketing and digital troubadors have all come to characterize Brazilian music, which remains ahead of global curves.

Brazilians often use the word *tribos*, or tribes, to refer to the nation's varying musical subcultures. But these tribes are neither exclusive nor cohesive, and young Brazilians in particular skip from one to another with little fear of ostracism or retribution. This salutary promiscuity of taste owes a debt to a lingering inspiration of *Maluco Beleza* – the nickname of pioneering rocker Raúl Seixas, the guiding spirit of a movement that reconfigured the popular musical market over the course of the 1980s.

Geração '80

Elis Regina's 1979 recording of "O Bêbado e a Equilibrista" (the Drunk and the Tightrope-Walker), the theme song of political amnesty, served as the opening fanfare for a generation that felt that its arrival on the national stage had been unjustly delayed by dictatorship. But an even younger generation found this attitude in itself oppressive. "O Bêbado" left its own hangover, which young Brazilians struggled to shake off. This generation, reaching its teenage years in the early 1980s, had not experienced "the leaden years" of the late 1960s and early 1970s as ones of oppression and fear, and its members tended to resent the self-importance of the returning exiles. As the generation of '68 assumed command of the nation, it inevitably began to alienate a significant portion of the generation of the 1980s, or what became known in the Brazilian culture world as *Geração '80*.

Like any ascriptive identity based on a decade, this one was frayed around the edges and not necessarily felt by many of those who came to be perceived as its icons. But the term did point to an important shift: as figures like Chico Buarque and Gilberto Gil became canonical, deliberately countercanonical manifestations emerged – particularly in popular music, always nurturing the vanguard of Brazilian culture. As a result, popular music became one of the most vibrant areas of invention and transformation in post-1989 Brazil.

Rock music displayed a global pedigree of youth rebellion since the late 1950s, but had not yet taken on that guise in Brazil. Cultural nationalism across the political spectrum generated suspicion of overt adoption of international models, and a laudable tendency towards the creation of inventive hybrids yielded new forms and styles. These, like the tropicalismo of Gil, Caetano Veloso and Os Mutantes in the late 1960s, had contestatory power, but, the use of electric guitars notwithstanding, were not considered rock. That label, and the intentionally disparaging homegrown term of *iê iê iê*, from the Beatles' yeah yeah yeah, was reserved for Roberto Carlos, the king of early Brazilian rock and roll. Roberto Carlos famously sang *"quero que você me aqueça neste inverno, e que tudo mais vá pro inferno"* (I want you to keep me warm this winter, and let everything else go to hell), but even in his youth he was far from a rebel. His compositions and recordings were finely cut and polished. His control and restraint, not qualities normally associated with leading rockers, only grew more evident as his long career unfolded.

Over the course of the 1970s, a new rocker emerged at the margins of Brazilian popular culture. Raúl Seixas was everything Roberto Carlos was not – wild, experimental and iconoclastic. His album-oriented rock of the 1970s drew heavily on psychedelic influences, both in its use of distorted guitar sounds and in its lyrics of vague but

impassioned questing. Many of these were written by his collabora-
tor, Paulo Coelho, who was later to apply a similar formula to the
printed page with more commercial success. In the late 1970s Seixas
recorded two anthems that summed up his career, "Metamorfose
Ambulante" (Walking Metamorphosis), and "Maluco Beleza" (Crazy
Beauty). The first gloriously intoned "I prefer being this walking
metamorphosis to having that same old pre-formed opinion about
everything" – a sentiment that would later be invoked to question
the terrible certainties of the generation of '68. The latter, more
celebratory, scoffed the mainstream and opted instead for the more
noble destiny of crazy beauty. This romantic sentiment was typical of
'70s global rock, but was not otherwise given much play in Brazil.

"Maluco Beleza" became Seixas's nickname, and the sentiment
behind it fueled a rock boom that changed Brazil's musical landscape
over the course of the 1980s. Seixas himself became more popular,
in sometimes surprising ways – he became particularly beloved in
the favelas of Rio de Janeiro, for example. These neighborhoods
were historically linked to the cultivation of samba and had begun
to nurture the new style of carioca funk. But the same favelado
youth who tried out for the samba school's drum corps and danced
to funk's sampled beats knew all the lyrics to Seixas's "Sociedade
Alternativa," singing along, "every man and every woman is a star."
Loosed from its restraints, rock had begun to take on unpredictable
contestatory manifestations.

The spirit of *maluco beleza* also informed the two defining trends
of Brazilian rock in the 1980s – the celebratory, "let's have fun and
forget about politics" style of rockers like Blitz, Kid Abelha and
Lulu Santos, and the passionate and occasionally defiant, "don't
trust anyone over forty" sound of groups like Legião Urbana, Barão
Vermelho, Titãs and Paralamas do Sucesso. The former was often
called *rock besteirol*, or nonsense, slapstick rock, the latter *rock
cabeça*, or, literally head rock, music for thinking about. Because it
was supposedly apolitical, rock besteirol posed a bigger challenge
to the cultural architecture of Brazilian popular music.

The broad category of Música Popular Brasileira had emerged
in the mid-1960s among Marxist–nationalist cultural theorists in
order to accommodate figures like Chico Buarque. It initially desig-

nated a musical approach deeply rooted in Brazilian tradition, but incorporating the harmonic ambition of bossa nova and the political strivings of the international folk movement. The category of Música Popular Brasileira, or MPB, as it came to be known, allowed participants in the Centro Popular de Cultura, a Marxist-nationalist culture club, to admire music that had some international influences and was part of a capitalist market – Chico Buarque sang on network TV, after all. Over the 1960s and '70s, MPB expanded to include new approaches, such as the music of Milton Nascimento, Caetano Veloso, Maria Bethânia and others. This expansion made the banishment of Raúl Seixas to the margins even more striking. MPB, rather than being defined by rhythm or instrumentation, came to be understood as music that was Brazilian and serious without ceasing to be popular.

By the 1980s, MPB had become the canon that rock besteirol came along to disrupt. With slangy and often comical lyrics about surfing, high-school love and consumer pleasures, supplemented by guitar-riff hooks and liberal doses of hair gel, these groups advocated a politics of earthy humor and good times. Although Lulu Santos was himself too cool to be considered besteirol, his "Como Uma Onda no Mar" became the scene's iconic hit. Written by Santos and Nelson Motta, the smart producer who recognized the market potential of the new generation, it declared at the outset, "Nothing that was will ever be again the way it was one day." Again, this was a familiar rock sentiment speaking pointedly in response to its local context.

The rock cabeça crowd, for its part, questioned whether the generation of '68 was truly prepared to do much to change Brazil. Many of its members came from Brasília and were members of the first generation to grow up in that city of revolutionary design and stultifying practice. Many of them were the sons of civil servants and recognized the corrupt clientelism that lay behind the façade of democratizing renovation. They had also witnessed firsthand, if not necessarily personally, the stifled dreams of the migrants that made up Brasília's reserve labor force and the growing violence of its satellite cities.

Legião Urbana, the most successful of the Brasília bands, had the iconic hit of the rock cabeça scene with "Faroeste Caboclo," a title that can at best be loosely translated as "Halfbreed Western." The nine-minute story-song recounts the violent life and death of João de Santo Cristo, who flees the poverty of the parched hinterlands for the capital, where he becomes a carpenter's apprentice and then a drug-dealing kingpin before a rival shoots him in the back. Although few recognized it at the time, "Faroeste Caboclo" is MPB – its structure, narrative and melody recall the repentista style honed by northeastern fok troubadors recounting heroic duels, its characterization of corruption among the "high bourgeoisie" and class struggle follow the political handbook of engaged left, its Christlike imagery reveals poetic aspirations, and its electric guitar makes it modern. For these reasons, "Faroeste," and rock cabeça more generally, would ultimately fit comfortably in the expanding category of MPB. But when the song was first unveiled, in 1987, it still seemed to be outside and opposed to increasingly staid MPB, and was taken as evidence that Brazilian rock had achieved the substance and the authority to address national issues.

The two strands of BRock, as '80s Brazilian rock came to be known, came together at the 1985 Rock in Rio festival, held in grounds developed specifically for the event in the distant suburb of Jacarepaguá. The festival featured Brazilian bands opening for past-their-prime international acts like Iron Maiden, Queen and AC/DC. Rock in Rio proved that Brazil could do overblown rock festivals as well as any first-world nation, and it brought home two truths to Brazilian rockers – first, they were in a position to put their own stamp on rock, rather than simply following a successful model; and, second, while they had the talent to compete with the foreigners (and with Foreigner), they were badly outclassed in power and showmanship. At Rock in Rio, the BRockers got a crash course in rock theatrics that would have profound consequences on the packaging of popular music in Brazil in the ensuing decades.

Most of the foundational BRock groups broke up in the early 1990s. As everywhere, the ravages of rock took their toll and several of their key members died young. Cazuza, lead singer of Barão Vermelho, broke with the band and embarked on a brief solo career before dying of AIDS-related illnesses in 1990. Renato Russo, lead singer of Legião Urbana, similarly left his rock band and pursued more diverse solo projects, including romantic pop sung in Italian. Like Cazuza, Russo died of complications related to AIDS, in 1996.

Cazuza and Russo, at the vanguard of Brazilian rock, were also at the vanguard of a more candid approach to homosexuality – both singers openly acknowledged same-sex activity, defying the Brazilian audience to show prejudice. In 1994, Russo recorded an album titled Stonewall Celebration Concert, in homage to the foundational moment of the North American gay rights movement. Androgyny and sexual ambiguity had been common in the Brazilian popular musical world since the tropicalist movement of the late 1960s, and long before that the homosexuality of several musical stars had been an open secret. But Cazuza and Russo tore off the veil. They were joined in this regard by other figures such as Ney Matogrosso, Edson Cordeiro, Cássia Eller, Marina Lima and Ana Carolina – an all-star roster of Brazilian rock and pop. The commercial success of these artists suggests their importance in setting the tone for the increasing acceptance of open homosexuality in urban Brazil in the 1980s and '90s. By the early twenty-first century, alleged bisexuality, at the very least, had become an important tool in the self-marketing of aspiring pop stars.

In the meantime, the surviving members of the '80s BRock scene invested their energies in a wide range of projects in the musical market of the 1990s and beyond, playing a strong role in most of the major transformations from the 1990s onwards.

While Rio, São Paulo and Brasília became three points of a BRock triangle, rockers in other parts of the country developed their own local scenes. Belo Horizonte nurtured a heavy metal scene that shared BRock's suspicion of the category of MPB and its political and cultural implications, but that stood one step further from national media networks. The catalyst for this scene and its most successful act was Sepultura, a death metal band that sung in English and that gradually cultivated an international fan base. Sepultura made the jump to the United States in the early 1990s and became one of the primary exponents of thrash metal, blending the frenetic tempo and political topics of hardcore punk with the gothic touches and key changes of heavy metal. By the mid-1990s, the individual band members, embarking on different projects, began to reclaim Brazilian influences, recording in Portuguese and incorporating Brazilian percussion instruments. Sepultura's international success was one of the first indications that Brazilian popular music was beginning to outgrow the constraints of the Rio–São Paulo distribution axis.[35]

Sertaneja

"Faroeste Caboclo" narrated an iconic migration from the dusty backlands to the fallen city, a passage that intrigued an urban audience, befitting a band called urban legion. Meanwhile, out in the countryside, a different kind of musical phenomenon was unfolding, and recent migrants from country to city tended to look to that music and its idealized vision of rural Brazilian life for their musical enjoyment. The genre of sertaneja music had been around since at least the 1930s, when singing cowboys from the interior of São Paulo, accompanied by guitar or *viola caipira* – a small, ten-string guitar – came to the state capital to sing songs of love and cattle on the radio. Sertaneja music had remained popular everwhere in Brazil that nurtured a ranching economy, but was not nationally popular and had never won over the cultural metropolis of Rio de Janeiro.

In the 1980s, as agrarian economies began to expand into a new ranching frontier, the rural audience expanded and its demands triggered rapid transformations in a style that had been largely unchanged for decades. Aspiring sertaneja stars looked to foreign rural genres – particularly to US country and Mexican *ranchera* – for new ideas. The slide guitar suddenly found its way into sertaneja music, as did the melodramatic vocal style of ranchera. The ten-gallon hat, previously a rarity in Brazil, became standard accoutrement for sertaneja performers, and recordings quickly gained the polish of multitrack studios with overdubbing and sweeping synthesized flourishes.

These innovations were incorporated seamlessly into a genre that glorified the past. The target audiences for the new sertaneja music were the residents of the new agrarian frontier, on the one hand, and the recent migrants from the country to the city, on the other. Both proved enthusiastic consumers of music that extolled the moral, romantic and familial virtues of a timeless rural life. Successful acts overwhelmingly consisted of male duos, either real or symbolic brothers. They sang harmony with a perfection that suggested deep emotional kinship. Women were the objects of the romantic songs, and were not on stage – a characteristic of the genre that endured into the early twenty-first century. The open homosexuality celebrated in BRock was strictly off-limits in the sertaneja world, where manly defense of traditional gender roles was considered an unquestioned value.

A small segment of the audience rejected the innovations, preferring the hard-won virtues of the older rural style. This approach now became known exclusively as caipira music, a style marked by rigorous musicianship on demanding instruments like the viola caipira, and suspicion of market gloss. Sertaneja and caipira, once used fairly interchangeably to describe rural styles, now defined separate approaches that at least the fans of the latter imagined to be completely opposed.[36]

Sertaneja fans had the comfort of numbers and therefore less need for purism. The industry grew, at first in the shadows of metropolitan culture. Rodeos became increasingly popular and lucrative in the 1980s and 1990s. Fans and participants trekked from all over the interior to attend the annual rodeos in provincial cities like Barretos and Presidente Prudente, São Paulo. Smaller rodeos could be found in every major rural region, every weekend. Rodeos were an ideal venue for the new sertaneja performers and largely through them sertaneja found venues, a marketplace and a distribution network. By the time the metropolitan media titans were prepared to pay attention, sertaneja was primed and ready to boom.

In 1990, the Manchete network, owned by the media entrepreneur Adolpho Bloch, aired a telenovela called *Pantanal*. Manchete was a junior competitor to the dominant Globo network, generally trailing Globo by a wide margin in audience polls. Bloch gambled the future of his network on showing a different side of Brazil – where Globo's novelas tended to be set primarily in the milieu of upper-middle-class Rio and São Paulo, Bloch saw the opportunity to portray the new rural Brazil. *Pantanal* was named for the vast wetlands of Mato Grosso, home both to a unique biosphere and to a booming ranch economy. In real life, these facets may have been at odds, but in the novela they combined in an alluring recipe of striking eco-footage supporting a gothic plot encompassing land, heritage and revenge.

The soundtrack was predominantly sertaneja, with incidental caipira flourishes. Sertaneja star Sérgio Reis – an early rocker in the Roberto Carlos crowd who had reclaimed his rural roots – played one of the key roles. Almir Sater, renowned among caipira fans for his viola prowess, played another.

Pantanal was a hit: it was one of only a handful of novelas since the 1970s to beat Globo's competitor in the ratings. And it brought the new sertaneja music into the living rooms of Brazil. When *Pantanal* ended, Manchete followed it with another rural-themed novela, *Ana Raio e Zé Trovão* (Ana Lightning and Joe Thunder), which lasted most of 1991. The two main characters were rodeo stars in rival troupes, offering the ideal plot justification for plentiful location footage of the rodeo circuit. Like Pantanal, the new novela's soundtrack featured rising sertaneja stars. Globo had customarily ruled the pop charts through the popularity of its novela soundtracks. Manchete now did the same with the success of *Pantanal* and *Ana Raio e Zé Trovão*. As a result, sertaneja duos like Leandro and Leonardo and Zezé di Camargo and Luciano now transcended the rodeo circuit to become megastars.

In 1998, Luiz José Costa, better known throughout Brazil as the Leandro half of the famed sertaneja duo Leandro and Leonardo, died after a sudden onset of a rare cancer. Hundreds of thousands of fans gathered for his funeral in his home state of rural Goiás. The outpouring of grief following Leandro's death showed the strength of the sertaneja boom even more decisively than the success of the rural novelas. This was not a fad, but a growing market segment: seven years later, in 2005, Zezé di Camargo and Luciano became the subject of a glowing biopic chronicling their rise from early poverty to glorious stardom, based on brotherly love and harmony. *Dois Filhos de Francisco* (Two Sons of Francisco) became the top-grossing film in Brazilian history (until 2007, when it lost that distinction to *Tropa de Elite* – Elite Squad – the urban nightmare opposed to *Francisco*'s rural ideal).

Salvador

Sertaneja, partly because of its link to the rodeo circuit, was diffused over a broad stretch of the interior even before its boom. Other styles that came to the fore in the 1990s were nurtured in local scenes before rising to national prominence. Salvador da Bahia was the first of these to gain extensive national and international exposure.

Salvador had always been a center of musical invention, but not one of reproduction and distribution. That changed over the course of the 1980s and '90s, largely due to the success of *bloco afro* and its offshoots. In 1974, a group of drummers from the working-class, predominantly Afro-Brazilian neighborhood of Liberdade formed a *bloco*, or carnival parade band, named Ilê Aiyê. Its founders were part of a black movement that flourished in Rio de Janeiro, São Paulo and Salvador in the 1970s. Many of the intellectual leaders of this loosely organized movement were strongly steeped in Marxist, pan-Africanist cultural theory, and looked with disfavor on carnival as a tourist industry. They sought to recover an idea of a less commercial carnival, where Afro-Brazilian cultural roots could be more effectively nourished and displayed. For the founders of Ilê Aiyê, this meant a bloco that would emphasize Salvador's historic cultural links to West Africa, through use of African-inspired clothing, a Yoruba name which loosely translates as "black clay," and emphasis on African rhythms. They called their project a bloco afro, and limited participation to black Brazilians.

In a city that had often been cited as the primary example of the supposed existence of racial democracy in Brazil, this was a provocative undertaking. In the carnival of 1975, Ilê Aiyê took to the streets with signs reading Black Power, in English, directly challenging the predominant understanding of carnival as an apolitical, sensual celebration. Many Bahians were scandalized, but more were inspired. Ilê Aiyê became one of the most popular blocos in the city and a model to be imitated. Musically, the group emphasized cross rhythms played by the *surdos*, or bass drums, and the *repiniques*, or tom-toms. In contrast to the increasingly frenetic sound of the Rio samba schools, Ilê Aiyê emphasized a marching pace, marked by thunderous bass rolls, enlivened by the crisp patterns of the repiniques. The bloco's sung refrains always featured liberal use of Yoruba terms and exaltations of black Bahia.

By the end of the 1970s, Ilê Aiyê had a new competitor, Olodum. This new bloco was more festive and better-located – its roots in the historic Pelourinho neighborhood positioned Olodum to take advantage of local tourism. Perhaps for this reason, Olodum was less wary of the market than Ilê Aiyê. In keeping with the pan-Africanist foundations of the bloco afro phenomenon, Olodum looked to the reggae of Jamaica, and of Bob Marley in particular, for inspiration. It adopted the colors of red, gold, green and black, and incorporated the loping rhythm of Marley's reggae into its music. The result soon became known as samba-reggae, gradually spreading beyond both carnival and the bloco format.

Olodum itself expanded, putting together various subunits – they could parade in a bloco of hundreds, play in a theater with thirty drummers, or in a bar with ten drummers and a keyboardist. They created a children's band and a theatrical company. And Olodum also began to run local education programs. By the late 1980s, it was half NGO, half musical enterprise, running a community center that supported the commercial ventures of its performing groups, and vice versa. In 1990, Paul Simon recorded the album *Rhythm of the Saints* with Olodum's collaboration, and bloco afro suddenly went international. Olodum developed a global fan base, while purists opted for the vintage sounds of Ilê Aiyê. Olodum also used its fame to pursue funding for its NGO activities, winning support from the Ford Foundation and other international funders.

The success of bloco afro and samba-reggae triggered demand for similar music in a format more conducive to recorded music and TV appearances. Wesley Rangel, owner of the local recording studio WR Discos, stepped into the void, producing records not only of the blocos, but of smaller groups who adapted their rhythms to the stricter structural confines of the pop song. The result became known as "axé music," mixing Yoruba and English, a reminder that this was a product meant for export as well as internal consumption. Margareth Menezes, one of the early WR stars, was soon picked up by David Byrne's record label, acquiring an international audience. Within Brazil, Daniela Mercury became the most successful axé star of the '90s, omnipresent in Brazil-MTV videos and shampoo commercials ("my hair is part of my show"). Bloco afro had come a long way from its non-commercial roots.

Successful as it was, axé soon paled in sales to Bahian *pagode*, a

variant of samba featuring sexualized double-meaning lyrics match-
ing suggestive dances. The term pagode had originally denoted any
informal samba party, but in '70s and '80s Rio, pagode came to mean
a melodic, romantic samba, sung by a group of musicians playing
acoustic instruments and taking turns as lead vocalist. In the early
1990s, the success of the band Grupo Fundo do Quintal (The Back of
the Garden) brought Rio's pagode sound out of the informal settings
of suburban Rio and into the national spotlight.

WR Discos and other Salvador producers adapted the trend, crafting a Bahian variant. They simplified the harmony, sticking to a basic
pattern of three major chords endlessly strummed by a *cavaquinho*,
or ukulele, and reduced the syncopation of the *pandeiro* and the
cuíca, samba's traditional percussive instruments. Most importantly,
in live performance they brought scantily clad dancers upstage, usually with their hindquarters oriented towards the audience, shaking
at approximately 120 beats per minute. Bahian pagode was a natural
for the Sunday-afternoon variety shows that have long been a staple
of Brazilian TV. By the mid-1990s, Bahian pagode groups like É o
Tchan were inescapable.

Recife

A few hundred kilometers to the north of Salvador, a more vibrant
scene emerged in Recife, Pernambuco. Like Rio and Salvador, Recife
and its surrounding hinterlands had long nurtured local forms combining African and European influence in unique ways. But while
the *maracatu*, *ciranda* and *samba de côco* of Pernambuco were widely
known, they had not yet become a focus for national attention nor
incorporated significantly into the recording and broadcasting industries. That changed over the course of the 1990s, as a cohort of
young musicians interested in putting a modern, globalized stamp
on Pernambucan identity began combining these local forms with
elements of punk rock, heavy metal and hip-hop.

The principal catalyst of this scene was a young musician and
tastemaker who called himself Chico Science – a moniker that
alluded to hip-hop argot, where dropping science meant disseminating knowledge. Chico dropped serious science, first on his peers
in Recife and its sister city across the river, Olinda, and then on

global audiences. He was *antenado*, tuned in, to thrash, funk, indie comics and other artifacts of global punk chic, trading records and magazines within a small circle of like-minded peers in Recife in the late 1980s. But he was also deeply familiar with Olinda's traditions of ciranda – a ring-dance animated by drums, brass and participatory singing of simple refrains – and maracatu – a parade music, featuring snare and bass drums and a syncopated cowbell. His genius was to recognize that the combination of these influences could yield new forms that would be distinctly Pernambucan without being pigeonholed as folklore.

This approach followed the recipe honed by Caetano Veloso and Gilberto Gil in the tropicalist movement of the late 1960s, blending traditional local forms with foreign influences in a format where both would be instantly recognizable but inextricably combined, used to underline lyrics which often described political and personal disjuncture in dense symbolic terms. But Chico Science and cohort brought new elements to the tropicalist palette, through incorporation of maracatu, ciranda, thrash metal and sampling. More importantly, they crafted an identifiable local brand, calling their style *mangue bit*, mangue for the swamplands surrounding Recife and bit for digital bits or the homonym, in Brazilian Portuguese, of funky beats – *mangue beat* soon became the more commonly used term. In 1992, Science's colleague Fred 04 issued the mangue beat manifesto, "Caranguejos com Cérebro" (Crabs with Brains), suggesting that mangue beat practitioners were like sly, resourceful crabs flourishing in the tropical muck while making mental connections to hip-hop and "the collapse of modernity."

The manifesto's rapid-fire montage recalled previous documents in Brazilian cultural history, such as the manifesto of the Pau Brasil poetry movement in 1924, and that of the anthropophagist movement of 1928. This self-branding demonstrated that the mangueboys and manguegirls, as they called themselves, were keenly aware that their moment had arrived and that they were prepared to seize it. It also provided ready explanation and interpretive armature to critics within Brazil and beyond, helping to pave mangue beat's path to critical success. In contrast to sertaneja and bloco afro, mangue beat would win over hip journalists first and then a popular audience.

The mangueboys had the musical chops to back up their media strategy. Chico Science and Nação Zumbi had their biggest hit with a recording of Jorge Mautner and Nelson Jacobina's "Maracatu Atômico," a tropicalist artifact first recorded by Gilberto Gil in 1974. The lyrics offered striking symbolist combinations of elements of natural tropical fertility and modern urban life. Gil's original recording had featured his trademark acoustic guitar style, light percussion and synthesizer, and only a distant evocation of the maracatu rhythm referred to in the title. Chico Science and Nação Zumbi's version, in contrast, featured searing electric guitar locked in a driving rhythmic pattern with thunderous maracatu percussion, overlaid by sampled fragments in a dizzying blend that could be taken in any of several directions – the band's 1996 CD, *Afrociberdelia*, featured four versions of "Maracatu Atômico," all mixed to evoke different national and international influences. This experimentation showed that mangue beat was both a realization of initial tropicalist approaches and a transformation of them into something intriguingly new.

For Chico Science and his band, Nação Zumbi, the media strategy and the musical invention paid off in an invitation to open for Gilberto Gil at New York's Central Park Summerstage series in 1995. While few in the audience could understand what Chico Science was saying, his snarled vocals, backed by distorted guitars and maracatu drums, made an unforgettable impression. They received rave reviews in the *New York Times*, altering the traditional path to stardom – in the past, Brazilian acts achieved international fame only after first winning over a national audience from a base in Rio or São Paulo. Chico Science and Nação Zumbi were darlings of the international press when only a few Brazilians outside of Recife had heard of them.

Fred 04's group, Mundo Livre S/A, shared in the attention, as did other emerging Recife acts. Mangue beat had gone from local curiosity to global phenomenon, fulfilling the far-fetched but brilliantly executed designs of its originators. Precisely because the mangue beat concept embraced the combination of disparate elements, it incorporated or became linked to a wide range of musical phenomena. Many of these focused with greater intensity than had Chico Science and Nação Zumbi on Pernambuco's traditional forms.

Groups playing orthodox renditions of maracatu became part of the mangue scene even though their music prized fidelity to tradition above all. The Recife crowd had at least temporarily overcome one of the greatest obstacles to the preservation of local forms, finding a way to pass on traditional styles that could only be learned through painstaking apprenticeship without turning them into fusty museum pieces. Old hands like Mestre Salustiano, a musician with over forty years of experience mastering the subtleties of Pernambucan music on the *rabeca*, a rustic homemade violin, became treasured interlocutors of the mangue scene.

The fertility of this scene survived the death of its most important progenitor – Chico Science was killed in a car crash during carnival of 1997. Nação Zumbi carried on, as did the Recife scene. Chico Science's survivors on that scene sustained its vitality by reaching in two directions – towards the Pernambucan hinterland and towards an international critical audience. The group Cordel do Fogo Encantado created a cultural lifeline between the Recife scene and the dusty hinterland town of Arcoverde, a stronghold of rural Pernambucan music. The group Cascabulho did much the same for Carpina, another hinterland town with a tradition of forró, an accordion-based popular dance music, combining this form with the noise and energy of punk rock. Both Cordel do Fogo Encantado and Cascabulho also cultivated ties on the international festival circuit, becoming representatives of Pernambuco's vitality without having to use Rio or São Paulo as a springboard.

Funk and hip-hop

In the 1970s, Rio and São Paulo had nurtured burgeoning soul music scenes. This scene was demographically, politically and musically innovative. Its initial target audience was working-class youth of the urban periphery. It drew heavily on the rhetoric of black power, and it brought the music of performers like James Brown and Isaac Hayes into the Brazilian lexicon. The soul dances of the mid-1970s were usually held at social clubs in the working-class suburbs, and would alternate live performances of artists such as Tim Maia and the Banda Black Rio with a DJ spinning soul records. The dances became so successful that upscale clubs held their own soul dances, with a more mixed audience. By the early 1980s, the music at these dances was primarily disco, and black power was no longer part of their market appeal.

Out in the suburbs, the social clubs kept holding weekend dances, beneath the market's radar. Many of these continued to feature soul music and nurtured the early careers of crossover soul performers of the 1980s such as Luiz Melodia and Sandra de Sá. By the late 1980s, they had also begun to make room for the experiments of MCs rapping over sampled beats.

In São Paulo, aspiring MCs tended to be overtly political, condemning police violence and racial discrimination. They worked with DJs, assembling a collage of dissonant beats and samples. They looked to international models such as LL Cool J and Public Enemy for inspiration, and called their music hip-hop or rap (incongruously pronounced as "happy" in Brazilian Portuguese). They were the hip-hop equivalent of rock cabeça. In Rio, MCs tended to be apparently apolitical, exhorting the crowd to get up and get moving, often reciting highly sexualized lyrics in a semi-comical sing-song, while DJs pumped simple drum and bass beats behind them. They called their music funk, although it had little in common with the funk of James Brown, and were the hip-hop equivalent of rock besteirol.

Over the course of the 1990s, São Paulo's hip-hop and Rio's funk came out of the shadows, gradually seizing market share and media attention. Racionais MC's (Rational MCs) was the prototypical São Paulo group, as their name suggests: *Racionais* indicated their cabeça political posture, *MC's* both their debt to international hip-hop and their rebellious attitude towards punctuation. They hailed from the working-class suburb of Capão Redondo, an area plagued by violence and police brutality in the 1990s. As a result, Racionais MC's arrived on the market with a built-in street credibility. They reinforced that reputation with a 1994 performance at a street festival in downtown São Paulo, where their set ended in a crowd skirmish and the band members were arrested for inciting violence against the police. Racionais subsequently became the unofficial spokesmen for the marginalized periphery, much in demand not only at suburban dancehalls but for interviews with the *Folha de São Paulo*.

In Rio, meanwhile, the soul dances that had once been concentrated in suburban social clubs migrated to more public spaces, most notably the *quadras*, or courts, of favela samba schools and resident associations. These favela *bailes funk*, or funk dances, became the most feared popular cultural manifestation of Rio in the '90s. Rio's daily newspapers depicted them as drug bazaars created by criminal networks for the purpose of marketing cocaine. Funk dances and funk itself became inextricably linked in the public mind with the plague of urban violence. This exaggerated, but not entirely off-base, coverage triggered an equally exaggerated response among academics, who began to theorize the funk dances as a space of resistance against marginality.

In reality, many different kinds of funk dances proliferated throughout the city. Some of these had obvious links to criminal networks and were characterized by an atmosphere of potential violence. Dances of the late 1980s and early 1990s occasionally featured semi-organized brawls, where rival groups faced off across a "death corridor" – anyone who crossed the corridor initiated a rumble. This practice faded as turf wars became more entrenched – the possibility of rival crews meeting in the same quadra diminished. Most dances were characterized by no greater violence or drug dealing than one might find at many Rio de Janeiro discotheques, and many by considerably less. The weekly *baile charme* of Madureira, for example, featured *charme*, or R&B, as backing music, and drew an audience decked out in its finest evening gear, looking for a night of style and romance, with no threat of violence and no overt drug use.

The location of most funk dances nonetheless tied them to the turf battles between rival criminal networks and the police. Even where criminal networks were not producing the dances, they often looked upon the crowds as a captive market. At the weekly dance in Chapéu Mangueira in the mid-1990s, attended by many youth from surrounding middle-class neighborhoods, one of the key sources of profit was parking: drivers were charged princely sums for parking along the favela's only road. Most violent episodes associated with funk dances happened neither within the dances nor within the favela, but in the liminal zones between the favela and adjacent neighborhoods, where participants passed from one zone of authority to another.

By the end of the 1990s, however, the association between funk and the criminal networks had become a self-fulfilling prophecy. MCs seeking to cultivate favor with local gang leaders extolled the glory of their exploits. Because any statement presenting an *apologia do crime* (a justification of crime) is technically illegal in Brazil, these funk lyrics could not be legally recorded and distributed, giving rise to the subgenre of funk *proibidão*, or really prohibited funk. Proibidão circulates in underground CDs and MP3s, and on YouTube.

While proibidão became the newest *bête noire* of funk-fearing cariocas, the larger genre of funk subdivided and recombined with other styles of popular music, including samba. Rio began to nurture its own overtly political hip-hop scene, led by figures like MV Bill, from the historically peripheral neighborhood of Cidade de Deus. Like Racionais MC's, MV Bill drew a street credibility from his background, which he subsequently used to speak as a self-styled representative of favela youth, condemning police violence and marginalization.

The Rio de Janeiro collective Afro-Reggae – primarily a hip-hop band, despite its name – followed Olodum's lead in the combination of musical spectacle and NGO fundraising. Afro-Reggae is likely the world's most-sponsored popular musical group, with ongoing funding from Petrobras and project funding from the Ford Foundation, Pão de Açucar Supermarkets, Telemar telecommunications, Globo TV, the city and state governments of Rio de Janeiro, and many other state and private entities. Playing music is a relatively small part of Afro-Reggae's agenda – the group dedicates most of its energy to running community outreach programs and public relations campaigns. Afro-Reggae has, in effect, built a recognizable brand through successful marketing and fundraising, oriented towards a mixture of musical production and community service, supported primarily by Brazilian taxpayers. As in Olodum's case, this has undermined the group's ability to create fresh and compelling popular music.

Since 2003 the party funk that had always been the genre's most prominent tendency in Rio grew up, leaving behind, for the most part, the grating incantations and droning beats of the mid-1990s for a denser layering of samples. Groups like Malha Funk began to draw on a larger meaning of the term funk, sampling grooves that recalled both US funk and Brazilian soul-samba of the 1970s.

Musicians formerly or primarily associated with other genres also stepped into the once isolated funk and hip-hop territory. Fernanda Abreu, onetime backing-vocalist for the rock besteirol band Blitz, reinvented herself as a fierce hip-hop MC, rapping over a sound collage rich in nuggets of US and Brazilian soul. Farofa Carioca united *sambistas* and old-school *funkeiros* with members of the younger crowd to create an updated soul-samba sound. The vocalist and composer Seu Jorge demonstrated a similar ability to bridge '70s soul-samba and late-'90s funk, creating a successful trademark sound. And the São Paulo band Funk Como le Gusta re-created and extended 1970s horn-based samba-funk, adding a DJ sampling and mixing. Funk and hip-hop, in other words, were folded into the process of hybridization that has continually domesticated influences and enriched Brazilian popular music over the course of its history.

The critical category of MPB, already broad and ill-defined in the mid-1980s, expanded further to include at least some of these regional and stylistic variations. Artists working within this category consequently had a broader palette from which to draw. Techno-bossa nova became a rich forum for this approach. The early experiments of the São Paulo DJ Suba in the mid-1990s turned into an intercontinental scene, where DJs and singers book gigs in São Paulo, London and Los Angeles with equal ease. DJs like Meme and Marcelo da Lua of Rio de Janeiro and Nuts of São Paulo draw on archives of source material, sampling and mixing them in identifiable styles that have become coveted brands on the international club circuit. The techno-bossa wave also facilitated the return of older bands like Azimuth and the rise of new ones like BossaCucaNova, combining live instrumentation and sampling.

The techno-bossa wave coexists amicably with revival scenes for bossa nova, samba and choro, where younger performers craft highly faithful renditions of older styles and once forgotten journeymen return to live performance. Bossa-jazz pioneers like Durval Ferreira, Maurício Einhorn and J. T. Meirelles, all of whom had gone decades without recording, made new CDs in the early twenty-first century, showing they had merely been waiting for the audience to catch up to them again. Samba performers like Teresa Cristina and Nilze Carvalho re-created the sound and energy of dancehall samba of the 1950s, headlining popular weekly gigs in downtown Rio.

All these tendencies showed that performers and producers had learned to draw on a living archive of Brazilian popular music, catering neither to an artificial sense of purity nor to an impetus towards novelty for its own sake. The stylistic innovations that had disrupted and expanded the category of MPB, and the regional scenes that had disrupted and expanded the Rio–São Paulo production axis left a popular musical market of extraordinary diversity and vigor. Brazilian popular music of the early twenty-first century has a debt to the past, and artists often make repayment of that debt an explicit part of their performance. But participants in the current fragmented but overlapping musical scenes have no cause to envy the innovation and vitality of their forebears.

As diverse as this panorama seems, it fails to take account of one of the fastest-growing sectors of Brazil's music market, that of religious popular music. Singers linked to Pentecostal churches, in particular, have become among the top-selling artists in Brazil. The growth of those churches and its consequences is the subject of the next chapter.

5 | The Pentecostal boom

Brazil used to be known as the world's largest Catholic country, but is now the world's largest Pentecostal country. Catholics still considerably outnumber members of Pentecostal churches – according to a 2007 study by Datafolha, one of Brazil's premier polling organizations, 64 percent of Brazilians declare themselves Catholic and approximately 17 percent declare membership in Pentecostal churches.[37] Most Brazilian Catholics, however, are nominal believers – their faith may or may not be deeply important to them, but they do not attend mass regularly, do not donate to the Church, and do not make Catholicism a strong part of their daily social and political life. Most Brazilian Catholics have Catholic parents, and were baptized in their infancy. Catholicism is primarily an inherited condition, one with roots in Portuguese colonization and the establishment of Catholicism as the religion of the Brazilian empire in the nineteenth century. The reverse is true of Brazil's Pentecostal churches – almost all members are committed churchgoers and active participants in church social and political networks. Many donate a significant portion of their income and savings to their church. Most have left another faith or church in order to join their current Pentecostal church, and most of these churches are themselves relatively new creations.

Redemocratization has coincided with the massive growth of Pentecostalism. That growth was underway by the 1980s, but has proliferated at a rate and in diverse manifestations few predicted at that time. This proliferation reflects Brazil's broader transformations: the Pentecostal denominations have grown as Brazil has urbanized, pushed into new frontier zones, and undergone profound economic and political changes. The rise of these denominations is not the only novelty in Brazil's religious market. The Catholic Charismatic Renewal – the Church's response to Pentecostalism –

has flourished, while the Christian Base Communities – politically mobilized grassroots organizations in poor neighborhoods, associated with liberation theology – have dwindled, with many of their leaders entering the formal political arena and cutting direct ties with the Church. Traditional Afro-Brazilian religions like *umbanda* and *candomblé* have also attracted greater numbers of participants, as have eastern religions. But the Pentecostal churches, designed to attract believers in the midst of transition, have drawn the most energy from larger economic and political transformations. Their increasing prominence is one of the most striking and consequential developments of the new democracy.

Brazil has now become an exporter of Pentecostalism – Brazilian churches establish successful franchises around the globe, ministering both to expatriate Brazilian communities and to local populations. Within Brazil, meanwhile, the Pentecostal boom, transformative as it has been, has been folded into older political and cultural traditions. As Brazil has become Pentecostal, Pentecostalism has become Brazilianized.

Protestant Brazil

Traditional Protestant denominations were present in the nineteenth-century Brazilian empire, but their presence was minimal and restricted primarily to those not born in Brazil. This began to change with the inauguration of the republic in 1889, and its clear separation of Church and State. Methodist missions to Brazil became increasingly common. At a time when most Latin American republics were still characterized by close relationships between Church and State, Brazil was moving to diminish these, if not entirely sever them, thereby creating space for other denominations. Several of the new Protestant missions were informed by the "holiness" or "perfection" schools within Methodist thought, returning to the teachings of John Wesley and their emphasis on ecstatic purification of the heart.

By the early twentieth century, these schools had given rise to independent denominations, which emphasized speaking in tongues as the manifestation of holiness – a practice that became the hallmark of Pentecostalism. In 1911, missionaries spreading this doctrine formed a new church in Belém do Pará, in the Brazilian Amazon. By the end of the decade, they had taken the denomination Assembléia de Deus, or Assemblies of God, roughly at the same time independent branches of this denomination were being founded in the United States and other countries. Assembléia spread gradually from the Amazon throughout Brazil. Other Pentecostal churches followed suit, slowly gaining ground in Catholic Brazil.

Getúlio Vargas's Estado Novo renewed the alliance between the state and the Catholic Church – while other faiths were not constrained, state subsidies for the Catholic Church bolstered Catholic centrality. Government funding for Catholic social services to the poor, in particular, helped to reinforce the Church's appeal among this population. In subsequent decades, these services, separated from state funding, would play a key role in the development of liberation theology as a pastoral practice.

The Second Republic, between 1946 and 1964, witnessed a renewed expansion of Protestant conversion, both to traditional and to Pentecostal denominations. The Igreja Quandrangular (Foursquare Church) and Igreja Deus é Amor (God is Love Church) began to grow in these years, becoming Assembléia's primary competitors for converts to Pentecostalism.

The military regime once again depended on close but by no means consistently warm relations between the Catholic Church and the state. Most churchgoing Catholics supported the coup against Goulart, but support waned as the dictatorship hardened and endured.[38] In the 1970s, the Church's "preferential option for the poor" flourished, particularly in favelas and among the landless rural poor, who responded by forming thousands of Christian Base Communities. In the mid-1980s, these base communities began to lose participants. Their emphasis on collective struggles alienated many parishioners who were seeking to overcome grinding economic circumstances and triumph over difficulties within their own families. These communities' increasing connection to political parties alienated parishioners who were making other political choices in the context of redemocratization. And the Church itself withdrew funding for base community pastoral initiatives and began to restrain liberation theology's theoreticians.

Pentecostal conversion had continued to pick up pace during

the dictatorship, as the major existing denominations all opened new churches and expanded their congregations. This conversion was particularly strong among the urban poor, the primary target of the base communities. In contrast to the base communities, these Pentecostal churches emphasized not communal problems such as insufficient infrastructure and lack of political representation, but individual problems, such as alcoholism, adultery, and unemployment. Whereas the base communities flourished briefly during the period of incipient redemocratization and then either faded or separated from the Church as democracy consolidated, the Pentecostal churches addressed the kinds of problems that would become more pressing as poor and working-class neighborhoods changed. Liberation theologists tended to attribute rising urban violence to social injustice, offering only a communal struggle for redistribution of power and wealth as a means of confronting violence. This approach proved less attractive as economic stratification within these neighborhoods deepened and a sense of communal mission frayed. Pentecostal churches, in contrast, appealed to the poor and working-class women whose families were at risk of being torn apart by rising crime and violence. They preached that wayward souls – husbands troubled by drink, sons drifting into the wrong circles – could be saved through faith-healing, a message that proved deeply powerful.

Neo-Pentecostals and mega-denominations

In 1977, a new contender emerged – the Igreja Universal do Reino de Deus (IURD), or Universal Kingdom of God Church, founded by Edir Macedo in the suburbs of Rio de Janeiro. Macedo maintained all the salient practices of Pentecostalism – speaking in tongues, rapid training of local pastors, direct approach to individual difficulties – but added new emphases and new strategies. He brought the exorcism of evil spirits to the fore of his pastoral method, insisted on generous tithing from his congregation, and promised that true believers would be rewarded with material wealth. In contrast to liberation theology, Macedo preached prosperity theology, holding that wealth is a sign of God's blessing, that believers have a right to the best the world has to offer, and that God has the obligation to provide. Whereas leaders of base communities advocated radical redistribution in support of social justice and Pentecostals advocated tackling broad social ills one family at a time, the IURD accepted the exacerbation of social ills as inevitable features of an unsaved world. The believer's duty was not to his community or even his family, but to himself and to God, via his pastor.

In this doctrine, believers earned the right to place demands on God through fulfillment of their own obligations, primarily offering the *dízimo*, or tithe. The amount was not to be determined as a percentage or sum, but needed to be a significant sacrifice. Macedo urged his followers to donate whatever savings they had, for only by doing so would they be in a position to receive God's rewards.

In the IURD, the obstacle to enrichment was not social injustice but *encosto*, a term that implies not necessarily possession by evil spirits but the unfortunate approximation of the believer to evil spirits, which become effectively stuck to the believer, bringing misfortune upon him. Only a session of *descarrego*, discharging or unburdening, can separate the believer from these spirits. Any renewed approximation, however unintentional or unconscious, can create a new situation of encosto, requiring another descarrego.

The doctrine of encosto and descarrego resonates with universal experiences of Brazilian life, where one's path towards mundane and necessary goals – acquisition of an identity card, withdrawing a social security payment, parking on a city street – is blocked by obstacles that can be removed only through the intervention of a paid fixer. In legal circles, the fixer is a *desembargador*, or remover of embargos. In everyday life, he is a *despachante*, or dispatcher. And in the IURD, he is the pastor who offers descarrego. The doctrine also echoes similar practices in umbanda, also called descarrego. This is not surprising, for Macedo and subsequent IURD pastors honed their strategies in open competition with umbanda. For Macedo, coming into contact with an umbanda *terreiro*, or house of worship, or any of its practitioners, was precisely the kind of action that might lead to encosto. The IURD thus developed a doctrine that spoke directly to Brazilian experience and competed aggressively on local terrain.

Encosto has nothing to do with sin. The victim has not necessarily done anything wrong, and there is no penance to be paid: a hefty tithe and a quick descarrego are enough to set matters to right. But nor is there atonement. Continued impoverishment can be the result only of continued or renewed encosto, and failure to recognize this is the surest sign of encosto.

Macedo trained his pastors to preach this doctrine forcefully. They accepted nothing less than immediate cash contributions, chastising those who failed to give, and carried out on-the-spot descarregos that appeared to prove the truth of their words. When pastors asked for testimony in confirmation, nearly every member of the parish could attest that his fortunes had improved since joining IURD. They were a self-selected group of strivers, learning to believe that they were on the path towards enrichment; to admit otherwise was to admit to encosto.

IURD spread like wildfire in the expanding peripheral neighborhoods of Brazil's major cities, and then began reaching into more established neighborhoods and out to the countryside. Macedo became a wealthy and powerful man, as did several of his pastors. This success prompted the foundation of competing denominations operating on a similar business model, including the Igreja Renascer em Cristo (Reborn in Christ) and the Igreja Sara Nossa Terra (Heal Our Land). These new denominations, often characterized by exorcism, aggressive demands for tithing and variations on prosperity theology, became the fastest growing religious sector in Brazil in the 1990s. The most successful among them sent pastors across Brazil and then across the world, founding new and increasingly prosperous churches. Many more never grew beyond one or two churches – they remained essentially neighborhood operations, with a local clientele.

There is considerable theological and political diversity among these denominations, and among individual churches within the larger denominations. Scholars of Brazilian religion often describe any denomination founded after 1977 as neo-Pentecostal, using that term to refer to the greater propensity of newer churches to practice exorcism, demand tithing and build congregations through media ownership and exposure. Pastors at older denominations like Assembléia and Quadrangular echo this distinction, forcefully condemning denominations like IURD and Sara Nossa Terra for their

putative similarity to umbanda. But many of the newer denominations share greater similarities with Quadrangular than they do with
IURD. Relatively few of the new denominations own radio or TV
stations, or have any kind of media presence.

The expansionist success of IURD and Renascer, meanwhile, has
prompted older Pentecostal denominations to follow their tactics,
particularly in seeking media exposure. Traditional denominations
like the Methodist and Presbyterian Churches have also been deeply
affected by the Pentecostal boom, and have seen the rise of Pentecostal wings, characterized by greater emphasis on spiritual ecstasy
and some form of faith-healing. The Catholic Charismatic Renewal
also falls into this category, and like the expansionist Pentecostal
denominations has built up an impressive media portfolio.[39]

The leaders of IURD and Renascer em Cristo have been prosecuted
for fraud, international money-laundering schemes and tax evasion.
(Both denominations have weathered these charges and continue
to expand, and few believers have been driven away by unfavorable
press coverage.) But pastors from older Pentecostal denominations
as well as traditional denominations have also been linked to political scandals: the "neo-Pentecostals" have no monopoly on religious
corruption.

More salient than the Pentecostal and neo-Pentecostal distinction is that between mega and micro-denominations. IURD's rapid
growth in the context of redemocratization transformed the religious
marketplace, prompting more aggressive competitive practices, a
struggle to differentiate religious brands, and a race to control media
resources.[40] Within this competitive marketplace, both older and
newer denominations have found it expedient to collaborate in
certain contexts. The period from the mid-1980s has seen the rise
of an interparty *bancada evangélica*, or Protestant bloc, in Brazilian Congress, whose members have allied to protect each other's
denominations and to advance common interests. IURD sells airtime
on its television network to other denominations, giving them a
strong interest in that network's continued expansion. This practice
is also common on the most influential Protestant radio networks.
The mega-denominations have been the big winners in this process,
the micro-denominations the little strivers.

Participants, for their part, tend to self-identify primarily as *crentes* or as *evangélicos*. The first term literally means "believer," the second may denote a member of any Protestant denomination. As terms of self-identification both are limited predominantly to Pentecostals. Their practical usage in that sense again connotes perceived common characteristics, distinctions between denominations notwithstanding.

Who are Brazil's crentes?

While the rapid growth of the urban periphery in the 1970s and '80s facilitated the expansion of the mega-denominations, all have grown significantly beyond that periphery. There are now Pentecostal churches catering to nearly every subsector of the Brazilian population, and many survive by carving out market niches – building congregations primarily of surfers, truckers, or professional athletes. Many international football fans are familiar with Atletas de Cristo because of its most famous participant, midfielder Ricardo Izecson dos Santos Leite, better known as Kaká. Those who have seen any of Brazil's victories in recent international competitions may have noticed many of the players tearing off their canary yellow national jerseys to reveal t-shirts reading 100 percent Jesus: for these celebrants, religious affiliation is both deeper and more deserving of public acclamation than national identity.

A recent study by the Center for Social Policy of the Fundação Getúlio Vargas, one of Brazil's foremost research institutions, drawing on census data collected by the Instituto Brasileiro de Geografia e Estatísca, Brazil's government-funded demographic data institute, offers a detailed picture of Pentecostalism's rising arc. The percentage of Brazilians identifying themselves as Protestant rose from 9 percent in 1990, to 18 percent in 2003. Within this 18 percent, 12 percent were Pentecostal. This makes for approximately 24 million Pentecostals, a figure that vastly outnumbers any other nation. Assembléia has about 5 million adherents in Brazil, IURD about 1.5 million. Quadrangular has just under a million. The micro and medium-sized Pentecostal denominations collectively have over a million followers.[41]

More women than men declare Pentecostal affiliation. Young

Brazilians are also increasingly Pentecostal. In 2003, over 14 percent of Brazilian children under ten were Pentecostal, showing that the Pentecostal denominations are expanding steadily through natural reproduction as well as conversion.

Average declared income remained significantly lower among Pentecostals than among Catholics – 1,500 *reais* per month in comparison to 2,000, in the data from 2003 – demonstrating that Pentecostal denominations remain strongest among poor and working-class Brazilians. Pentecostals nonetheless far outdo members of other faiths in tithing, offering 44 percent of total religious donations in 2003.

Although Pentecostals tend to be poorer than Brazilians in general, they are not, for the most part, among the very poor. Only 10 percent of those making less than twice the minimum wage, or 760 *reais* per month, are Pentecostal, while 15 percent of those making between twice and four times the minimum wage are Pentecostal. This gap demonstrates primarily the continued urban base of Pentecostalism and its relative weakness among the poorest Brazilians in the rural northeast. It also may attest to the importance of Pentecostalism in low-income urban wage labor, where being a crente is often a significant job qualification.

Pentecostalism remains strongly rooted in the urban periphery. Over 20 percent of Brazil's Pentecostals live in the periphery of major cities, and 17 percent of residents of these peripheries are Pentecostal, compared to only 9 percent of rural Brazilians. But Pentecostal denominations are strong in new frontier regions, making up 20 percent of the population of Rondonia, and 18 percent of that of Roraima, Amazonian states with low population densities and rapid frontier expansion. This strength in the Amazon reflects both Assembléia's roots in Belem do Pará and the powerful attraction of Pentecostal denominations among populations in transition.

Among Brazilians who self-identify as black, 17 percent are Pentecostal, compared to 13 percent who self-identify as parda, or brown, and 10 percent who self-identify as white. Given the strong correlation between phenotype and wealth in Brazil, this confirms Pentecostalism's success among poor and working-class Brazilians. But it also suggests larger transformations in the meaning of blackness in Brazil, as self-consciously black organizations in civil society increasingly overlap with Pentecostal church groups.[42]

Rede Record

In 1989, a group of investors paid 45 million dollars for the purchase of TV Record. Subsequent investigation revealed that these investors were for the most part lower-middle-class residents of suburban Rio de Janeiro, with minimal collective assets. They were apparently the *laranjas*, or oranges – the felicitous Brazilian term for the front that provides cover for osbcure financial dealings – for Laprovita Vieira, an IURD pastor, who soon afterwards became the principal owner of the station. Vieira did not have 45 million dollars either: he had apparently borrowed much of the down payment from sheltered funds established in international tax havens. Vieira, in turn, was allegedly the laranja for Edir Macedo. Under Brazilian law, churches are tax-exempt non-profit entities, prohibited from owning TV and radio stations. Over the next several years, exhaustive federal investigations demonstrated that the station was a key node in an IURD financial empire.[43] Macedo, meanwhile, left Brazil and established residency in the United States, overseeing the IURD's Brazilian and international operations from there.

TV Record was just the beginning. Over the course of the 1990s, IURD pastors purchased TV and radio stations throughout Brazil, along with a publishing house, a magazine, real-estate holdings and other enterprises.[44] IURD pastors also became frequent candidates for state and federal office, depending on their congregations as voting blocs. Once elected, these candidates joined governing coalitions and acted to protect the IURD's interests. Partly through this painstaking construction of political alliances, TV Record, which soon became Rede Record, or Record Network, was protected from judicial fallout. Macedo was fined on several occasions for financial irregularities, but he never lost control of the network.

The IURD does not use Rede Record as a religious mouthpiece. Instead, Record features a range of entertainment and news programming similar to that offered by its major competitors. Record's investment in lavish telenovelas in recent years has made it the second most-watched network in Brazil. It remains far behind TV

Globo in the polls, but has begun to dig into Globo's advertising base. Not surprisingly, Globo has been a fierce critic of both Record and Macedo.

Religious programming on Rede Record is limited primarily to hours after midnight and in the early morning, when audiences are smallest and advertising revenues lowest. While these programs are a relatively small portion of Record's overall offerings, they nonetheless play an important role in the Church. The IURD grooms pastors for stardom within the Church through appearance on Record's programs. And for pastors in the field, urging potential converts to tune into Rede Record's religious programs can function as a powerful reinforcement of their message. For crentes, particularly those in the urban periphery, where cramped quarters and habits of sociability make watching TV a semi-public act, tuning into the religious programs – those of the IURD or competing denominations – can be a way to make a public affirmation of their religious status.[45]

The IURD's most notorious moment came during one of these broadcasts: on October 12, 1995, Sérgio von Helde, an IURD pastor, kicked and punched a statue of the Virgin Mary, on one of TV Record's early-morning programs. More precisely, von Helde kicked a statue representing Nossa Senhora da Aparecida, the miraculous manifestation of the Virgin in early-eighteenth-century Brazil. Nossa Senhora da Aparecida is venerated by Catholics as Brazil's patron saint – a veneration long supported by secular authorities. October 12 is annually commemorated as the Dia da Nossa Senhora da Aparecida. Von Helde was essentially dropkicking Church and State in a highly calculated act. Kicking the Virgin was a way of aggressively demonstrating to believers that dalliance with other faiths could only bring encosto, and therefore needed to be shunned like the devil. And it was a way of ratcheting up the competition in Brazil's religious marketplace.[46]

Relatively few Brazilians would have seen the act had it not been for TV Globo, which repeatedly aired the tape in order to characterize its upstart competitor, TV Record, as anti-Catholic and anti-Brazilian. While many Brazilians were appalled, others were inspired: von Helde continued his ascent in IURD's ranks.

No other manifestation of Pentecostal media has been any-where near as inflammatory. Pentecostal TV and radio programs overwhelmingly broadcast to the converted and to those in the process of conversion. In this context, even sermons denouncing Catholicism and umbanda come across not as condemnation but as confirmation. And fiery sermons themselves are far less common than musical programming, particularly on radio stations like Rádio Melodia, the most popular religious radio station in Rio de Janeiro. Rádio Melodia primarily programs contemporary Brazilian Christian music, directly modeled on the US contemporary Christian pop. It features slick production of catchy melodies and a basic message of Christian uplift.

Rádio Melodia and similar stations across Brazil appeal to Prot-estants of all denominations. They also target most of their pro-grams particularly at working-class women. The morning talk shows tend to feature inspiring advice for callers experiencing difficulties with rebellious daughters, wayward sons and unreliable husbands. Regular programs offer advice for managing household budgets and announce low-wage employment openings.

Rádio Melodia also features political programming, hosted by Anthony Garotinho, former governor of Rio. Garotinho is Presby-terian, but early in his career made the astute move of cultivating a Pentecostal electoral base. Along with his wife and gubernatorial successor, Rosinha Matheus, he is an excellent example both of the growth of Pentecostal wings within traditional Protestant denomina-tions and the growth of Pentecostal voting blocs. Garotinho was a radio host before he was a politician or a religious leader, and his on-air patter is smooth and professional, transmitting a sense of confidence and familiarity.

Francisco Silva, a Pentecostal pastor and political ally of Garo-tinho, owns Rádio Melodia. For Silva, offering Garotinho a platform was a logical strategy to cultivate politically powerful allies, but the station's profits depend on entertainment.[47] Rádio Melodia's rela-tionship with Garotinho reveals a surprising feature of the rise of religious media and the emergence of the bancada evangélica. Both these innovations are characterized by continuity with Brazilian media and political traditions. Rádio Melodia is an entertainment station broadcasting pop music to a broad but well-targeted audience. Garotinho is a politician using his media know-how to cultivate an electoral base. These phenomena are decades old. That they draw energy and resources from the Pentecostal boom demonstrates the ways in which that boom has been integrated into the structures of power in Brazil. The Pentecostal boom has transformed Brazil's religious map, but tends to reinforce its political and economic status quo.

Nowhere is this more true than in Brazilian Congress. Pentecostal congressmen tend to keep a low political profile. They demonstrate little party loyalty and no consistent ideological tendencies. They generally vote in favor of the governing coalition, whatever it happens to be. They form interparty alliances based on regional and sectoral interests, and use those alliances to protect pet projects. In all these ways, they blend in smoothly with the pliable mass of Brazilian congressmen known as the *baixo clero* (the low clergy), a nickname particularly appropriate for the bancada evangélica. There are 513 members of Brazil's federal House of Deputies, of whom approximately 60 comprised the bancada evangélica between 2002 and 2006.[48] Like other interparty alliances, this gave them enough members to exert leverage over spending proposals and not enough to accomplish much else.

Also typical has been the bancada evangélica's involvement in scandal. Members of the bancada were disproportionately represented among the indicted in the Escândalo das Sanguessugas, or Bloodsuckers' Scandal of 2006.[49] Over several years, middlemen had bribed congressmen to vote for local funding for ambulances, then vastly overcharged for the ambulances or simply failed to deliver them. Although the quantities involved were relatively small in comparison with other recent scandals, they came directly out of a minimal federal health budget, lending the scheme a ghoulish air. In the wake of the scandal, several allegedly bloodsucking members of the bancada evangélica were not re-elected, thus shrinking the bancada for Lula's second term.

The only novelty here is the foundation of the Brazilian Republican Party, or PRB, in 2005. The PRB is a micro-party created by IURD leaders. Its party president and only elected senator – a nephew of Macedo – are IURD bishops. The existence of a party so closely identified with the most controversial Pentecostal denomination poses a small threat to disrupt the interdenominational workings of the bancada evangélica. But this seems unlikely for two reasons. Lula's vice-president, José Alencar, immediately joined the nascent PRB. Just as quickly, the new party's leaders declared it to be a leftist, nationalist party. These factors suggest that the PRB will also be integrated into the usual operations of Brazilian Congress, and is likely to prove no worse than other micro-parties.

The Pentecostal boom is a global trend. Pentecostal denominations have flourished all over the world since the 1980s, most strikingly in Central America, West Africa and Korea. Pentecostal growth in Brazil not only reflects this global trend but helps to drive it: Assembléia, IURD and several other Brazilian Pentecostal denominations have extensive overseas operations. In countries like the United States and Australia, these denominations begin targeting extensive Brazilian immigrant populations – recent immigrants, necessarily in transition, are the ideal target population for Pentecostal conversion. They then move on to the native population or other immigrant groups – IURD in the Los Angeles area, for example, is particularly popular with Central American immigrants. In countries with no significant Brazilian immigrant populations, the initial hurdles are higher, but by no means insurmountable – Brazilian Pentecostal denominations are successful in Russia, for example.

Brazilian pastors and denominations have proven so successful that they are now studied as models of religious expansion. In Nashville, Tennessee, a Brazilian immigrant and former pastor named Maurílio Amorim has created an influential consulting business, advising new denominations in successful religious branding. In other words, Protestant preachers in the US South now look to Brazilians to show them how it should be done. Crentes in Rio de Janeiro and Roraima will not find this the least surprising.

New international locations are franchise operations of multinational corporations. They bring a recognizable brand and a successful marketing strategy to local markets, and test the competition. As individual pastors typically take on much of the risk of new operations, the parent denominations have little to lose and much to gain by opening new churches. These business strategies, determined at the highest levels of the mega-denominations, give the Pentecostal boom its economic importance.

The believer in the pews has a radically different perspective. Joining a Pentecostal denomination can be a way of entering a job network, gaining a measure of perceived control over the unpredictable forces of modern urban life, and experiencing spiritual ecstasy, all at the same time. This explains how the Pentecostal boom can be both a big and occasionally corrupt business and a grassroots movement that gives believers from the margins of national life a central importance in Brazil's ongoing cultural transformation.

In this regard, the Pentecostal boom is a major facet of the larger pluralization of Brazilian culture. Old hierarchies have crumbled or lost their ability to command deference, making way for new actors and new modes of behavior. Pluralization is not necessarily democratization, however. The Pentecostal boom gives believers from the urban periphery a greater stake in national cultural life than they experienced previously, but authority within the Pentecostal denominations and their individual churches is rigidly hierarchical. The heady brew of pluralization may itself generate longings for rules and order. In all these ways, the Pentecostal boom is typical of Brazil in the period of redemocratization, characterized by dynamism and a tension between inclusion and fragmentation.

6 | Making culture in digital Brazil

There are three rules governing patterns of circulation in Brazil's cultural marketplace. The first of these is new, and can be called the Orkut Rule, after Google's social-networking site, a runaway hit in Brazil. The Orkut Rule holds that, wherever possible, Brazilians will avail themselves of the possibilities of digital media to create subcultural niches and crosscultural networks in ways that defy traditional hierarchies and the existing cultural canon. The consequences of the Orkut Rule are limited by two previously existing rules, each of which has been reconfigured for the digital age.

The Petrobras Rule takes its name from the state-controlled energy-services behemoth that is also Brazil's largest cultural sponsor. It holds that the federal government will seek to maximize its cultural influence through indirect sponsorship of favored mouthpieces, rather than through direct propaganda. A corollary of the Petrobras Rule is that the executive branch will use this indirect sponsorship to reward political allies and build party strength.

The Virtual Pistolão Rule takes its name from the *pistolão*, the letter of recommendation from a powerful patron, written on behalf of a family member or dependent, that has traditionally served as an entrance requirement for Brazil's job market. A hard copy is no longer required – any public statement of protective support by one of Brazil's cultural gatekeepers now serves effectively as a virtual pistolão. The Virtual Pistolão Rule holds that major media enterprises will continue to rely on the indications of a small cohort of anointed tastemakers, guaranteeing that stardom spreads viruslike through familial and affective networks. These three rules sometimes reinforce one another and sometimes conflict. Their interplay determines which cultural producers and which products rise from local relevance to national prominence in digital Brazil, and this holds true for all sectors of cultural production, including the Internet, cinema, the book market and popular music.

Brazil has the largest and most sophisticated electronic communications and entertainment industry in Latin America. It has more Internet users than any other Latin American nation, more cable TV subscribers, more cellphones.[50] Having the largest population obviously plays a decisive role in pushing these numbers, but given Brazil's notorious inequality, the rapid expansion of its digitalized population since 1990 is striking. It is not surprising, however, to students of Brazil's history over the twentieth century, attuned to the constant innovation of its electronic media, and the success of major media enterprises in steadily expanding their markets.

Globo TV and its parent company, Globo Organizations, generally play an important role in explaining this media currency: Globo continues to reign over primetime television, if not with the same dominance as in decades past, and exercises broad influence through its tentacular enterprises in related fields. But while Globo has accompanied the expansion of the new digital media, it has not led the charge. Globo and other major media congolomerates such as Abril and the Grupo Folha have a significant presence on the Web, but most *internautas*, as Web surfers are called, travel digital byways that skirt these major destinations. Brazil also has more independent record labels than any other Latin American nation, including several operating exclusively on the Web, more documentary filmmakers, and hosts more websites. This digital expansion has reconfigured Brazil's cultural market, broadening access to production and distribution of visual art, literature, journalism and particularly popular music, as discussed in Chapter 4.

Brazilians actively engaged in this expansion describe it as a democratization of culture – as a digital realization of the aspirations for greater equality in the postdictatorship period that have been achieved only partially in other spheres. High-ranking civil servants such as Minister of Culture Gilberto Gil have made digital democratization a major objective, crafting various policies to further the "digital inclusion" of Brazil's poor and working-class citizens. Some of these programs have been strikingly successful, others less so, and a few have been linked to corruption schemes. But their collective influence has helped connect a generation of residents of the favelas and peripheries of Brazil's major cities to the Web. Low-interest layaway plans at chainstores like Casas Bahia and Ponto Frio, meanwhile, have made entry-level computers common features of working-class urban households.

Broad digital access gives the Orkut Rule its power, and fuels much of the dynamism in Brazil's cultural market. The Petrobras and Virtual Pistolão Rules respond to and direct that dynamism. They combine to produce a unique cultural marketplace. Brazil's domestic cultural industries are strong enough to run no risk of being forced into the undignified role of merely re-transmitting international corporate culture: on the contrary, Brazil is as success-ful an exporter of pop culture as it is of soybeans. At the same time, specific sectors in Brazil, such as cinema and publishing, do depend on public funding: this is vital to their survival. The particular ways in which public funding is distributed, however, often fulfill narrow political objectives, rather than enriching cultural offerings.

The Orkut Rule

Orkut, launched in 2004, allows users to create a digital profile, communicate individually with other users and join virtual com-munities. Users typically post photos of themselves, link to friends and surf communities based on affinities of taste, geography or any fleeting inclination. Orkut is similar to Facebook and MySpace, which took off at about the same time, with greater emphasis on the "communities" feature. Orkut arrived in Brazil before Facebook or MySpace, giving it a leg up on the competition (this "first-mover advantage" has proven crucial in digital markets, and consequently, in markets where Facebook and MySpace took off first, Orkut has been less successful). By early 2006, over 60 percent of users were Brazilians. The United States was second, with about 15 percent of users, a number slightly misleading because of the high number of Brazilian expatriates who access the network from the United States. Portuguese, oddly, is the lingua franca of the service. When Orkut Büyükökkten, the Turkish programmer who designed the service, made a triumphal visit to Rio de Janeiro in 2006, he was greeted as a pioneering hero. By late 2007, there were well over 40 million Orkut accounts registered in Brazil. Some users create multiple accounts, and it is impossible to ascertain precisely how many Brazilians use Orkut on a regular basis. But it is apparent that the vast majority of urban Brazilians under fifty have Orkuted.[51]

The communities they have created reveal a diversity that reflects Brazil's cultural transitions since the 1980s. There are communities not only for the Rio de Janeiro working-class suburb of Duque de Caxias, for example, but for frequenters of the Bar do Zeca, a local dive there. There are communities for lovers of Brazilian rodeo and of funk, for fans of Paulo Freire and Chico Science, for girls named Jussara. There are communities for skateboarders and for members of the Igreja Quadrangular, and for skateboarding members of the Igreja Quadrangular. While many of these communities have only a handful of members, they often generate heated exchanges, inscrutable to the casual visitor, but – if one is to judge by the number of exclamation points and bold caps – of intense interest to participants.

While passionately defended, taste and affinity on Orkut are value-neutral. On this terrain, members of "Eu Amo Vila Madalena," a community for fans of the upscale São Paulo neighborhood of Vila Madalena, have no more social capital than those of "Skatistas Diadema," for skate punks from the industrial working-class suburb of Diadema. There is no center and no periphery, and the communities dedicated to popular forms once scorned by Brazilian tastemakers, like hip-hop and thrash metal, vastly outnumber those for established genres like bossa nova and choro. For that matter, the members of "Skatistas Diadema" vastly outnumber those of "Eu amo Vila Madalena." One of the most vibrant arenas for cultural debate and social connections has thus grown outside the cultural canon and the social hierarchy, immune to their restrictive covenants.

Orkut, as a result, has served as an effective means for the creation of subcultural networks. Aspiring popular musical acts no longer need a recording contract or radio coverage to start building a national and international audience; they can do so through Orkut, which facilitates trading not only photos but audio and video files, as well as links to other websites.

Orkut's uses are not always salutary. As Brazilian usage of Orkut grew, communities honoring criminal networks became common, and Brazilian authorities alleged that Orkut was also being used to facilitate child prostitution and sexual tourism. On several occasions, authorities in various Brazilian municipalities persuaded local judges to issue injunctions against Google, temporarily shutting down local access to the site. Federal prosecutors threatened to bring suit against Google unless it turned over records of individual users involved in suspect communications. After initially insisting that Google's database, stored outside of Brazil, could not be subject to Brazilian investigation, Google's lawyers negotiated. In mid-2006, Google struck a compromise, exercising greater leverage over Orkut content in return for continued self-governance and access to the Brazilian market.[52]

Digital inclusion and Casas Bahia

In the mid-1990s, just as the concept of a digital divide between rich and poor began to arise as a topic of international debate, a network of activists and policymakers were already moving to prevent such a divide from emerging in Brazil. They owed their early inspiration to Alternex, one of Brazil's first Internet service providers, a creation of the NGO and think-tank IBASE. As discussed in Chapter 1, Betinho and Carlos Afonso founded IBASE in the early 1980s to serve as a center for politically engaged sociological research and a shaper of journalistic and political debate. Betinho's strategy for realizing this vision lay primarily in the creation of large-scale campaigns (against hunger, for ethics in politics, and so on) and the cultivation of old-media journalists. Carlos Afonso, a statistician drawn more to the technological cutting-edge, saw the opportunity to create a network of activists and researchers communicating digitally. He created Alternex in the late 1980s, primarily to link Brazil's emerging NGOs with international counterparts.

Over the next few years, as Brazilians began to make their first forays onto the Internet, Alternex developed a reputation as a reliable service provider that offered, as a bonus, information on NGO activism difficult to find anywhere else. Alternex became a key early participant in the Association for Progressive Communication, a global network of wired digital activists. Alternex's support for the operations of Eco '92, the environmental conference that drew global green activists to Rio, boosted its reputation domestically and internationally. Coming out of Eco '92, Alternex found its services increasingly in demand by both NGOs and individual users.

By the mid-1990s, Alternex had outgrown IBASE – the need to constantly hire and supervise new technical staff to run Alternex threatened to overwhelm IBASE's administrative capacity. IBASE spun off Alternex, initially retaining partial ownership, and ultimately cutting ties. Alternex continued to prosper, but many of the politically engaged techies who had joined its ranks left to join new NGOs. Alternex had linked the concepts of the Internet and social justice in Brazil, and spawned a cohort of wired activists. In 1997, the members of this cohort created the Rede de Informações para o Terceiro Setor (RITS), or Network of Information for the Third Sector. RITS carried on Alternex's original mission, shifting its operations to the Worldwide Web. Many of the NGOs participating in RITS offered Web access to residents of poor communities before "digital inclusion" was a term of political currency. RITS's own funding, from sources like the Ford and Kellogg Foundations, enabled it to support those ventures.

Domestic funding for such projects, both from private entities such as Globo and state-controlled entities such as Petrobras, increased with Lula's election in 2002. Lula's nomination of Gilberto Gil as Minister of Culture accelerated this trend. Gil had long been interested in digital networking, particularly in the creative energy waiting to be unleashed through linking poor and working-class Brazilians to the Web. He became Brazil's foremost connector, encouraging corporations to fund digital inclusion programs through his own ministry and independent NGOs. Municipal goverments in São Paulo and Porto Alegre also sponsored *telecentros*, providing free Web access and computer training in working-class communities.

Perhaps inevitably, digital inclusion projects became connected to kickback schemes and fraud. The Bloodsuckers' Scandal of 2006 (briefly described in Chapter 5) featured a digital component: the Ministry of Science and Technology had paid for "Digital Inclusion Buses," intended to bring wireless Web access to poor communities, but investigations revealed that much of the funding had been siphoned off and that many of the buses never functioned.[53] "Digital inclusion" has since become a much-lampooned cliché, particularly in the puns of *O Globo* newspaper's pseudonymous satire columnist Agamemnon Mendes Pedreira, who rarely fails to refer to the importance of vigorous digital inclusion in what he describes as Brazil's "collective psychoproctology."[54]

Fortunately, most Brazilians were not waiting for the digital inclusion bus, but instead bought their own computers. Casas Bahia, a furniture and appliance retailer, built its reputation on providing low-interest credit to workers in Brazil's massive informal sector.[55] By the late 1990s, computers constituted a sizable portion of Casas Bahia's annual sales. Other retailers followed suit.

Under Cardoso, the government drastically reduced its tariffs and controls on the tech sector, leading to lower retail prices and expanded availability of imported computers. Lula subsequently created a federal program offering low-interest loans for purchase of an entry-level computer specifically created for the program by approved suppliers.

These measures and developments did not entirely prevent the emergence of a digital divide in Brazil, but that divide is more one of geography than class – rural Brazilians, particularly those of the north and northeast, have much less access to the Web than their urban cousins. Digital inclusion programs have been concentrated in the cities, because that is where the voters are: Brazil is over 80 percent urban, and the peripheries of its major cities are teeming with new computer users.

Overmundo

The first thing many of these users do when they get online is to create an Orkut profile. Most soon supplement this with other kinds of surfing and connecting. Brazilian participation in the blogosphere spans the political spectrum and accommodates every popular cultural interest. Brazilian blog pioneers such as Alexandre Inagaki, of the blog *Pensar Enlouquece* (Thinking Makes You Crazy) began constructing a Brazilian network within the blogosphere in 2000, and served as the prime connector, inspiring a broad range of cultural producers to begin blogging over the next several years. The

invention and collaborative spirit of this early network notwithstanding, most Brazilians first found out about blogs through the sudden
notoriety of Bruna Surfistinha, the professional name of a São Paulo
prostitute who recounted her nightly adventures in the clubs and
hotels of that city on her salacious blog. Surfistinha's candid account
of a middle-class childhood leading to a life of drugs and prostitution titillated internautas over the course of 2005. She parlayed her
mounting Web hits into fleeting fame, publishing a tell-all memoir to
complement her tell-all blog, and getting her picture in publications
ranging from porn magazines to the *New York Times*.

These individual creations proved inspiring, but fit largely into
global models. Collective enterprises soon proved a way to put a more
Brazilian spin on the blogosphere, at times speaking powerfully to
local concerns. In 2006, the Rio daily newspaper *O Globo*, part of
the Globo media empire, began hosting a blog on local crime on its
website. Readers posted such an abundance of indicators of where
and how street crime occurred that it prompted the blog's administrator to create a crime map of diverse neighborhoods in the city,
with content created and updated by readers. The crime map offered
an effective, informative response to Rio's failed security policies – a
fascinating example of digital citizenship. Participants consistently
expressed relief that someone was finally paying attention to their
warnings regarding encroaching criminal use of public space.

One of the most compelling collective ventures to emerge is Overmundo, a collaborative site founded in early 2006, dedicated to Brazilian popular culture. Overmundo's mission is to disseminate popular
culture – musical, literary, visual, cinematic – with particular emphasis on culture produced outside the Rio–São Paulo axis. Its content
features stories on topics such as community radio in Porto Alegre, a
puppet museum in Olinda and passion-fruit sausage in Mato Grosso
do Sul. Anyone can file a story, but all stories remain forty-eight hours
in an editing-line, where readers can suggest changes. They then
move to a voting line, where readers vote on the content. Only stories
that receive sixty votes move to the front page. Those with more votes
stay on the front page longer. Stories are then archived under various
subheadings, grouped into announcements and reviews, guides to
local culture, short fiction and other categories.

Overmundo subscribes to the Creative Commons doctrine of Internet use – all published material is available for any non-commercial reproduction, lending Overmundo material to strategies of viral marketing. The site counts on collaborators from every state in Brazil. Contributions from the major poles of Rio and São Paulo are by no means barred, but have to pass through the same kind of field testing as other posts. Consequently, the stories from Rio and São Paulo that do survive tend to be items such as poetry from a contributor in the working-class Rio suburb of Mesquita, or a guide to the best hamburgers in the neighboring suburb of São João de Meriti. Overmundo strives to cut out the middleman – the press relations and advertising industry centered in Brazil's two largest cities.

Overmundo is thus relentlessly populist – the majority always rules, and lone voices disappear quickly – and also lends itself to corporatism – well-organized subgroups can always muster the votes necessary to keep their stories alive. But its offerings have been sufficiently diverse, at least in its first years of operation, that they do not succumb to the pitfalls of these tendencies. This success owes much to the vision of the site's founders, whose understanding of popular culture is anti-folkloric. They are interested in seeing the latest popular music from Maranhão not because they believe that state is a wellspring of a timeless essence of local color, but because they believe that Maranhenses are capable of producing music just as hip as anything from Rio or São Paulo, and that given the context such music cannot help but reveal an awareness of global media and an affinity with local surroundings. Contributors and readers have embraced this vision. Maranhense reggae is more likely to gain traction on Overmundo than is bumba-meu-boi, the local folkloric festival.

Hermano Vianna, one of the site's founders, expressed this vision most clearly in a manifesto – posted on Overmundo, of course – arguing that the most compelling tendency in Brazilian culture since the mid-1990s has been the emergence of the urban periphery as a center of production.[56] He issued the manifesto in conjunction with the debut of *Central da Periferia*, a Globo TV series, shown in primetime on Saturday evenings. Vianna is a consultant for the series, which often features talent lifted directly from Overmundo. Every week, the show's host, Regina Casé – a veteran of Rio's besteirol scene and a longtime Globo host – leads the proceedings from a different poor or working-class suburb on the outskirts of a major city. The provincial suburb-Overmundo-*Central da Periferia* pipeline thus marks – at least from one perspective – the periphery's conquest of a coveted slot on Brazil's most powerful media outlet.

From another perspective, this is business as usual – Overmundo serves as an efficient groomer of minor-league talent for Globo's big business. Nor is Overmundo itself free of corporate and government interest: it was started with a million-dollar grant from Petrobras. Overmundo used the Petrobras funding for initial costs and to pay early collaborators, then moved entirely to voluntary contributions. Overmundo's representatives state that they have not accepted further funding from Petrobras, but the corporation's logo is still on their homepage, and in Petrobras's ample portfolio.

Petrobras and company

Sponsoring Overmundo is just a tiny fraction of Petrobras's cultural spending. In 2006, Petrobras Holding spent over 100 million dollars on cultural programs, ten times as much as the next music-generous sponsor. In fact, second place went to the Banco do Brasil, another state company, followed by a third, Eletrobras. BNDES, the national development bank, was also in the top five, and two more state companies, Correios (the Post Office) and the Caixa Econômica Federal (a federally owned bank) also spent lavishly. Petrobras Distribuidora, the distribution wing of the state oil company, run as a separate company, has also been one of the top ten cultural sponsors. The most generous private company, Companhia Vale do Rio Doce, was a state company until 1996, and spends on cultural programs as part of its strategy to fend off calls for its re-nationalization.

All these corporations fund culture primarily through the Rouanet Law, a tax code revision of the early 1990s that allows corporations and individuals to support approved cultural programs in place of paying a percentage of their tax bill. According to the terms of the law, the President of the Republic sets that percentage each year – typically the Rouanet Law has been more indulgent in this regard than similar tax incentive laws in other countries. Since the mid-1990s, several subsequent tax code revisions have encouraged more direct sponsorship of specifical cultural sectors, such as cinema and publishing. In the case of state companies, then, the funding provided through these tax deductions is doubly public: in theory, Petrobras is owned by the people of Brazil, and owes its taxes to those same people. Petrobras's lavish cultural funding is certainly in its own interest, as is the less lavish spending of its fellow state companies – cultural sponsorship is a highly effective way to advertise, build brand recognition and reward allies.

This funding has obvious positive consequences, and less obvious political ramifications. It contributes to compelling cultural productions that otherwise would not survive. São Paulo's diverse and inventive theater scene, for example, has depended on federal and municipal tax incentives, and has used these in ways that not only have produced interesting spectacles, but that have helped to draw economic activity back to downtown neighborhoods.

At the same time, in a context in which democratization and transparency have become buzzwords of political debate, funding under the Rouanet Law is not necessarily democratic or transparent. Petrobras claims that three-quarters of its cultural funding goes to "public selections," and only one-quarter to "direct choice" by the Petrobras Cultural Council. But the Petrobras Cultural Council names the committees that make the "public selections," choosing them from a narrow range of politically allied candidates. The executive directors of Petrobras, in turn, name the majority of members of the Petrobras Cultural Council, with the Ministry of Culture and the President of the Republic directly naming one apiece. The president also appoints the executive directors of Petrobras, the Minister of Culture, and the top-ranking administrative personnel in both Petrobras and the Ministry of Culture. These connections add up to extraordinary leverage by the executive branch in determining the nature of Petrobras's cultural sponsorhip. The problem here is not one of state incentives for cultural production, but of the political power of a few officeholders over what kind of culture gets produced.

Lula has increased the number of the "*cargos de confiança*" – a term for direct executive appointment that is best translated as "trusty posts" – by over 20 percent, bringing the total to over 22,000 civil servants named directly by the executive branch.[57] The use of these trusty posts to place political loyalists at every level of the bureaucracy – a strategy the opposition describes as *aparelhamento*, or machine takeover – gives the executive branch a powerful tentacular reach. Of the trusty posts, President of Petrobras is the most coveted, not so much for its salary, but for its power – Petrobras plays a decisive role in Brazil's economy and its political scene. Indirect control over the corporation's cultural budget is a relatively small portion of that power, but hugely influential in Brazil's cultural market.

Cultural sponsorship by state companies has risen in direct proportion to the number of trusty positions created by Lula. Petrobras Holding spent 25 million dollars on sponsorship in 2002, Cardoso's last year in office, and quadrupled that amount by 2006, when Lula successfully ran for re-election. As these numbers suggest, the executive branch, and Lula in particular, have seized on cultural spending through state companies as a way to build loyalty and reward clients.

What kind of projects get funded? Overmundo is a rare example of an innovative cultural endeavor that draws participation from every corner of Brazil, primarily from unsung collaborators. There is no political censorship on the site, and although its focus is cultural it is not unusual to see posts criticizing some aspect of federal policy. Most other funding recipients are more disciplined. In several cases, the recipients of Petrobras's greatest largesse since 2004 have been among Lula's most vocal supporters – a tendency that starts with Petrobras's president, José Gabrielli, who was one of the most generous individual contributors to Lula's 2006 campaign.[58]

Cinema

The largest share of Petrobras's cultural funding goes to film. Brazilian cinema is state cinema, funded by Petrobras. Nearly every Brazilian feature film depends on Rouanet Law funding from one or several state companies, as do most short films and documentaries, and Petrobras is by far the largest contributor. Petrobras also sponsors Brazil's major film festivals and some of the theaters where Brazilian films are shown. Many Brazilian films, in effect, are never commercially released in Brazil: they never get significantly beyond the narrow sponsored-festival and subsidized-theater circuit.[59]

Brazilian film insiders have traditionally blamed poor distribution on Hollywood's leverage: for many years, Hollywood distributors refused to release blockbuster films to overseas theaters unless theater owners consented to dedicating much of their screen time to less successful films. This enabled Hollywood to make up for domestic losses with overseas gains, and made it difficult for Brazilian producers to find screen time. Although current Hollywood practices are less restrictive, Brazilian films still confront a bottleneck: many theaters have closed down, and an ever-larger share of the market consists of video and DVD rentals. Tiny advertising budgets (often not covered in the Rouanet projects) make it difficult for Brazilian films to compete in the video store. But Brazilian film of the Rouanet period has adapted thoroughly to this regime, rarely making any attempt to reach a broad public. Appealing to the Petrobras Cultural Council is a recipe for continued funding in the world of Brazilian film. Appealing to a popular audience is not.

One of the curiosities of this development is the involution of Cinema Novo, the movement that transformed Brazilian film in the 1960s. Cinema Novo directors such as Nelson Pereira dos Santos and Glauber Rocha developed methods to make compelling films on shoestring budgets, challenging political conventions and creating dense inquiries into Brazilian politics and culture. But the challenges of the 1960s have become the conventions of the twenty-first century, an inversion most evident in the reification of Cinema Novo's three preferred genres, the denunciation of dictatorship, the feudal struggle in the backlands and the tale of urban degradation and marginalization.

During Cinema Novo's peak years in the late 1960s, the existence of a real dictatorship meant that film could only denounce dictatorship allegorically. Current filmmakers do not face this restriction, and take full advantage of their freedom to denounce the dictatorship that fell from power twenty years ago. Films about the regime constitute a thriving genre, but not one marked by great achievements. *Zuzu Angel, O Ano em Que Meus Pais Saíram de Férias* (The Year My Parents Went on Vacation), *Sonhos e Desejos* (Dreams and Desires) and other films about the regime share a common perspective, portraying the dictatorship and its supporters as monolithically reactionary and oppressive and the youthful opposition as heroic and inspiring, if occasionally undermined by minor flaws.

Given that the most successful members of that opposition now control the purse strings upon which Brazilian film depends, this comes across as shameless pandering. *Hércules 56*, made in 2006, is a feature-length documentary by the director Sílvio Da-Rin about the ex-*guerrillheiros* involved in the kidnapping of US Ambassador Charles Burke Elbrick in 1969. Da-Rin interviewed the political prisoners freed by the action, including Lula's former chief of staff, José Dirceu, as well as several of the kidnappers, including current Minister of Social Communication Franklin Martins. But *Hércules 56* is not an investigation of the transformation of guerrilheiros into politicians, it is a commemoration of a foundational moment in the rise of the left. Although Da-Rin's team conducted exhaustive research in archives in several countries, the film includes no interviews with veterans of the military regime, nor with personnel from the US embassy or surviving members of Elbrick's family. Da-Rin limited his interest in the episode to its effect within what was once Brazil's radical left and is now its commissariat.

Petrobras sponsored the making of *Hércules 56*, and also sponsored the film festivals where it primarily showed. *Hércules 56* was also shown in a private screening in the presidential palace, with Da-Rin on hand. Late in 2007, Da-Rin was named Secretary of the Audiovisual Sector within the Ministry of Culture, where he will play a decisive role in determining which future films benefit from the Rouanet Law.[60] *Hércules 56* played on only a handful of screens, but its key audience was at the screening in the presidential palace, and that audience was enough to guarantee Da-Rin's ascent.

In the Cinema Novo films set in the sertão, exploitation and religious millenarianism drove feudal conflict. In the current spate of films shot in Brazil's northeastern interior, causes of conflict are more diverse, but other aspects of the genre remain constant. In the 1960s, Glauber Rocha argued for an "aesthetic of hunger," suggesting that low-budget, politically engaged filmmakers had a duty to film low-budget lives of political marginalization. The "aesthetic of hunger" as it has developed in the backlands films of the Cinema Novo period and the Rouanet years prizes stark landscapes, long-tracking shots, minimal dialogue and use of natural sound. The Petrobras Council esteems these characteristics, guaranteeing an ever-renewing crop of slow and frequently inaudible films shot in the sertão.

Cinema, Aspirina e Urubus (Cinema, Aspirin and Vultures) of 2006 is a typical example. *Cinema, Aspirina* was produced for only a million dollars, but looks and sounds cheaper. Its washed-out landscapes, jittery camera movements and mumbled dialogue are meant to evoke the air of a home movie of the early 1940s, and do so with striking success. The hero is a German salesman, roaming the northeastern sertão during World War II, peddling aspirin for a German company with a factory in southern Brazil. He sets up shop in dusty villages with a movie camera, showing a short film extolling the miracle of aspirin to impoverished sertanejos. But the real miracle is the film-within-a-film, which amazes the villagers, prompting them to plunk down the savings they don't have to buy medicine they don't need. The hero remarks that the sertanejos will get a headache for the first time just so they can have an excuse to buy aspirin. This allows meditation on two of Cinema Novo's favorite themes: the magic of cinema and the evils of capitalism. This is a recipe for a prizewinning film, and *Cinema, Aspirinas* duly garnered the 2007 Grande Prêmio do Cinema Brasileiro, Brazil's version of the Oscar. The film was sponsored by Petrobras, BNDES and Brasil Telecom, among other supporters.

Brazil's best films of the Rouanet years have emerged in the genre of urban marginality, which, like its real-life models, has shifted increasingly to the theme of urban violence. *Cidade de Deus* (City of God, 2002) and *Ônibus 174* (Bus 174), in particular, are powerful and politically complex films. The first, directed by Fernando Meirelles and Katia Lund, is a harrowing portrait of an enormous housing project in suburban Rio from its foundation in the 1960s to the peak of the drug wars in the 1990s. This account breathes with details taken from the Paulo Lins novel that inspired the film. Its sensationalistic violence threatens to overwhelm the substance of this historical interpretation, but is never more than accurate.

Ônibus 174, directed by José Padilha, is a documentary about a fatal bus hold-up in Rio de Janeiro in 2002. Sandro de Nascimento boarded a city bus in hopes of executing a quick stick-up and was surprised by the immediate arrival of the police. Nascimento took the passengers hostage just down the street from Globo TV's headquarters, and its film crews captured the unfolding crisis, leading to the death of one of the hostages and Nascimento's own suffocation in the back of a police van. The documentary combines this live footage with a sustained, clear-eyed investigation of Nascimento's background. The result is a compelling and open-ended investigation of urban violence in Brazil.

More broadly, the urban marginality genre – proliferating in numerous releases every year – has created a vivid local realism, stimulating broad debate about urban violence and the shortcomings of redemocratization.[61] Even when these films are unsuccessful aesthetically or commercially, they are part of a vibrant cultural debate. This is local film at its most vital.

Cidade de Deus and *Ônibus 174* by no means stand alone: Brazil produces over fifty feature films annually, and every year a handful of them are excellent. The current system is far preferable to that prevailing between the close of the dictatorship and the mid-1990s, when hyperinflation and dwindling arts funding brought Brazilian cinema to its knees. But the current system, where taxpayer funding is routed through state companies and councils stocked with political loyalists, yields a cinema of distorted contours and strange silences.

While in the late 1960s films could only confront the dictatorship allegorically, in the Rouanet period the subject that cannot be named is precisely the dependence of filmmakers on the state, and the connections between funding for the arts and party politics. Jorge Furtado's 2007 film *Saneamento Básico* (Basic Sanitation) begins to broach this subject, although, taking a cue from Cinema Novo, it does so allegorically. The film's protagonists are villagers who need a new cesspool, but their municipal administration can provide them only with money for a local film project, funded through a federal arts program. Misunderstanding the terms of the grant, the villagers attempt to make a science-fiction film about a genetic mutant lurking in their fetid creek while using the bulk of the funds to upgrade the cesspool. They make a charmingly disastrous video – the magic of cinema strikes again – and the cesspool is never built. This light-hearted allegory raises half of a pressing question, implicitly asking whether taxpayer money should be spent on cinema rather than health and sanitation. The thunderous applause of villagers for the film-within-a-film – evidence that footage of a topless beauty will overcome many cinematic shortcomings – offers a positive response, suggesting that film helps show us who we are, and that local film is a key to local self-discovery.

The other half of the question – whether the political use of arts funding undermines its beneficial effects – goes unaddressed. This is not surprising, given Furtado's career path. He is one of Brazil's most-sponsored directors, and *Saneamento Básico* itself is sponsored by Petrobras, BNDES and Banrisul, the former state bank of Rio Grande do Sul. Furtado has also directed electoral infomercials for PT candidates. His films are fresh, multi-layered and accessible, but his ability to secure public funding has noticeably coincided with his public support of the right candidates.

Publishing and music

The Rouanet Law has been less decisive, but its record just as dubious, in other sectors. Brazil's book market is notoriously limited – there are only 1,500 bookstores in Brazil, a country of over 5,000 municipalities. There are even fewer libraries, and most existing libraries, with the laudable exception of São Paulo's university libraries, have minimal funding for new book purchases. Brazil's book market is consequently relatively small for the size of its population – France and Italy, for example, publish and sell significantly more books than Brazil, despite having populations about one-third the size of Brazil's. Although major corporations often make use of the Rouanet Law to sponsor publications, the book market has actually shrunk as this sponsorship has expanded. In 2000, some 45,000 titles were published in Brazil. In 2005, only 36,000 titles were published. The number of copies sold dropped by nearly a quarter.[62]

A large portion of book purchases are made by the federal and state governments, primarily for educational purposes. These government purchases have remained roughly constant since 1996, while individual purchases on the open market have dropped by nearly 50 percent.

During these same years, cutting-edge bookstores in Brazil's major cities improved dramatically. Bookstores like the Travessa chain in Rio de Janeiro now offer a wide range of books, knowledgeable service and compelling events. But these stores, important as they are, serve a tiny fraction of the Brazilian market. While the cosmopolitan upper middle class is increasingly well served, the book-buying public continues to shrink. These trends are not independent of one another.

Many of the books stocked by Travessa, particularly the gorgeous coffee-table books prominently displayed near the front doors, are published under the auspices of the Rouanet Law. *Brasil Rito e Ritmo*, for example, is a book of images and essays on Brazilian popular music, published by the boutique house Aprazível Ediçoes in 2004. The insurance company Bradesco Seguros sponsored publication, allowing Aprazível to publish it for ninety dollars per copy. The sponsorship also paid for 2,000 copies to be delivered to libraries and cultural institutions, which otherwise could not have afforded it. The book is by no means overpriced – the small print run, lush image reproduction and the inclusion of two CDs make it expensive to produce. But its price effectively puts it beyond reach of all but a tiny fraction of Brazilians, of whom no more than a few thousand are likely to purchase it.

Brasil Rito e Ritmo is typical of the workings of Rouanet publications. Brazil now publishes art books, a new trend since the mid-1990s, funded through the Rouanet Law and beyond the reach of typical Brazilians. Consequently, while upscale bookstores become more pleasurable and enriching, the remainder of the book market reaps no benefit.

Houses like Aprazível publish only sponsored books, which drastically reduces their risk. Many publishers no longer review manuscripts – only authors who arrive with sponsorship are considered. Many sponsored books, in turn, are not intended for the open market: up to half the small print runs are given away by the sponsors in *brindes*, or tokens of appreciation, to employees and clients.

In 2004, Congress passed a new law ostensibly intended to expand the reading public. Bookstores were exempted from a portion of their taxes, and were required instead to pay 1 percent of gross intake into a Pro-Reading Fund, which supports public campaigns extolling the benefits of reading and pays for the "formation of agents for reading mediation" – in other words, for training reading teachers. While the Pro-Reading Fund may have some positive consequences, it is unlikely to change the dynamics of Brazil's book market. Funding for libraries might have been more successful in this regard.

Maecenas' clerks

Rouanet funding from Petrobras and other companies has created a niche for producers who can connect authors looking to pitch manuscripts, corporations interested in Rouanet tax credits and Ministry of Culture personnel who approve projects. *Brasil Rito e Ritmo*, for example, was shepherded to publication by RKF Produções, a Rio de Janeiro production and consulting firm founded in 1999. Such firms typically make their services available from the initial pitch through the production, publication or release. The pitch phase is by far the most important, and companies with a record of success are in a position to demand significant concessions from creative talent.

In late 2007, the directors of two such firms, Mecenas – aptly named after Maecenas, the first-century Roman patron of the arts – and G4, were arrested for extorting a cut of Rouanet funding from their clients. The promotional middlemen worked with an insider in the Ministry of Culture – also arrested – to block funding for projects, then persuaded their clients that payment of a percentage of the grant would start the money flowing.[63] (Like the phenomenon of encosto in the Igreja Universal do Reino de Deus, the scheme exploited the common Brazilian practice of paying fixers to remove obstacles to the accomplishment of a necessary task, often put in place for that very purpose.) They concentrated their efforts on major projects, likely to receive several hundred thousand dollars in sponsorship.

To its credit, the Ministry of Culture uncovered these irregularities and brought them to the attention of the Federal Police. The episode nonetheless pointed to larger problems in the overlap between cultural funding and government propaganda. In the same week that Operation Mecenas, as the Federal Police called it, hit the news, Lula and Franklin Martins were pushing through plans to create a new government TV station, called TV Brasil. Federal and state governments have had their own television and radio stations for decades, but these concentrate primarily on educational programming. The new station, with funding of hundreds of millions of dollars per year, is ostensibly dedicated to deeper analysis of cultural and political issues. But a strong emphasis on political loyalty within the station has made for sterile programming, attracting negligible viewership. TV Brasil, in its early months, appears to bear great similarities to the *Hora do Brasil*, one of the radio programs created by Getúlio Vargas's Estado Novo. Like the old *Hora do Brasil*, TV Brasil does not presume to manipulate culture, but appears to exist primarily in order to reward an inner circle. In the meantime, indirect state sponsorship plays a more influential role in the cultural market.

The virtual pistolão

Petrobras may sponsor Overmundo, but the democratizing tides of digital expansion often run against the centralizing currents of state influence. Major media enterprises negotiate these treacherous waters by relying heavily on the guiding compass of the pistolão, or its new virtual versions.

Consider Bebel Gilberto and Maria Rita, two of Brazil's recent Latin Grammy winners. Bebel is the daughter of bossa nova superstar João Gilberto and singer Miúcha Buarque de Hollanda. Bebel's uncle, Chico Buarque, is one of Brazil's most influential popular composers. Maria Rita is the daughter of bossa nova superstar Elis Regina and pianist Cesar Camargo Mariano. These family connections proved decisive in garnering the favorable media attention that propelled them to stardom. Or take pop singer Preta Gil: being the daughter of the Minister of Culture certainly eased her path to overnight stardom in 2003. Martn'alia, recording artist and daughter of samba superstar Martinho da Vila, joined the inner circle of celebrity that same year. The success of these young media darlings and many others hinged heavily on the early endorsement of famous relatives.

None of this familial success results from conspiracy or from aggressive backstage campaigning on the part of famous parents, a practice surely more common in the United States. Brazil's media market has been configured to work in this way, in accordance with the traditional rules of the Brazilian job market. Flautist Danilo Caymmi has probably not gone far out of his way to promote his daughter, Alice. Promoters are preconditioned to descend on this teenaged singer because her father is Danilo and her grandfather is Dorival, her uncle is Dori and her aunt Nana (all famous performers). They do not want to turn her into the next Dorival Caymmi, but into the next Maria Rita. And because of her parentage, they can be guaranteed that she will be covered amply and favorably, at least in the beginning, in all Brazil's media outlets. On the basis of such market predispositions, sixteen-year-old Alice was chosen to sing the inaugural theme for the 2007 Pan-American Games in Rio.

The use of the pistolão in the entertainment industry has been common practice since the 1930s, at least. But the rapid proliferation of the practice in genres and styles associated with the democratizing aspects of the digital boom, like funk, hip-hop and techno, has been particularly notable. See, for example, the instant success of Simoninha and Max de Castro, sons of pop star Wilson Simonal, both of whom were showered with media attention before recording their first CDs in the techno-soul-samba subgenre. Hip-hop icon Marcelo D2 is nurturing the emergence of his pre-teen son Stephan in the same genre.

These practices are by no means unique to Brazil's media market – examples from Hollywood to Bollywood abound. They do seem to be particularly prevalent in Brazil, where the growth of vibrant domestic cultural industries combined with entrenched practices of nepotism to produce familial networks of stardom. Quantifying such practices would be impossible, however, and it is more revealing to observe the ways in which they have been reinvented in the digital age.

The virtual pistolão – the well-circulated endorsement by a cultural patron – allows both the state and private media enterprises to draw on the energies of digital expansion. Hermano Vianna, brother of rock star Herberto Vianna and friend of Minister of Culture Gilberto Gil, won Petrobras's support for Overmundo. He then worked with his old friend Regina Casé, granddaughter of pioneering variety-show producer Ademar Casé, to create the Globo TV series *Central da Periferia*. In a case like this, the traditional powers of Petrobras and Globo are linked through a web of familial and affective connections to the decentralized communication of cyberspace and the emerging culture of the working-class suburbs.

When Vianna and Casé invite a hip-hop duo like Cidinho e Doca to appear on *Central da Periferia*, they are ushering them into the magic circle of Brazilian celebrity, where potential conflicts become harmonious synergies. To capitalize on these relationships, Cidinho and Doca have stopped performing proibidão, the ostensibly banned funk in praise of criminal activity that circulates primarily through CDs recorded and sold on the informal market. The virtual pistolão, like its traditional predecessor, effectively disciplines the client, who avails himself of the access it guarantees.

Like other media markets, Brazil's star industry generates fresh personalities annually, the majority of whom are fated to travel the arc from obscurity to fame and on to obsolescence in a season or two, with no chance to name their own successors – Bruna Surfistinha, for example. Then there are figures like Caetano Veloso, who earn the power of the pistolão and maintain it for decades. Since the mid-1990s, new genres like hip-hop and new media pursuits like blogging have generated their own superconnecting godfathers, and these are always only a click away from established icons like Veloso. DJ Marlboro – who got his first drum machine from Hermano Vianna – is the pre-eminent tastemaker in funk. Cidinho and Doca are on his label. When Regina Casé throws a party attended by Veloso, Marlboro, and one or more of their protegés, society columnists document the event with names in bold type and the spinning wheels of fame suddenly have a new spoke.

The success of the protegé then becomes further evidence of the patron's stature – true for the traditional pistolão and its virtual versions. When the young Globo actor Jorge de Sá is pictured in celebrity magazines alongside his mother, Sandra, a popular soul singer of the 1980s, it helps prove she is still a star in her own right.

In consequence, Brazil's celebrity culture is as clannish as the quasi-aristocratic society it replaced.

Savvy children of the old gentry have perceived this trend and made the jump from the kinds of activities that once guaranteed their progenitors wealth and influence into pursuits more likely to bring new media celebrity. Eduardo Smith de Vasconcellos Suplicy chose not to imitate his grandfather, a coffee-exporting titan, nor his father, a senator for the PT, but instead made his foray in the world of rock, billing himself as Supla – different enough to avoid being confused with his dad, similar enough to remind people he is from one of São Paulo's leading families. His media success, however, probably owes more to his mother, Marta Teresa Smith de Vasconcellos Suplicy, a daughter of the old elite who rose to celebrity as a sex advice personality before becoming mayor of São Paulo for the PT. Supla's cousin, Jayme Monjardim Matarazzo, is a successful film director, celebrated for his biopic on the life of communist revolutionary Olga Benario Prestes. The success of the latest generation of the Suplicy Monjardim Matarazzo clan brings to light the familial fibers that connect old money, new cultural sectors and the rise of the political left.

Walter and João Moreira Salles offer more prominent examples of this phenomenon. They are scions of the founder of Unibanco, one of Brazil's most successful banks. Walter directed *Central Station*, a film that combines the urban marginality/backlands drama genres of Cinema Novo, and subsequently made *The Motorcycle Diaries*, a heroic portrait of the youthful Ché Guevara. More recently, he has become an influential patron in Brazil's film industry, connecting young directors to producers.

João Moreira Salles has directed a number of excellent documentaries, including *Notícias de uma Guerra Particular* (News from a Private War), on violent conflict between police and drug traffickers in Rio de Janeiro. He also made *Entreatos*, a documentary of Lula's 2002 presidential campaign, released in 2004. According to Moreira Salles, he effectively had unlimited access to the campaign – no one ever asked him to stop filming or to keep certain comments off the record. But the film nonetheless comes across as an unusually polite treatment of backroom politics, perhaps because, as Moreira Salles noted later, he and his crew took it upon themselves to stop filming when matters became too sensitive.[64] As one of Lula's advisers notes during the film, "They can be trusted." Dirceu, more cautious, opines, "They can be trusted. But no one can be trusted absolutely."

In a striking coincidence, Moreira Salles and *Entreatos* were nominated for Best Director and Best Documentary in the 2005 Grande Prêmio do Cinema Brasileiro shortly before the mensalão scandal broke. Coverage of the scandal revealed evidence of extensive illegal campaign practices by Lula's 2002 team, subsequently confirmed by high-ranking members of the PT. The celebration of *Entreatos* and the mensalão coverage seemed to exist in parallel universes, offering completely distinct perspectives on Brazil's political and cultural reality.

As these examples show, ties of family and friendship continue to structure and discipline representations of both politics and popular culture in Brazil's media marketplace. The virtual pistolão can eliminate the potential tensions between pluralistic cultural expansion and the restraining influences of state leverage. In doing so, it counterbalances both of these phenomena. The Brazilian cultural market is not shattering into a million digital bits, nor is it falling under the shadow of the state, nor is it controlled by a tight-knit circle of the anointed. Instead, all three of these tendencies are evident, sometimes pulling against one another, sometimes reinforcing each other in unexpected ways.

This makes Brazil's cultural market unique. Brazil is like India in that over many decades it has nurtured a domestic media industry that remains capable of feeding the demands of its wired population. But whereas India produces hundreds of feature films every year with little state funding, Brazil produces relatively few, and these are dependent on the state. This funding is completely necessary to the continued vitality of Brazilian film, but its political usage itself poses a threat to that vitality. Brazilian TV, meanwhile, with its high-gloss popular entertainment, featuring melodramas and variety shows, is more like Indian film than is Brazilian film.

Brazil has some similarities with Russia and Italy in the highly political use of media, both state and private, by the executive branch. But Brazil's cultural market is more diverse and freewheeling than that of Russia, and freedom of speech is under no immediate danger. As in Mexico, media titans have parlayed political connections into massive wealth and predominant market share. But whereas Carlos Slim of Telmex and the Azcárraga family of Televisa have expanded and consolidated control in the era of deregulation, the Marinho family has gradually decreased its own role in Globo operations. Globo has diversified along with the rest of the media market. It is more profitable than ever and remains highly influential, but no longer exercises the tidal pull over Brazilian popular culture that it did in the 1980s. Digital democratization, for all its pitfalls and qualifications, has been too successful for that.

Brazil's famous cultural vitality and its tendencies towards hybridity gave it a leg up in the process of creating a vibrant cultural market. The early expansion of media industries and state investment in domestic media capitalized on these tendencies, making Brazilian media self-sufficient and oriented towards cultivating and disseminating domestic products.

Since the fall of the dictatorship, a host of new producers and talents have come to the fore, ushered onto the stage by an older generation of patrons. Their energies and experiments ensure that Brazil remains culturally vital. These qualities, intangible as they are, transcend the guiding and limiting tendencies of state direction and familial networks. Neither Orkut, nor Petrobras nor the virtual pistolão explain what remains perpetually interesting and inventive within Brazilian culture. Orkut, current enthusiasm notwithstanding, will probably give way to new forms of digital democratization before long. In future administrations, Petrobras may cease to be the nation's foremost cultural sponsor. But the expansion of popular participation and strong state influence are likely to remain defining features of the cultural marketplace. The virtual pistolão, flexible and always in fashion, is more likely to endure. And the interaction of these phenomena will continue to determine the ways in which cultural invention finds its way to the national and international public.

Conclusion

Brazil has now been "redemocratizing" since the mid-1980s. Has democracy been consolidated, and how can we know? As these pages have made clear, "redemocratization," in truth, required the creation of a new democracy, rather than the rehabilitation of an old one. The current Brazilian Republic incorporates and gives some measure of power to more diverse sectors than any preceding version, and is grander both in its democratic aspirations and its accomplishments. The struggle to expand and consolidate those accomplishments is contentious and open-ended, but has now advanced to the point that Brazil can accurately be described as a democracy, and not merely as progressing through a transitional phase towards democratic aspirations.

Like all democracies, this one contains and must seek to control elements that endanger it. The flourishing pluralism of redemocratization has given rise to a dynamic society, but has also unleashed corroding forces. These forces – urban violence, political corruption, and environmental destruction, to name three – cannot be eliminated, but only beaten back, in the same way the *Real* Plan beat back inflation to tolerable levels. As with the *Real* Plan, successful confrontation of these forces will require not merely well-crafted policy but a laborious process of political persuasion leading to a larger social buy-in. Affected interest groups and the broader population need to be convinced that new policies will redound to their benefit, and those parties who stand to lose – criminal networks, corrupt police and politicians, illegal loggers, for example – must be effectively extricated from the political system and marginalized. This is easier said than done, but so was holding off inflation.

In the 1990s, "citizenship" was the buzzword of Brazilian politics. Reformers and activists who recognized that the 1988 Constitution had only laid the formal groundwork for universal citizenship without making it a reality organized to expand popular political participation and to confer the benefits of democracy on a greater number of Brazilians. The rhetoric of citizenship was occasionally self-serving, disingenuous, and misleading, thinly veiling partisan projects. But, lo and behold, by the early twenty-first century citizenship and its benefits had indeed expanded, in ways that depended partly on policies and projects, but also on economic growth and the gradual decomposition of social and cultural hierarchies.

"Impunity" is the new buzzword, and like its predecessors it occasionally serves unwholesome purposes. No one can be counted on to rail against impunity as fiercely as a micro-party deputy up for re-election. And the ascription of national ills ranging from deforestation to rising drug addiction to vaguely defined "impunity" is as unconvincing an oversimplification as their prior ascription to weak citizenship. But Brazilians increasingly recognize that corruption has astronomical costs that must be borne collectively. These costs include exorbitant interest rates, the proliferation of private security forces, the explosion of informal commerce with links to criminal networks, correspondingly high tax burdens in the formal market, and low returns on social spending – the Bloodsuckers' Scandal brought this home to many Brazilians in a visceral way.

Growing awareness of these costs has led to widespread expressions of indignation and demands for accountability, and to the formation of civil society organizations designed to combat it. In the 1990s, cutting-edge NGOs organized around citizenship, and advocated for delivering citizenship to the poor by funding digital inclusion programs and upgrading of favela infrastructure, for example. Today they often organize around issues of accountability, and undertake close inspection of municipal budgets. The mood of civil society has begun to shift.

Will this lead to significant progress in the fight against corruption? To put it somewhat differently, will these isolated and occasionally partisan efforts in the name of fighting impunity coalesce and find reinforcement in the kind of economic and social transitions that previously helped turn the rhetoric of "expanding citizenship" into actual expanded citizenship? There are a few encouraging signs, including the creation of independent government bodies and civil society organizations with authority to audit public accounts, but it is too early to say whether these will yield enduring transformation.

In this regard, as well, Brazil brings local particularities to global patterns. Democracies characterized by the inconsistent rule of law, persistent political corruption and high levels of inequality are the global rule, not the exception, and this rule applies to both fully emerged as well as emerging nations. To determine that these are not democracies despite their constitutional pretensions might provide some frisson of purist vindication, but would leave a very small democratic club, and would overlook the real, if inconsistent, representative practices of these polities.

In Brazil, in a strange way, to suggest that the nation is still redemocratizing but not yet arrived at democracy would also be to let the young republic off the hook for the ways in which it falls short of its own aspirations. Blaming the legacy of the dictatorship for political problems – the persistence of the regional machines, for example – may have been convincing in the late 1980s, but no longer holds water. Historical legacies bequeathed by the dictatorship and its antecedents doubtless shaped the challenges faced during redemocratization, but the responses to those challenges, in both their successes and their failures, have been determined by actors within the new democracy and not by ghosts from its past.

Overthrowing the dictatorship and dismantling its remains provided one of the grand narratives of Brazilian history since the 1970s. Brazil's path in this regard was necessarily particular, although parallel in many ways to those of Latin American neighbors emerging from authoritarian regimes in the same period. The quest for economic growth in the context of the Washington Consensus and the drive to emerge as a player of the first rank in the world economy provided another grand narrative. Brazil's adherence to the gospel of growth, efficiency and market capitalization was something it shared with a great many peers, and its emergence as an economic power, at least in some key sectors, it famously shared with Russia, India and China.

Unusually, Brazil achieved greater prominence in the world economy without deepening inequality at home, and indeed Brazilian inequality has gradually declined since the early 1990s.[65] This is an important achievement, and one that challenges assumptions that the Washington Consensus proved overwhelmingly negative for Latin America in general. The Brazilian case may be *sui generis* within the region in this regard, but it is a case large and important enough to merit close consideration. At the same time, it is not necessarily cause for jubilant celebration: Brazil has gone from being a member of the highly selective club of most unequal nations to being merely very unequal. This is nothing to turn up one's nose at, but is somewhat underwhelming as the conclusion of a grand narrative.

The dictatorship is now a part of history, the Washington Consensus still prevalent rhetorically but no longer capable of exerting much in the way of discipline. Will another grand narrative emerge, one that will carry the young democracy towards further improvements? Or does the burgeoning pluralism of the last twenty years indicate that grand narratives themselves are hopelessly out of fashion? If the latter, what will hold this experiment together? As these pages have shown, there is no longer a shared popular culture drawing Brazilians into a common embrace. There is, however, a strong and persistent belief in cultural vitality itself as a common attribute. Time will tell if this is enough to provide a grand narrative. It is certainly enough to provide a good soundtrack.

Further reading

A growing number of scholars have begun to consider Brazil's broad transformations since redemocratization in the 1980s. Particularly recommended among these general works are Marcelo A. Font's *Transforming Brazil: A Reform Era in Perspective* (2003) and the volume edited by Mauricio Font and Anthony Peter Spanakos, *Reforming Brazil* (2004). Francisco Vidal Luna and Herbert S. Klein's *Brazil since 1980* (2006) is particularly strong on economic transitions. James Holston's *Insurgent Citizenship: Disjunctions of Democracy and Modernity in Brazil* (2008) is a compelling analysis of changing patterns of civic mobilization within persistent structures of inequality.

A number of excellent works cover key portions of the political transformation since the 1980s, and of the rise to power of former opponents of the dictatorship in particular. Timothy J. Power's *The Political Right in Postauthoritarian Brazil* (2000) details the adaptation of regional political machines to the democratic context. Margaret Keck's *The Workers' Party and Democratization in Brazil* explores the formation of the PT and its early evolution. Alfred P. Montero's *Brazilian Politics: Reforming a Democratic State in a Changing World* (2006) provides rich analysis of the recent political arena. Rebecca Neaera Abers offers a case study of the movement for greater popular participation in municipal government in *Inventing Local Democracy: Grassroots Politics in Brazil* (2000).

Urban violence and criminal territorialization, and corresponding fortification have been the subject of rich and extensive analysis. Among the best works in English are Enrique Desmond Arias's *Drugs and Democracy in Rio de Janeiro: Trafficking, Social Networks and Public Security* (2006) and Teresa Caldeira's *City of Walls: Crime, Segregation and Citizenship in São Paulo* (2001). On the roots of these arrangements, see Brodwyn Fischer's *A Poverty of Rights: Citizenship and Inequality in Twentieth-Century Rio de Janeiro* (2008).

Finding balanced coverage of agrarian issues is more difficult. Sue Branford and Jan Rocha's *Cutting the Wire* (2002) provides a well-documented history of the landless workers' movement. Zander Navarro's "Mobilization without Emancipation: Social Struggles by Brazilian Landless Families," in Boaventura Sousa Santos's *Another Production is Possible: Beyond the Capitalist Canon* (2007) offers lucid critical analysis of MST strategies. On settlement in the Amazon region, see John O. Browder and Brian Godfrey's *Rainforest Cities: Urbanization, Development and Globalization of the Brazilian Amazon* (1997). On further challenges in the region, see Mark London and Brian Kelly, *The Last Forest: The Amazon in the Age of Globalization* (2007).

Brazilian popular music inspires a rapidly proliferating body of critical work. Key contributions in English are Idelber Avelar and Christopher Dunn, eds, *Brazilian Popular Music and Citizenship* (2009) and Charles A. Perrone and Christopher Dunn, *Brazilian Popular Music and Globalization* (2001). Alexander Dent's *Country Critics: Rural Music and Performativity in Brazil* (2009) explores the patterns and meanings of sertaneja and caipira music. Philip Galinsky's *Maracatu Atômico: Tradition, Modernity and Postmodernity in the Mangue Movement and the New Music Scene of Recife, Pernambuco, Brazil* (2002) analyzes the mangue beat movement. For good general overviews, see John P. Murphy, *Music in Brazil: Experiencing Music, Expressing Culture* (2006), the revised edition of Christopher McGowan and Ricardo Pessanha's *The Brazilian Sound: Samba, Bossa Nova and the Popular Music of Brazil* (2008), and Larry Crook, *Brazilian Music: Northeastern Traditions and the Heartbeat of a Modern Nation* (2005).

Andrew Chesnut provides an acute analysis of Brazil's religious marketplace in *Competitive Spirits: Latin America's New Religious Economy* (2007) and of Pentecostalism in particular in his *Born Again in Brazil: The Pentecostal Boom and the Pathogens of Poverty* (1997). Cecilia Mariz explores similar phenomena in *Coping with Poverty: Pentecostals and Christian Base Communities in Brazil* (1994). John Burdick's *Blessed Anastacia: Women, Race and Popular Christianity in Brazil* (1998) focuses on the religious choices made by women of color in an increasingly pluralist Brazil.

On the production dynamics of recent Brazilian film, see Randal Johnson, "TV Globo, the MPA and Contemporary Brazilian Cinema," in Lisa Shaw and Stephanie Dennison, eds, *Latin American Cinema: Essays on Identity, Gender and National Identity* (2005). On Casas Bahia and expanding digital access through the market, see C. K. Prahalad, *The Fortune at the Bottom of the Pyramid* (2005). On Brazilian blogs, see Idelber Avelar, "Cultural Studies in the Blogosphere: Academics Meet New Technologies of Online Publication," in Erin Graff Zivin, ed. *The Ethics of Latin American Literary Criticism* (2007).

Notes

1 Francisco H. G. Ferreira, Phillipe G. Leite and Julie Litchfield, "The Rise and Fall of Brazilian Inequality, 1981–2004," World Bank, Policy Research Working Paper, WPS 3867 (2006), and Francisco H. G. Ferreira, Phillipe G. Leite and Martin Ravallion, "Poverty Reduction without Economic Growth? Explaining Brazil's Poverty Dynamics, 1985–2004," World Bank, Policy Research Working Paper, WPS 4431 (2007).

2 Mário Sabino, "As Mortes de Brizola," *Veja*, 1860, June 2004.

3 Susan Okie, "Fighting HIV: Lessons from Brazil," *New England Journal of Medicine*, May 2006, 1977–81.

4 CIA World Factbook, Brazil, Communications, 2006, <https://www.cia.gov/library/publications/the-world-factbook/geos/br.html#Comm> (accessed May 15, 2008).

5 Nice de Paula, "A interminável Era Vargas," *Jornal do Brasil*, 24 June 2001, <http://www.fgtsfacil.org.br/newsclip/NewsShow.asp?Materia=1497&Editoria=3&Pagina=47> (accessed May 15, 2008).

6 See, for example, André Campos, "Vale do Rio Doce anuncia corte de fornecimento a siderúrgicas," *Reporter Brasil*, August 23, 2007, <http://www.reporterbrasil.org.br/exibe.php?id=1153> (accessed May 15, 2008).

7 On local and international reactions to Cardoso's attempted pension reform, see Diana Jean Schemo, "Social Insecurity in Brazil for Its Government Retirees," *New York Times*, January 24, 1999.

8 Instituto Brasileiro de Geografia e Estatística, *Pesquisa Nacional por Amostra de Domicílios* (Rio de Janeiro: Pnad, 2004).

9 Kathy Lindert, "The Nuts and Bolts of Brazil's bolsa família Program: Implementing Conditional Cash Transfers in a Decentralized Context," World Bank Working Paper, WBP 39853, 2007.

10 Lindert, "The Nuts and Bolts," Fábio Veras Soares, Sergei Suarez Dillon Soares, Marcelo Medeiros and Rafael Guerreiro Osório, "Cash Transfer Programmes in Brazil: Impacts on Inequality and Poverty," International Poverty Center, Working Paper 21, 2005, and Marcelo Medeiros, Tatiana Britto and Fábio Soares, "Programas Focalizados de Transferência de Renda no Brasil: Contribuições para o Debate," Instituto de Pesquisa Econômica Aplicada, Texto 1283, 2007.

11 João Ubaldo Ribeiro, "O Presidente Lula Beijou a Mão de Jader Barbalho," *Estado de São Paulo*, September 9, 2006.

12 Mário Sabino, "Me considero de esquerda," interview with Fernando Henrique Cardoso, *Veja*, March 22, 2006.

13 "Discurso do presidente da República, Luiz Inácio Lula da Silva, no ato político de celebração aos 15 anos do Foro de São Paulo," Presidência da República, Secretaria de Comunicação Social, Secretaria de Imprensa; available at <http://www.info.planalto.gov.br/download/discursos/pr812a.doc>.

14 Luiz Carlos Bresser Pereira, "A New Management for a New State: Liberal, Social and Republican," John. L Manion Lecture (Ottawa, Ontario, Canada, 2001).

15 Brodwyn Fischer, *The Poverty of Rights* (Stanford, CA: Stanford University Press, 2008).

16 Carlos Amorim, *CV-PCC: a irmandade do crime* (Rio de Janeiro: Ed. Record, 2006).

17 Enrique Desmond Arias, *Drugs and Democracy in Rio de Janeiro* (Chapel Hill: University of North Carolina Press, 2006).

18 *Caros Amigos*, PCC, Special Edition, May 2006.

19 See Tom Phillips, "Blood Simple," *Observer* Magazine, September 17, 2006.

20 Juliana Linhares, "PT, PCC e peruas, tudo a ver?" *Veja*, June 28, 2006.

21 Mariana Cavalcanti, "Of Shacks, Houses and Fortresses: An Ethnography of Favela Consolidation in Rio de Janeiro" (PhD dissertation, University of Chicago, 2007).

22 Bruno Paes Manso, Maryluci de Araújo Faria and Norman Gall, "Do faroeste para a vida civilizada na periferia de São Paulo," Braudel Papers no. 37, Instituto Fernando Braudel, 2005.

23 See, for example, Ted Goertzel and Tulio Kahn, "Brazil: the Unsung Story of São Paulo's Dramatic Murder Rate Drop," *Brazzil*, May 18, 2007. Rates have continued to drop.

24 Sue Branford and Jan Rocha, *Cutting the Wire: The Story of the Landless Movement in Brazil* (London: Latin American Bureau, 2002).

25 *Constituição da República Federativa do Brasil*, December 5, 1988; available at <http://www.planalto.gov.br/ccivil_03/Constituicao/Constituiçao.htm> (accessed May 15, 2008).

26 Kenneth Maxwell, "Chico Mendes," in *Naked Tropics: Essays on Empire and Other Rogues* (New York: Routledge, 2003).

27 Amnesty International, AMR, "Brazil: Corumbiara and Eldorado de Carajás: Rural Violence, Political Brutality and Impunity," January 19, 1998; available at <http://www.amnesty.org/en/library/info/AMR19/001/1998/en> (accessed May 15, 2008).

28 See, for example, Bernardo Mançano Fernandes and Cristiane Barbosa Ramalho, "Luta pela terra e desenvolvimento rural no Pontal de Paranapanema," *Estudos Avançados* 15:43 (September–December 2001), available at <http://www.scielo.br/scielo.php?pid=S0103-40142001000300018&script=sci_arttext> (accessed May 15, 2008); and Rachel Bertol, "Como os sem-terra se inventaram pela mídia: a novidade social nos anos 1990," CPDOC, *Estudos Históricos*, "Mídia," 31/1: 1–22.

29 Anthony Pereira, "Brazil's Agrarian Reform: Democratic Innovation or Oligarchic Exclusion Redux," *Latin American Politics and Society*, 45/2 (Summer 2003): 41–65.

30 Alana Gandra, "Vale vai suspender fornecimento de minério de ferro a empresas que desrespeitam

legislação," *Agência Brasil,* April 6, 2007.

31 Leandro Beguoci, "Bolsa Família esvazia MST, dizem analistas," *Folha de São Paulo,* November 4, 2007.

32 Leandro Beguoci, "Invasores de terra diminuem com avanço do Bolsa Família," *Folha de São Paulo,* November 4, 2007.

33 Alessandra Milanez, "Monsanto irá cobrar royalties de soja transgênica," *Folha de São Paulo,* June 11, 2003.

34 José Maschio, "Justiça decreta prisão de seis por mortes na Syngenta," *Folha de São Paulo,* December 11, 2007.

35 Idelber Avelar, "De Milton ao Metal: Política e Música em Minas," International Association for the Study of Popular Music Conference, Rio de Janeiro, November 2004, <http://www.hist.puc.cl/historia/iaspm/rio/Anais2004%20(PDF)/IdelberAvelar.pdf> (accessed May 15, 2008).

36 Alex Dent, *Country Critics: Rural Music and Performativity in Brazil* (Durham, NC: Duke University Press, forthcoming, 2009).

37 Datafolha, "64% dos brasileiros se declaram católicos," *Opinião Pública,* April 14, 2007, <http://datafolha.folha.uol.com.br/po/ver_po.php?session=447> (accessed May 15, 2008).

38 Kenneth Serbin, *Secret Dialogues: Church–State Relations, Torture and Social Justice in Authoritarian Brazil* (Pittsburgh, PA: Pittsburgh University Press, 2000).

39 Andrew Chesnut, *Competitive Spirits: Latin America's New Religious Economy* (New York: Oxford University Press, 2003).

40 Ibid.

41 Fundação Getúlio Vargas, Centro de Políticas Sociais, *Retratos das Religiões no Brasil,* Rio de Janeiro, 2005.

42 All figures in this section are from the Fundação Getúlio Vargas study, Retrato das Religiões no Brasil, 2005, and from its continuation, Fundação Getúlio Vargas, Centro de Políticas Sociais, *Economia das Religiões, Mudanças Recentes,* Rio de Janeiro, 2007.

43 See, for example, Bernardo de la Peña, Cesar Tartaglia and Toni Marques, "Crivella será ouvido pela PF por evasão," *O Globo,* July 3, 2004, and Gilberto Nascimento, "A tevê que caiu do céu," *Revista Isto É,* July 15, 1998.

44 See, for example, "Igreja Universal com império empresarial," *Folha de São Paulo,* December 15, 2007 and Gilberto Nascimento, "As contas secretas da Igreja Universal," *Revista Isto É,* May 25, 2005.

45 Martijn Oosterbaan, "Divine Mediations: Pentecostalism, Politics and Mass Media in a Favela in Rio de Janeiro" (PhD dissertation, University of Amsterdam, 2006).

46 Eric W. Kramer, "Law and the Image of a Nation: Religious Conflict and Religious Freedom in a Brazilian Criminal Case," *Law and Social Inquiry,* 26/1 (2001): 35–62.

47 Consuelo Dieguez and Marcelo Carneiro, "Tem até bombeiro no chuvisco," *Veja,* April 12, 2000.

48 Felipe Recondo, "Deputados elegem hoje novo presidente da Câmara," *Folha de São Paulo,* September 28, 2005.

49 Letícia Sander and Rainer Bragon, "58% da propina foi para evangélicos, diz CPI dos Sanguessugas," *Folha de São Paulo,* August

12, 2006, and Adriana Ceolin and Leonardo Souza, "82% dos sanguessugas são da base aliada," *Folha de São Paulo*, July 19, 2006.

50 See the International Telecommunication Union website for 2006 figures, <http://www.itu.int/ITU-D/icteye/Indicators/Indicators.aspx#> (accessed May 15, 2008).

51 For Orkut usage, see Orkut (www.orkut.com) Demographics. For Brazil's Orkutmania, see Seth Kugel, "A Website Born in US Finds Fans in Brazil," *New York Times*, April 10, 2006.

52 Dayanne Mikevis, "Google faz acordos extrajudiciais com órgãos de investigação e denúncias," *Folha de São Paulo*, March 10, 2006.

53 See, for example, Andreza Matais, "Esquema dos sanguessugas pode ter desviado mais de R$100 milhões," *Folha de São Paulo*, August 10, 2006.

54 Agamemnon Mendes Pedreira and his psychoproctologist Jacintho Leite Aquino Rêgo are the creation of humorists Hubert and Marcelo Madureira. See Hubert and Marcelo Madureira, *Agamemnon Mendes Pedreira, o homem e o minto* (Rio de Janeiro: Livraria Só Letrando, 2002).

55 See C. K. Prahalad, *The Fortune at the Bottom of the Pyramid: Eradicating Poverty through Profits* (Philadelphia, PA: Wharton School Publishing, 2004).

56 Hermano Vianna, "Manifesto de Hermano Vianna," *Overmundo*, originally posted June 14, 2006; accessed May 15, 2008.

57 See, for example, Maria Celina Soares D'Araujo, "Governo Lula: contornos sociais e políticos da

elite do poder," Centro de Pesquisa e Documentação, Fundação Getúlio Vargas, July 2007; and "Profusão de cargos de confiança," *Estado de São Paulo*, editorial, June 21, 2007.

58 Sílvio Navarro and Fábio Zanini, "Setor bancário deu maior doação à campanha de Lula," *Folha de São Paulo*, November 29, 2006.

59 See Randal Johnson, "TV Globo, the MPA and Contemporary Brazilian Cinema," in Lisa Shaw and Stephanie Dennison (eds), *Latin American Cinema: Essays on Modernity, Gender and National Identity* (Jefferson, NC: McFarland, 2005).

60 Marcelo Cajueiro, "Silvio Da-Rin is Brazil's Culture Czar," *Variety*, October 26, 2007.

61 Beatriz Jaguaribe, *O Choque do Real: estética, mídia e cultura* (Rio de Janeiro: Editora Rocco, 2007).

62 Flávio Sá Earp and George Kornis, *A Economia do Livro: A Crise Atual e uma Proposta de Política*, Instituto de Economia, Universidade Federal do Rio de Janeiro, Working Paper 004, 2005, <http://www.cbl.org.br/pages.php?recid=57> (accessed May 15, 2008).

63 Mônica Bergamo, "PF prende cinco acusados de acelerar projetos que pleiteavam recursos da Lei Rouanet," *Folha de São Paulo*, November 6, 2007.

64 Alessandra Bastos and Spensy Pimentel, "Lula diz não querer ver *Entreatos* para manter liberdade dada ` a produção, diz Salles," *Agência Brasil*, December 7, 2004.

65 Ferreira, Leite and Litchfield, "The Rise and Fall of Brazilian Inequality, 1981–2004."

Index

7 DAYS TO A BYLINE THAT PAYS

10658724

Michael Ray Smith

Foreword by two-time
Pulitzer winner Manny Garcia

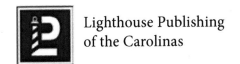

Lighthouse Publishing
of the Carolinas

7 DAYS TO A BYLINE THAT PAYS BY MICHAEL RAY SMITH
Published by Lighthouse Publishing of the Carolinas
2333 Barton Oaks Dr., Raleigh, NC, 27614

ISBN: 978-1-941103-48-7

Available in print from your local bookstore, online, or from the
publisher at: www.lighthousepublishingofthecarolinas.com

For more information on this book and the author, visit:
http://writingtipsthatwork.com/

Brought to you by the creative team at Lighthouse Publishing of the
Carolinas:
Shonda Savage, Brian Cross, and Eddie Jones

Library of Congress Cataloging-in-Publication Data
Smith, Michael Ray.
7 Days to a Byline That Pays / Michael Ray Smith 1st ed.

Printed in the United States of America

DEDICATION

For Madison and Abigail

PRAISE FOR 7 DAYS TO A BYLINE THAT PAYS

7 Days to a Byline That Pays is a terrific guide for aspiring journalists. It's written by a veteran journalist who is now giving his time and talent to develop the next generation of award-winning journalists. Michael Ray Smith has successfully culled the best ideas from colleagues and published a book that is essential reading for anyone who wants to succeed in journalism. It's creative, clear, fun and timeless. He hits all the fundamentals.

~ Manny Garcia
Two-time Pulitzer winner

The good Lord made the world in six days. Not being divine, Michael Ray Smith needs one additional day in his staggeringly excellent book, *7 Days to a Byline That Pays*, to take a person from a wanna-be to published journalist. Journalism is reinventing itself with a new paradigm that integrates its storied past with a dynamic future. This book charts the way forward. Smith understands that the 21th-century journalist needs grounding in the historic fundamentals as well as mastery of the latest digital tools. But the human condition has not changed. Smith endorses a model of empathic narrative, which touches people and moves them to re-engage with present-day challenges.

~ Tim Morgan
Senior editor, global journalism, *Christianity Today*

Budding journalists aren't the only ones who should read Michael Ray Smith's *7 Days to a Byline That Pays*. His advice—at once sensible and stirring—benefits writers of any stripe.

~ Lori Haskins Houran
Children's book editor and author of more than 25 books

Teaching, at its best, does much more than instruct. It engages, excites and even inspires students with specific, practical guidance about how to do the job right. In *7 Days to a Byline That Pays*, Michael Ray Smith delivers on all of these dimensions. At a time when young journalists confront a marketplace filled with new challenges and constant upheaval, this book can help them get into print fast. Its breezy approach gets readers right to the point with dozens of useful suggestions that are well organized and highly accessible. Most importantly, this book goes beyond the "what and how" and clearly explains why young writers should heed these valuable tips.

~ Robert P. Patchen, Westat

In *7 Days to a Byline That Pays*, Professor Michael Ray Smith outlines practical steps to write a compelling story well and find an outlet to publish it. Whether reading from beginning to end or using as a reference, his book will help any writer wrestling with how to begin a story to craft it to completion.

~ Meagan Clark
Writer for International Justice Mission
Former writer for International Business Times

In *7 Days to a Byline That Pays*, Smith has designed an easy-to-follow step-by-step method that will help the beginning writer get into print fast. His smooth, quick pacing urges the reader on, building confidence along the way. The book will also help veteran writers keep up with the changing feature marketplace. The contributions by the writers in the bonus section are just that: a bonus."

~ Dennis Bounds, Ph.D.
Adjunct professor in Communication at Christopher Newport University and Virginia Wesleyan College

Michael Ray Smith has impeccable credentials, having worked in journalism all his professional life. He has been a college professor, newspaper editor/columnist and author of many books. He puts a lifetime of writing, editing, and the teaching of writing into this book: *7 Days to a Byline That Pays*. The book every writer needs to read.

~ Astrid Rivera
Journalist for Spanish TV and Creator of LatinBlah.com

"Smith writes in an easy, conversational style that carries with it nuggets of insight to help a writer get published quickly— like being able to sit down and pick the brain of a top journalist. The offerings by other writers award the reader an additional treasure trove of bang-on advice that I appreciate both as a writer and an editor."

~ Andrea Miles Di Salvo
News Editor, *Heppner Gazette-Times*

An excellent, cleverly-organized introduction to journalism by an outstanding professor and former practicing journalist.

~ John Vernon Lawing
Journalist Professor Emeritus, Regent University and illustrator of Terry Lindvall's *A Mirror of Fools.*

7 Days to a Byline That Pays delivers. The text combines the journalistic essentials—from defining news to conducting interviews—with an entrepreneurial eye to getting the product to market. A chapter on Internet resources and pitfalls is particularly useful, as is one comprised of advice on topics ranging from photography to building relationships.

~ Brad Nason
Associate professor in Department of Communication &
Literature of Media
Pennsylvania Technical College

7 Days to a Byline That Pays is a great tool for professionals trying to get valuable messages across to their stakeholders in clear, compelling and creative ways. It will also serve the layperson whose great ideas often go unsaid because he doesn't know how to put them in writing.

~ Edward I. Fubara, Ph.D.
Educator, administrator and minister
Author of *Lessons from the Life of a Bald-Headed Blind Clown*

Do you have a great idea for a story, but you're not sure what to do with it? If so, then Michael Ray Smith's latest book—*7 Days to a Byline That Pays*—is sure to become one of your favorite writing resources. As a successful writer himself, Michael shares with you the easy-to-follow, step-by-step process of turning your idea into the kind of story editors want to publish. *7 Days to a Byline That Pays* is sure to become a favorite among new and experienced writers alike.

~ Edward A. Johnson
Mass communication professor

Michael Ray Smith has pounded pavement as a reporter, "chased" down leads, interviewed politicians and paupers, won journalism awards, and earned a doctor's degree in communication arts. He teaches from experience, not vapid theories.

~ **Dr. Dennis E. Hensley**
Chairman of Department of Professional Writing,
Taylor University
Author of more than 50 books

It's as if Michael Ray Smith has gathered an elite team of America's most talented, most experienced—and especially most plain-spoken—journalists in one room. They're there with one goal: to systemically explain the essential basics for envisioning, writing, and selling a story. Smith's seven-day plan from assignment to byline is an inspiration.

~ **Bill Newcott**
Features Editor, AARP Media
Host, Movies for Grownups Radio Show
Former Expeditions Editor, *National Geographic* magazine

7 Days to a Byline That Pays is sure to become one of your favorite writing journeys: to the point, practical, funny, clever, insightful, and not too heavy. It works as a primer for a beginning writing class and a nifty prompt for the experienced writer. I loved the witty contributions and advice from a host of published writers. This is good stuff. Get it. And don't leave home without it.

~ **Robert Darden**
Associate Professor of Journalism, PR & New Media at
Baylor University
Author of more than two dozen books, including *Nothing But Love in God's Water: Black Sacred Music from the Civil War to the Civil Rights Movement, Volume I*

Prof. Smith has distilled his years of newsroom and classroom experience into an excellent introduction to becoming a journalist. It's clear, readable, and packed with more than enough helpful information to make this book useful long after your first reading.

~ **Dr. Les Sillars**
Patrick Henry College
WORLD Magazine

Ben Franklin would have highly approved of this book. He celebrated as we do an era where information has been democratized, which requires writers, reporters and editors to see, before they define, while trusting readers/citizens with information they need to know that makes democracy and self-governance more possible.

~ **Bruce Evensen**
DePaul University professor
Author of *The Responsible Reporter: Journalism in the Information Age, Truman, Palestine, The Press, When Dempsey Fought Tunney, God's Man for the Gilded Age*

From advice about Twitter to old-fashioned notepads, Michael Ray Smith's new field guide covers it all. From getting the first interview to putting the finishing touches on a story, Dr. Smith provides a quick and clear manual free of extraneous detail and muddled ambiguity. The product of Smith's years of experience as a mentor to journalists, *7 Days to a Byline That Pays* compiles the very best information and most helpful recommendations. The title aims for a byline in seven days, but anyone who follows Dr. Smith's advice will hit it in six.

~ **Adam C. English**
Campbell University professor
Author of *Theology Remixed* and
The Saint Who Would be Santa Claus

This book is an ideal basic training manual for aspiring journalists. It delivers all the practical advice new (and some old) writers need. It is user friendly, a brilliantly fun read packed with real-life nuggets. Eons ago, one of my journalism professors was quite fond of saying, "What's the one thing we KNOW about communication? We tend to get it wrong!" But this book can help you get it right. It takes a special kind of person to be a journalist. This book can guide you successfully around some of the minefields and pitfalls every writer encounters along the journey of a writing life. For those journalists seeking to improve their communication skills and get published, this book is a must-read.

~ Deborah Strong, Ph.D.
Missionary and journalist of Nepal Disability Relief
Founder/Director "A Voice for the Voiceless"

Don't wait on the Muses to begin writing because often the Muses need a jump start. This is the perfect book to wheedle the Muses and release the creative chattels within.

~ Ran Whitley, Ph.D.
Professor of Music, Campbell University
Author of *Melodious Counterpoints*

7 Days to a Byline That Pays is a quick, easy read that contains valuable information to help writers get published. As I read it, I couldn't help but wish that I had it when I started my career more than 27 years ago.

~ Steve DeVane
Journalist, *Fayetteville News*
Winner of Frank Burkhalter Award for news writing

In *7 Days to a Byline That Pays*, aspiring writers will find fodder for the imagination along with important nuggets on how to write. Smith continues to develop his instructive guidance that leads writers from the idea stage to a completed magazine article that will impress editors. The book is chock full of examples of what works well. Even people who think they already know how to write will find a wealth of new strategies in this book.

~ Stephen D. Perry, Ph.D.
Associate Dean for Academics
Professor, Regent University School of Communication & the Arts
Author of *A Consolidated History of Media*

FOREWORD

The hardest task for a journalist is to find the right story to tell. How to interview, identify your protagonist, create a narrative that is riveting, fun, a must-read for an ever-changing world of consumers.

That's what Dr. Michael Ray Smith's book is about. Telling a story. It means taking raw material, learning to write, using new approaches, across platforms, that connect with our audiences.

The hard work of telling a story clearly remains the platinum standard in journalism today. Most of us are not born writers. It takes training and this book can be a start. *7 Days to a Byline That Pays* is a terrific guide for aspiring journalists. It's written by a veteran journalist who is now giving his time and talent to develop the next generation of award-winning journalists.

Smith has successfully culled the best ideas from colleagues and published a book that is essential reading for anyone who wants to succeed in journalism. It's creative, clear, fun, and timeless. He hits all the fundamentals.

Manny Garcia
Investigative Reporter, Pulitzer Prize-winning journalist and editor

TABLE OF CONTENTS

Extra Day

WHAT OTHER WRITERS WANT YOU TO KNOW TO SNAG A BYLINE

INTRODUCTION

You're a writer in a hurry. You can't help it. Writer Walter Fisher says we are *homo narrans*, storytellers, and these stories give order to life. Master raconteur G. K. Chesterton once wrote, "I had always felt life first as a story—and if there is a story, there is a storyteller," while Frodo sighs, "I wonder what sort of tale we've fallen into?" in J. R. R. Tolkien's *The Lord of the Rings*. "All of life is a story," notes Madeleine L'Engle of *A Wrinkle in Time* fame.

So, you are in good company, and you want to write a story, a factual one, that includes the drama of Tolkien, perhaps, but a nonfiction piece that someone will buy and someone will read. This book is your secret weapon to getting published quickly. The ideas are not new, but the presentation is deliberately breezy and compact to help you work fast. I've worked with writers and editors across the country to compress the salient points in an easy-to-grasp approach that you can tackle.

We think you can accomplish the goal of writing a salable article in seven days by using the ideas in the pages ahead. Other books will provide ideas on which to write. This book is written with the assumption that you have a specific idea and you need to flesh it out. Perhaps you have access to a woman who survived a car-jacking episode, and she is willing to tell you her story. Some periodical or website may want this piece, but each will have a different angle. One may want to include tips on avoiding car-jackings. Others may want you to include a state-by-state summary on where these kinds of crimes occur. Yet another approach explores ways for people to overcome the trauma of that kind of crime.

Let's say you have contacted an editor who said she will take a look at the article on speculation, on spec, we say. You quiz her a little, and she gives you a little guidance. With that, you tell her that you can sew up the piece in a week. You do the interviews, check documents, visit the library, call sources, check the Web and, voila, you have an article. You re-read it and make changes and edit out the wordy parts and now it's ready for submission. Plus you send her an irresistible, first-class digital photograph and the sale is nearly certain. How did you do it? You followed the outline in this manual, one chapter a day, to secure your byline. Let's get started.

Day 1

THE CHOCOLATE-COVERED ALMOND

CHAPTER AT-A-GLANCE

Understanding conflict is essential in storytelling

Identifying the news peg or news angle in an article

Using the five Ws to answer questions that are important in an article

In many ways, writing for publication is like foil-wrapped
chocolate.

The foil wrapping can be viewed as the central idea of the story.
Beneath the foil is a luscious piece of chocolate, detail that supports the main idea. But inside that hunk of chocolate is a sweet
almond, a colorful expression that makes your writing sing.

This chapter will provide an overview of the steps writers
use to unearth the sweet spot that's part of every story assignment. These techniques will serve writers well, whether
it's crafting a news release in public relations, creating a tight

argument in advertising, or writing a crisp news story. They all begin with selecting the main idea.

THE MAIN IDEA

Find the **conflict**, and you'll find the main idea.

Imagine that the library is installing a new system that will scan books using your identification card. What's the conflict? The conflict could be the time and inconvenience needed to make the change. Or, the conflict could be the amount of money the system will cost. Maybe people are just fond of the old system and don't want to see it abandoned.

Literature, film, life. All require conflict. Where is the sparkle without conflict? The same idea is true in media writing, but don't be deceived into thinking that a writer imposes conflict where none exists. Don't make up the conflict; just ask yourself, "What issues does this story suggest?"

Throughout this book are **Tips**. TIP, an acronym meaning "to insure promptness," once was the payment given to someone in advance of his or her service. For our purposes, **TIP** can stand for **"To Insure Publication."** The tips that you will find in the pages ahead are ideas that may help you refine your editorial edge, to become the writer that is only a byline away.

Tip: To gain an appreciation for news writing, type . . . literally, type . . . the first three paragraphs of a news article from a newspaper or news aggregate website. *Drug arrests on college campuses jumped 34%, but burglary and other property crimes fell for the second year in a row, says a news report.* That's a lead, a first sentence, from "Drug arrests up, property crime down at colleges", an article by Anita Manning and Tamara Henry[1] in *USA Today's* Life section. Or, this one. "Problem: You hate your job. It's not that the work itself is particularly awful. But the boss—oh, sheesh—the boss doesn't get it." Mike Krumboltz wrote that sweet lead for Yahoo! News, September 30, 2013. Or this hard-hitting indictment lead with the headline, "Righteous Fury: The American who indicted a notorious African war criminal." "David Crane, a 63-year-old law professor at Syracuse University, sat in the sleek gray rectangular courtroom at The Hague and listened intently as the decision was delivered: the final verdict in the war-crimes trial of Charles Ghankay Taylor, the former president of Liberia," wrote Claire MacDougal, *Newsweek*, September 27, 2013.[2]

Find a lead that you like and type it and the next two sentences! Most people will ignore this technique, but for those who try it, they will gain a greater appreciation for the rhythm and cadence of good writing. The old master Benjamin Franklin taught himself the beauty of a well-turned sentence by copying and then rewriting essays that he found highly readable. It worked for Franklin, inventor, statesman, and writer, and it will work for you.

---

[1] Manning, A. and Henry, T. (1995, January 30). Drug arrests up, property crime down at colleges, *USA Today*, p. D1
[2] http://www.thedailybeast.com/newsweek/2013/09/27/david-crane-s-indictment-of-former-liberian-president-charles-taylor.html

THE INTERVIEW AND CONFLICT

A typical assignment for news reporters and writers is to interview a person. Those making assignments, called **editors**, don't randomly assign writers to interview just anyone. People are interviewed because they've done something notable or can provide information about someone who has. The job of the writer is to unlock as much relevant information on the issue as possible while meeting that crucial deadline. Some assignments will require extensive preparation on the person's background and demand additional interviews with the subject's friends and peers. Other stories don't merit this attention and can be completed with a thoughtful, but quick telephone interview. In all cases, the writer must find the conflict that makes this article worth the reader's effort. Joseph Pulitzer told his reporters in the 19th century he wanted to read articles that caused him to say, "Gee, whiz!" To surprise the reader, the writer must work hard to mine for a conflict that is appropriate for the article and interesting to read.

Like the chocolate candy, conflict may have many layers. Imagine, for instance, you are in a community where two retired men spend the better part of two summers carving a 40-foot totem pole, complete with colorful depictions of bears, turtles and an airplane. You hear about the enterprise, contact an editor in your area, and sell her on a feature. The editor assigns you to write the article and gives you a firm deadline.

WHAT'S THE CONFLICT?

For this article, you make an appointment to meet the men and you show up on time, feeling relaxed but curious. As you think about the totem pole carving, your mind toys with the question, "What's the **conflict**?" The natural conflict is the men could have spent their days sipping hot tea and pondering the heavens, but they chose to use electric grinders to make a totem pole. Find out the reason for the labor and you've found the natural conflict.

The fact that no one paid them to work day after day on the pole, once an ordinary utility pole, is another layer of conflict. The conflict could include that choice of sites to show off the work of art; in this case, the finished totem pole was erected near the parking lot of a butcher shop. Let's say one of the carvers is related to the owner of the shop and carved a vulture on top of the pole as a joke. That element also suggests conflict between the businessman who wants his customers to value his meat and an artist who finds humor in a predator associated with decaying animal carcasses.

Whatever conflict the writer chooses must be one that can be sustained throughout the article. If the article is meant to be humorous, the vulture conflict may be the best pick, but if the men hope to make a political statement about Indian art in rural Pennsylvania, the vulture idea may interfere with the overall concept.

THE GOAL AND NEWS QUALITIES

To succeed, it is in the writer's best interest to pick the conflict that is a natural part of the story and stay with it throughout the article. Keep in mind that the conflict is supported by other demands of the article. All articles must satisfy readers' questions. In short, relevant articles possess **news qualities**.

When you pick the conflict, consider the characteristics of news qualities.

Ask yourself . . .

Is it timely? Some event happened and people are talking about it. The emphasis here is on the currency of the information. A tragedy last month is dated as a report for a daily newspaper; however, a feature writer with a creative bent can find a fresh angle to describe and use the incident to highlight the action. The September 11, 2001 disaster is of interest today as writers reflect on new angles such as the role of buildings as symbols of capitalism, security issues vs. personal freedoms, and the call to firefighting and police service as an act of commitment to a noble truth.

Is it close? The nearer the event to the audience, the greater the proximity, the more interesting the audience will find that information.

Will it affect a lot of people? The more impact, the newsier the story.

Is it unusual? About once a decade a man will bite a dog, and it's always news, but the reverse isn't news. Dog bites are common and aren't typically reported unless the attack is particularly severe, such as the case of an animal hurting a child. As you write, keep these ideas in mind as you refine the article's most salient point.

THE NEWS PEG

By ruminating on the timeliness, proximity, unusualness and other aspects of the ideas, you will help yourself find a **news peg**, the reason this article is being written now. Sometimes an anniversary is all that is needed to make an article idea fly. Sometimes it's a matter of pairing two ideas, such as restaurants along the Susquehanna River that are available by boat. Other times the news peg is a general awareness that the topic is hot, such as the trend to wear face masks in Asian countries during the Severe Acute Respiratory Syndrome panic of mid-2003. Many approaches are available for the news peg. Part of your job as a feature writer is to isolate the strongest news peg and use it to build a memorable article.

THE CLIPPER

Ever meet a person who clips funny sayings or illustrations and gives them to her friends? A women's magazine might be interested in an article on a person who entertains her friends with cutout phrases and illustrations. This idea is meant to be fun, and the writer would use a light tone to explain a playful person who shares humor in this way with friends, but does this story meet the requirements for news? What would you say?

Tip: Should your interview lag and you need to juice it up, try some of ABC TV's Barbara Walters's sure-fire questions.

What was your first job?

When was the last time that you cried?

What would you like your tombstone to read?

Did you ever . . . build a weapon, sing at a wedding, fall out of a tree? Ask any silly question that comes to mind. Usually, these questions get nothing but a laugh from your source; however, sometimes the source comes back with something very unexpected.

A news reporter speaking to a university class on these questions had one member of the class turn the question on him. The class conducted an interview as part of the host teacher's assignment. "What would you like your tombstone to read?" the student asked. The speaker paused and finally said that he wanted to be remembered for his faith in Christ. That answer surprised the class, and it opened up a number of follow-up questions that no one had anticipated. This tip worked for them, and it will work for you.

> **Tip:** In the seminal November 1991 issue of *Campus Life* magazine, Nancy Ricker Hoffman suggested that writers emphasize a central point, another name for conflict.
>
> Instead of writing about the list of activities with which a person may be involved, try capturing the central meaning of those activities.
>
> *Not: I spent the summer painting houses . . .*
>
> *Better: With each stroke of the paintbrush, I learned the truth about myself.*
>
> Hoffman also suggests that writers use concrete detail by showing the reader, not telling her.
>
> *Not: The car is attractive . . .*
>
> *Better: The fire-engine-red Renault convertible gleamed in the afternoon sun.*

THE 5 W's

Feature writing is a subset of writing that is meant to be more timeless, and, in general, more entertaining. Nonetheless, among the qualities all the articles share are answers to the 5 Ws. Master raconteur Rudyard Kipling said:

> I keep six honest serving men
>   (They taught me all I knew);
> Their names are What and Why and When
>   And How and Where and Who.

Answer these questions and you'll have the basis of an article.

In constructing your article, particularly a feature article based on a news story, the writer must answer all those questions, but not necessarily one at a time or all at once. The "what" question is important. To open your article, you may answer the question, "What's new?"

ANSWERING THE WHAT QUESTION

Here's an opening from *Christianity Today* magazine about a public school district in Central Pennsylvania that stopped Bible reading and prayer in late 1993.

For nearly 40 years, students in Pennsylvania's Warrior Run School District began classes with Bible reading over the intercom system. In December, the practice stopped.

Although it took two sentences to do it, this beginning, called the lead, tells us that a Bible reading practice—*the what*—stopped in December—*the when*. The question could be, "What's happening with the Bible reading?" The lead answers that question.

Another useful question is to ask, "Who did what?" In this case, the writer can plug in the correct answers.

For the Bible reading story, the lead could have been:

A Pennsylvania community school board official stopped Bible reading in his public school in late 1993 to avoid a lawsuit.

In this lead, part of the "why" question is answered. Why did the school board stop the Bible reading? The school board feared a lawsuit would ensue if it didn't stop the practice.

In later chapters, this book will focus on developing the news story, the use of quotations, and other techniques of mass media writing.

> **Tip:** When a media writer talks to a source, the first question that she should ask is the person's name. If the person won't give you her name, any other information is nearly useless. After you ask for the person's name, write it down and show what you've

written to your source. Ask, "Is this correct?" The person will spy any misspelling. People who use this technique will never have a source accuse them of shoddy work. Be accurate. Even a veteran reporter has misspelled a name out of carelessness.

CRASH COURSE

1) Your feature story needs a main idea or theme.

Look for the natural conflict in the story. Tell us in one sentence what the story is all about. Summarize.

2) Be brief. Be concise. Be terse.

Sentences can be 12 to 15 words long or longer, but alter the length for variety.

3) News and magazine columns can be narrow, sometimes a little more than two inches wide, so each paragraph should be short to avoid looking too gray when a story is published. No more than two sentences per paragraph.

4) Use quotations. Use lots of quotes.

"The new scanning system will make checking out a book easier for all the library staff," said Library Director Betty Bookbinder.

Make sure you punctuate the quote in the same way as the example.

Paragraph one is your lead. Paragraph two amplifies the lead and explains some of the feature components. Put a quotation high in the story at about paragraph three. End your story with a quote and put some quotes in between.

Day 3, *Free the Writing Spirit*, provides other ways to open your article, but this method is a good one to memorize.

5) Interview at least three people about the story.

Get quotes and background information from them. Ask at least three people about the issue, but don't necessarily ask each one the same question.

6) Always double-check the spelling of names. Even the name Smith can be spelled Smyth, Smythe, Smithe, and so on. Misspelled names are inexcusable. For students, include class status and major. Senior Joyce Mills, a psychology major, said, "I'd give the president a B for his foreign policy because it's always late and not very neat." For adults, provide some identification of their profession or vocation and address. Often, the person's age is included because readers tend to rank others in terms of their age.

7) Always type your story notes as soon as you finish the interview. You will think more clearly and write with more ease by following this simple edict.

8) Meet your deadlines.

9) Watch mistakes such as spelling demons, comma splices, and pronoun agreement. Use the spelling checker function on the computer.

Tip: Avoid trademark woes.

A warning!

Beware of the power of words, not just to uplift and comfort or inform and entertain, but also to violate the law. Note the precise language of this letter regarding trademark misuse. A general counsel for Kransco Group Companies in San Francisco, California, spotted a reference to one of its products in a little-known community newspaper in Shippensburg, Pennsylvania, a town near Gettysburg. The attorney wrote, "I am writing to you because one of our company's registered trademarks (Frisbee) appears in the above mentioned, a photograph that said, 'Frisbee frivolity.'"

The letter went on to give three guidelines to mentioning Frisbee. The common name "disc" should follow the trademark Frisbee, as in Frisbee disc. The attorney also suggested that the symbol for the registered trademark be used, but acknowledged that some publications do not have that symbol on the keyboard.

Finally, the attorney urged the publication not to use Frisbee as a noun as in "Let's play Frisbee" because the word is an adjective describing a specialized disc.

You may be wondering, so what's the problem? The problem is that promotion of trademarks is costly, and if they aren't protected, the trademarks can become generic names. For this reason, it is important for mass media writers to refer to products by precise names.

For instance, you might want to take two Bufferin tablets, or you might settle for two aspirins. Notice the capitalization. If you want to photocopy this page, you will use a photocopy machine or a Xerox machine if it's available. You don't want to make a Xerox. You can reach for a carbonated beverage, but be sure you want a Coca-Cola if you ask for this product using the formal name.

A FINAL WORD ON CONFLICT

Among the salient points in this chapter is the idea of conflict as a necessary part of any media artifact, particularly news, and that includes a feature article. Fictional newspaper editor, Bob Miles Jr. of *The Harmony Herald,* learned that his small town of Harmony wasn't much interested in conflict. "So Bob decided to get out of the news business and confine his reporting to weddings, graduations, church happenings, and gardening. A doomsday cult could poison the New York City water supply and kill a million people, and Bob would write about Bea Majors having Sunday dinner at her sister Opal's house."[3] Bob is meant to be a humorous caricature of a hard-driving editor to underline the idea that conflict may be overrated. That content might appeal to some readers, but most of us want some edge on our news.

It doesn't take much, just enough to make flesh-and-blood people wonder about the contest of life. Who is winning, who won, who should win? This simplistic idea of winning and losing is just another way to frame conflict. If it doesn't help you internalize the concept, discard it. Instead, retain the idea that your audience expects you to give them information of value. Be sure to ask yourself, "Why does this information matter?" Once you've written the piece, ask yourself, "Would I read this piece if I hadn't written it?" If the answers to those questions aren't satisfying, rework your piece. Don't settle for second-rate work if it's not up to your high standards. All writing is re-writing and no ink spot is satisfied with submitting a first draft for the audience she loves too much for second-rate prose. You will succeed, but you have to invest the sweat equity to make the article work well. You may never write the perfect book, perfect article, or even the perfect sentence, but with perseverance, you will go from mediocre to half bad to better than average, and with time, share words that seem to have a home in harmony.

SUMMARY

The chapter examined the role of conflict in an article. Without **conflict**, an article has no depth charges and is pinched and

---

[3] Gulley, P. (2000). *Home to Harmony*. Sisters, OR: Multnomah Publishers, p. 31.

narrow. It is weak and likely to take a break just to catch its breath. An interview with a source can help a writer identify the inherent conflict by thinking about the timeliness, the proximity, the impact, the unusualness, even the human interest of the topic or event. These elements also lead the writer to select the best **news peg** or **angle** to frame the article. Once the conflict has been identified, a writer can use a series of questions, better known as the 5 Ws, to collect the pertinent information that is necessary for all articles. Conflict is not something that we seek in our personal lives, but it is essential in writing for the mass media. Inhale it through the mouth and let readers enjoy a deep cleansing breath.

Now which way?

Day 2

GETTING STARTED AND MASTERING THE LEAD

CHAPTER AT-A-GLANCE

- Examining the summary lead
- Selecting the appropriate opening
- Considering fictional techniques in nonfiction writing

Writing for mass media is different from fiction, yet the best nonfiction relies on fictional techniques such as drama and dialogue. The most outstanding difference is that mass media writers never suffer from **writer's block**, the inability to formulate a developed idea. In mass media, the material for the assignment is defined by the assignment; therefore, the writer won't have to worry about what to say, only how to say it.

Throughout this book, feature story ideas and approaches will be explored in the context of news. Ideas abound, and part of your job will be to recognize them. Online enterprise alone allows any of us to formulate an idea and trot it out without a deep investment. One writer made a modest livelihood by writing about his experiences living on the street. Writer Kevin Barbieux's website is www.TheHomelessGuy.net.[4] Barbieux calls himself the homeless guy and once said his website received 15,000 hits after Yahoo.com mentioned his site on its new-and-notable list. Barbieux blogs, a term that means a free-form diarist style of Weblogs. From Nashville, TN, Barbieux blogs about his efforts to get off the streets and build a normal life. He talks about what it's like in the world of the homeless and offers his ideas on finding good meals. The site includes a "tip jar" button that allows visitors to use their credit cards to deposit money in his bank account, and he once received a donation of $1,000.[5]

Writing can pay, but you must be ahead of the curve. Take a lesson from Dr. Norman Vincent Peale of The Power of Positive Thinking fame. He suggests that all of us spend fifteen minutes a day in quiet contemplation. The idea is to make your mind still. When the mind becomes like a tranquil pool of water, deep and creative thoughts can form. His counsel is to avoid thinking; instead, allow the mind to rest. Out of this relaxed state may come ideas that you can use in your career, not just to write, but to soar with the angels.

As a writer, you are ever vigilant for article ideas. Next, you must think about the story that you are crafting and make the

---

[4] Kornblum, J. (2002, October 3). A homeless guy finds a refuge on the Internet. *USA TODAY*, p. 10D. In a related story, Ted "Golden Voice" Williams goes from homeless to voice-over announcer through an unlikely TV interview in Ohio. http://www.usatoday.com/story/news/nation/2013/11/13/man-with-golden-voice-ted-williams/3517937/
[5]

decision on how best to write it. The first portion of this book will examine the conventions of writing news to prepare you to take the feature approach, often considered the supplemental way of learning about topics, events, places, and people. A feature story can be the second view, often read or watched because the audience chooses this content. The news approach can be a warm-up for the main event, the feature article. For this reason, an understanding of news writing will be examined as the foundation for all the concepts that follow.

THE CONCEPT OF NEWS

One ancient idea about **NEWS** is that it stands for North, East, West and South,[6] the intelligence from all points of the compass. News may be defined as reports of information of interest to an audience. One of my editors liked to say news is what she said it was. True, but news can be generally understood to be concerned with people in high places, people in low places, and those in between, you and me. News concerns events, issues, the little known and overblown. It is about correcting false or distorted reports and reminding audiences of information that was lost or forgotten with an attempt to set the record straight. News is more about recent history, the now, rather than the past, timeliness. It's about events closer to home, rather than farther away, proximity. News is about the unusual and the controversial of the culture, along with the celebration and defeat of the human condition. It is about celebrity and celebrities, as well as conspirators and consequence.

That last category is the one that feature writers often consult to write profile articles, how-to pieces, and a different

---

[6] Hoffman, D. (2000). *Who knew? Things you didn't know about things you know well.* New York: MJF books, Pine Communications, p. 141.

view on a topic that is in the news. As you craft your feature article, remember that you are still providing news—you're telling an audience something that is new to them. Often the news is event-oriented. A speaker comes to town and you get an assignment to cover the speech or interview the person. In either case, the writer selects the information he or she wants to use based on an understanding of news. The article may take the form of a **profile** on the new mayor after her first 100 days in office, or it might explore a family who must endure loneliness as a parent fights in a war thousands of miles away.

Getting started means examining the essence of the assignment to determine the best angle for the presentation. Regardless of the form, whether it's a speech story or a personality profile, the writer will ask herself, "So what's new?"

What's new?

The best way to answer the "What's new" question is to role-play with yourself or a friend. Pretend you just went to a government meeting or met with a prominent businessman who is giving $10,000 to build a new shelter for homeless people. Your notebook is brimming with pithy quotes or descriptions of the scene.

You have so much information that you are hard-pressed to get started. That's when you turn to a friend and ask him or her to ask this question: "In one sentence, tell me what's new?" Getting a friend to ask this question will force the writer to clearly articulate a response; however, a writer can play this game in his or her head. Pose the question, and then answer it.

If this question doesn't do the trick, try a variation. Have your accomplice ask, "In one sentence, tell me what happened?"

If you still are fumbling to reduce the information to a statement, try yet another variation, this one a directive rather than a question. "In one sentence, tell me the most interesting action, fact, or idea that you just heard."

By compressing the story idea into one sentence, you are fashioning a crude lead, the first sentence of your report. Lead, also known as the lede, is the hook you hope will make your reader, and listener, want to stay with you. The lead is crucial to your report. These days readers often abandon an article after only six paragraphs, so it's our job to make them want to read on.

LEADS

Leads are like tools in a toolbox. A tool is designed for a specific job. While a screwdriver may be used to hammer a nail, it isn't recommended. In some cases, the wrong tool just won't work. Try using a claw hammer to remove a sticky screw. Nonetheless, some tools just get more of a workout by virtue of their usefulness. Hammers, for instance, fulfill a deep desire in many of us to strike objects, even when we're not trying to be constructive. This tool is used over and over and over again. In the worst case, a person with a hammer sees every article as a nail.

The hammer may be compared to a type of lead known as the summary lead. This lead packs the sentence with all the essential information to understand the article.

SUMMARY LEADS

A summary lead provides a one-sentence to two-sentence summary of the article. Summary leads may be up to 35 or 40 words in newspapers such as the *New York Times*, considered the premium newspaper in the United States. The *New York Times* is known for its international news coverage and its coverage of public affairs including reprints of speeches.

These summary leads are long because they are trying to answer all the questions mentioned in Day 1, *The Chocolate-covered Almond*, who, what, where, when, and sometimes how and why. The why question is particularly difficult to integrate into a lead. Imagine reducing the reason something happened to a short phrase. Generally, it will take a separate sentence or a paragraph to provide the most rudimentary explanation. For instance, answering the question, "Why did the fire begin?" may be answered briefly by saying, "An electrical short sparked a fire," to a more complicated explanation on the nature of charged energy and friction.

A more common approach to the summary lead is to say who did what. The lead could be a kind of formula where two or three of the W's are answered . . . but not all of them.

WHO-DID-WHAT LEAD

Who did what? The idea is to put a person's name in the first spot and the action in the second spot.

Virtual reality artist Brenda Bennett won first place today in an art contest.

Who? Virtual reality artist Brenda Bennett.

Did what? Won an art contest.

This type of summary lead only answers two of the five W's yet it does the job. When writing these leads, select a strong verb that conveys action or your lead will be limp.

For instance, avoid summary leads such as this one with a weak verb.

An alcohol-dumping party occurred over the weekend at Glendale's oldest college.

In this case, the *what* was the first element followed by the *when* answer.

The what? An alcohol-dumping party.

The when? Over the weekend.

The verb "occurred" is very weak. In addition to being the language's most frequently misspelled word, occurred doesn't convey specific action.

By substituting a stronger verb, the writer sometimes can solve other problems with the lead.

For instance, take our friend Bennett. You could write,

"Virtual reality artist Brenda Bennett spoke Monday night."

The lead answers two questions.

The who? Virtual reality artist Brenda Bennett.

The what? Spoke.

The when? Monday.

The problem: The lead doesn't tell me the topic. Since none of us knows anything about Bennett, knowing what she had to say in one abbreviated phrase would be a big help.

REVISED LEAD

Virtual reality artist Brenda Bennett denounced the lack of sacred images produced by the majority of artists in a speech before Colson College students.

In this case, the lead tells us who said what and it gives the reader some context for the remarks. This lead has the following arrangement.

Who said what?

21

EXAMPLES FROM NEW WRITERS

What kind of lead would you write if you were assigned to cover criticism of one elected official for her organization? Here's the background. That happened at Franklin College when junior Deanna Barthlow published a letter to the editor of the student newspaper and criticized her student organization for its ineffective approach to conducting business. At a meeting following the publication of her letter, the other members of the group, known as the Student Senate of Franklin College, listened to her read the letter and then responded. Some agreed; others didn't. Senate President Bob Tyson responded by listing a number of accomplishments of the senate in the last six months. He went on to say that the senate exists to improve student life and suggested that the letter might be the motivation his group needed to excel.

Here's one possibility for a lead.

Junior Deanna Barthlow stirred up some controversy around campus with her letter written about ineffective student government in the Jan. 20 issue of the Express student newspaper. (For news and feature articles, the month is abbreviated when with the date.)

While that lead sounds good, it's missing the latest news, that Senate President Bob Tyson wanted to use the critical letter to improve his organization.

See the difference?

By playing the game, "What's new?" the writer can focus on the latest and most important development of the story in the very first sentence.

Here's a better lead.

Student senate President Bob Tyson is denying that apathy lurks within his organization in response to a negative letter published in the recent issue of the student newspaper.

This lead is an improvement over the first one because it provides a partial answer to the "What's new?" question by saying that the president doesn't agree with the letter writer. However, this lead still fails to give the reader the absolute latest in the article, the idea that the president, despite his misgivings about the letter, hopes to use it to improve the senate.

Here's a lead that puts the latest news in the lead and uses an economy of words:

The student senate is running a negative letter to make some positive changes.

The story went on to say that the senate president urged the members to return to the next meeting with a fistful of ideas to rid the organization of its inefficiency.

Tip: While the lead above, 13 words total, may not look like the same kind of lead in the *New York Times*, it is. It summarizes the new story and gives the reader a clear idea of what to expect in the following paragraphs. Future chapters will describe other types of leads, other tools, and situations that demand an approach other than the summary lead. However, a good rule of thumb is the shorter the lead, the better. A corollary to that rule is to strive for 12 to 15 words to jumpstart your article.

Regardless of the type of lead or sentence word length, a lead must be supported by the rest of the article. An article that begins with a dispute about a critical letter must maintain that focus and not veer off into some unrelated issue such as a problem with dormitories, pollution, or the coming drought.

All the leads about the critical letter were written by students, writers who knew no more about publishing than the person who has read thus far in this book. By concentrating on answering the "What's new?" question, you, too, will be ready to write summary leads. Tell the most important information first and the summary will be both efficient and appropriate. For practice, read a newspaper such as the *New York Times* and identify 10 summary leads. Then, type, literally type, those ten leads on a typewriter or personal computer. Feel the rhythm of the words. Notice the syntax or the word order. After typing those leads, read them out loud and get accustomed to the sound that this kind of writing makes.

Be advised. Summary leads, like any tool, work best when they are used for a specific purpose. In breaking news, news that is unexpected and ongoing, the summary lead is very useful. A news story about a kitten that survived being sucked through the city's leaf-gathering equipment, while news, lends itself to a non-summary lead. In the case of the kitten, the maintenance crew adopted it and named it, you guessed it, Hoover.

Here's a summary lead from the November 29, 2008 *New York Times* about a football player.

Giants receiver Plaxico Burress accidentally shot himself in the right thigh while at a Manhattan nightclub early Saturday, hours after he was deemed unfit to play in Sunday's game at Washington because of a hamstring strain in the same leg.[7]

Here's another from the December 2013 issue of *Christianity Today:* "Journalist Kathryn Joyce caused a stir this year with her book 'The Child Catchers,' a sweeping indictment of the evangelical overseas adoption movement."[8]

---

[7] Branch, J. (2008, Nov. 29). Plaxico Burress shoots himself accidentally. *New York Times*. Retrieved Jan. 19, 2014 http://www.nytimes.com/2008/11/30/sports/football/30burress.html?_r=0

[8] Morgan, T.C. (2013, December). There is no silver-bullet solution for the challenge of orphan care. *Christianity Today*, 28.

More information on non-summary leads will be given in the next chapter.

EXERCISE

Read a publication.
1) Identify five "who-did-what" leads.
2) Write them out in longhand along with the next two sentences.
3) Now type them on a computer.
4) Study the leads. Sense the cadence. How does it sound?
5) Write a lead based on some experience that you had today.

SUMMARY

This chapter explored the classic opening to articles, the summary lead. While the summary lead is used most often for breaking news, it is considered the basic opening for writing; however, the lead is dependent on the type of article that you are constructing. The creative writer considers the goal of the article and fashions the appropriate opening. Among the leads that are available to writers is the summary lead, which often can be reduced to the phrase, "Who did what?" Be advised. The first draft of the article and the lead will need some work. Ernest Hemingway said all first drafts are rubbish. As a writer, you must discipline yourself to recast your prose, rework it until your reader's eyes glide over the sentences as if it were magic.

Glide into your piece with free writing.

Day 3
FREE THE WRITING SPIRIT

In most newsrooms around the nation, editors, reporters, writers, and producers keep in touch using electronic messaging, through which one person sends a typed message to another person using the computer system. These days that idea is practiced internationally with electronic mail, or email, systems using the **Internet**, a global information network.

A typical day for most writers begins with checking for messages in what is sometimes called the **messages queue** or **in-basket**. That's where an editor may send a message assigning a reporter to cover an event that day.

This system is so convenient that some editors send electronic messages for anything, even one urging the reporter to check on a bomb threat heard just that minute on a police scanner. The editor might flash a message to the reporter that suddenly appears at the top of a computer screen or send a longer version that shows up as "message pending" on the top of the screen. The point is that the editor might save some time by resorting to the low-tech method of alerting a writer to a story, yelling across the room. Shouting may be a bit old-fashioned, but it gets the job done in short order.

FREE WRITING

Old-fashioned methods survive because they work. Among the techniques that hold promise for callow mass media writers and veterans alike is a method of writing known as **free writing**. Author Ronald D. Smith says, "Free writing is a kind of stream-of-consciousness writing without stopping and without self-editing for a period of time. Its purpose is to get your initial thoughts on paper."[9] Some writers remember penning essays in which they wrote the first idea that came to mind, then the next, and so on until the idea reservoir was dry. This crude convention didn't produce memorable prose, but it freed the writer to get on paper a bevy of thoughts. That's *free writing*.

Here's how it works. Let's say your editor flashes you a message to bolt to a fire at the historic church on Center Square. You grab a notebook and two lead pencils, sling a flip camera over your shoulder and break for the door, your laptop computer in a pack snugly on your back. Within a few minutes, you're at the scene watching the spectacle.

---

[9] Smith, R. D. (2012). *Becoming a public relations writer, A writing workbook for emerging and established media*, (4th ed). New York: Routledge, 3.

Six firefighters wrestle hoses off an engine. Flames peek through a second story window. A crowd of shoppers forms at a safe distance. An elderly woman holds the arm of a man in an overcoat, crying silently. In the distance, you see a single-engine airplane veer toward the west and you suddenly become aware that a wind tosses your hair from side to side and the rank odor of smoke assaults your nostrils.

In short, your senses are bombarded. You want to capture the moment as a rough draft of the event, but you know that the story demands quotations from authorities, including the church leadership, firefighters, and eyewitnesses.

Back at the newsroom, you must select a lead that captures the tragedy of the moment, including the color appropriate for a fire that destroys some property, but doesn't cause any personal injuries. You may be writing a breaking news story, sometimes called **hard news**, but the technique works for both **hard, tragic** news and soft, feature news. This occasion suggests *free writing*. You take a long pull from a bottle of mountain water or hot beverage and get to work. For five minutes, you write non-stop. You dump all your impressions on the page. Stray thoughts are allowed.

"Flames bright orange and white-yellow. Get Honda brakes checked. The woman's crying sounded like a tinny toy sound. Confusion. Sadness. The fire chief spits when he talks fast."

You write and write and write until five minutes pass. You don't stop to correct spelling errors or punctuation. You write and write. Then you look at these random observations and mine for the one gem that could sum up the story as a summary lead might do, but with some passion and spirit. Circle words that you like. Circle phrases that you find suitable for the assignment.

In some cases, this process yields a winner. The goal of the exercise is not to, repeat, not edit the words as they appear. The goal is to reach deep into your mind for images, pictures, impressions that help reveal the story that you want to tell.

Once the words can be seen and read, the writer can eliminate most of them, but those rare, rich phrases that fall lightly from the lips and ring true in the ear may be the ones that will make the article sing. This technique is worth trying on occasion, for no other reason than it can be liberating. Should it produce no powerful results, slide the idea into your mental toolbox with a reminder to try it another time.

VARIATION ON THE SUMMARY LEAD

When it works, free writing may lead to a phrase that you want to stamp into the first sentence. Perhaps it's one word.

Determination.

That's a one-word lead for an article on a basketball team that fought back from a dismal season to snag a place in a tournament.

Delicious.

That's another one-word lead on a feature story about ice cream.

These leads are examples of **creative leads**, which work best for feature stories but can be used anytime. An article about a 10-year-old girl who writes reviews of children's books for an out-of-town newspaper is the kind of story that doesn't become stale if it isn't printed or broadcast right away.

These kinds of stories are known as soft news stories and tend to focus on lighter topics that entertain. Many depend on **human interest**, unraveling the human condition. Since this quality covers the spectrum of behavior, many of the approaches are considered standards and are written over and over again. Often, feature news is considered more **timeless**. It's even referred to as an **evergreen**, news that holds up no matter the calendar. It is always fresh and in bloom.

For instance, a person who rescues another person is the substance of dramatic stories. While the event can be written as hard news—news that must be printed or broadcast immediately or it loses its value—a more complete story would require a longer, feature touch.

Here's one from *The New Yorker* that uses a little story to open the article.

> *When Jonah Berger was a graduate student at Stanford, in the early aughts, he would make a habit of reading page A2 of the Wall Street Journal, which included a list of the five most-read and the five most-shared articles of the day. "I'd go down to the library and surreptitiously cut out that page," he recalls. "I noticed that what was read and what was shared was often different, and I wondered why that would be." What was it about a piece of content—an article, a picture, a video—that took it from simply interesting to interesting and shareable? What pushes someone not only to read a story but to pass it on?*[10]

The article goes on to say that Berger, now a professor of marketing at the University of Pennsylvania's Wharton School, and Penn professor Katherine Milkman found that articles that arouse positive emotion, even anger, are more likely to be circulated. If the reader became excited about the content,

---

[10] Konnikova, M. (2014, Jan. 21). "The six things that make stories go viral will amaze, and maybe infuriate, you." *The New Yorker.* retrieved Jan. 22, 2014 http://www.newyorker.com/online/blogs/elements/2014/01/the-six-things-that-make-stories-go-viral-will-amaze-and-maybe-infuriate-you.html

whether it was humorous or outrageous, he or she was more likely to pass the content on to friends and others.

WORD PLAY AND CREATIVE LEADS

More will be said about the feature story in future chapters. For now, let's return to the technique of fashioning a creative lead. These leads can draw on wordplay, but the goal is to suggest more than one meaning and intrigue the reader.

Here's one from the January 6, 2014 *New Yorker*.

> *Storyboard P, a Brooklyn dancer, comes from the 1300 block of Eastern Parkway, on the border between Crown Heights and Brownsville. When he was five or so, his grandmother tugged him onto the dance floor at a family gathering and, as reggae played, got him moving for the first time.*[11]

That lead uses exacting detail and sets a tone for the rest of the article that portrays the world of a street dancer as a serious one. The next lead, however, suggests a more playful tone.

> *When the world closes in on you and your head feels a size too small, what you need is a piece of mind.*

That lead is from *Mademoiselle* magazine in December 1993.

Ordinarily slang terms are avoided in mass media writing, but creative leads allow the writer to slip one in on occasion as this writer did:

> *Those clever Brits—they've discovered that having a belt or two every day can increase your resistance to the sniffles.*

---

[11] Weiner, J. (2014, Jan. 6). "Onward and upward with the arts, The impossible body, Storyboard P, the Basquiat of street dancing." The *New Yorker*, 22-28.

"Clear alcohols are for rich women on diets." So said Ron Swanson on "Parks & Recreation." But women these days are drinking more whiskey than vodka. So said a Wall Street Journal report, from the *Palm Beach Post*, February 5, 2015.

Yahoo.com offered this light-hearted approach on January 20, 2014. "The holidays are over but don't put away those shot glasses just yet. Lauren Slayton, nutritionist and author of *The Little Book of Thin*, says, 'Shots are the new vitamins,' and taking the right ones can give your health a serious boost."[12] The article goes on to provide a number of ways to ingest nutritional ingredients using the small portions found in shot glasses.

In this next example, the Associated Press wire service used vernacular in a piece from February 3, 1995.

In the City of Brotherly Love, even dead men can get ripped off.

The *Williamsport Sun-Gazette* that same day carried this lead about feuding elected officials:

The Lycoming County commissioners are acting like a dysfunctional family.

Wordplay relies on clever use of words that suggest the theme. An article on meals could use a food term such as the verb "cook," as the writer did in this *USA Today* lead from February 6, 1995.

---

[12] Wentworth, A. (2014, Jan. 15). "Take Your Vitamins With a Shot Glass." *Yahoo Shine*. Retrieved Jan. 20, 2014. http://shine.yahoo.com/dailyshot/take-your-vitamins-with-a-shot-glass-153711334.html?vp=1

Taco Bell has cooked up a new menu that could change the way fast food is sold.

Even without this special brand of wordplay, strong verbs can make an opening sentence sparkle, as the writer did in this March 1995 lead in *Sassy*.

Claire Danes was just about to tell me the wildest thing she's done lately when her car phone crackles, sputters and dies.

Perhaps the master publication of creative leads is *USA Today*, the pioneer of the short, breezy article topped off with a pithy lead. Note the lean but creative words in the following six-word lead from September 12, 1994.

NBC could get a second parent.

IMPERATIVE LEADS

Another useful lead in opening an article is the **imperative** or **command lead**. Ordinarily mass media writers avoid telling people what to do. Too directive. In some cases, however, the command lead drills the point home. The command may be a soft one, as in the case of this lead.

Look into the refrigerators of single men and women and you'll come away with some significant indicators of gender spending differences.

The reader can barely sense the command, but it's there. The writer said, "Look," but the lead reads more like a suggestion than a command. Subtle imperative leads are useful to aim your reader in the direction that moves the story flow in the direction the writer wants. Consider this lead in *Time* from February 7, 1994.

Imagine the five-and-ten on the corner.

Do you see the store in your mind? Eight words. Words can be powerful to evoke pictures. The beauty of mass media writing is that a wordsmith doesn't need an elaborate vocabulary, just an inner voice that suggests strong verbs for the thought you want to convey. You could have penned this *USA Today* lead.

Do what works.

MORE EXAMPLES OF IMPERATIVE LEADS

Hide your souls, this cat looks like he's out to steal them. Atchoum is the Internet's latest cat sensation, and the kitty couldn't look more sinister, from the *Palm Beach Post,* February 5, 2015.

It's time to celebrate for the New England Patriots! After a serious nail biter, the Patriots beat the Seattle Seahawks to win the title of Super Bowl XLIX champions! Shira Benozilio in *Hollywood Life,* February 1, 2015.

Do your workout first thing in the morning and you won't have to worry about getting to the gym after work, when you have a hundred reasons to skip it. This workout takes only 7 minutes, so you have no excuses! From Jenna Wolfe, writing for *TODAY,* February 3, 2015

You don't want to see this woman, carrying these black bags, approaching your door. Or maybe you do. In one bag she carries a vial from the river Lethe, in the other an array of medicines that might save your pet's life. Susan Luzzaro in the *San Diego Reader*, May 29, 2013.

"Use your hands. It creates a physical connection in addition to your lips,"says Jill Blakeway, clinic director at the YinOva Center in New York City (on kissing). Huffington Post, February 3, 2015.

Hit the weight room. Yahoo Shine. January 17, 2014.

Whatever that prize or goal may be, it's imperative that you learn how to keep your focus engaged therein. Entrepreneur, January 27, 2015.

Get ready for lower PC prices — and more choices on store shelves. USA Today, February 6, 1995.

If you can't beat them, steal from them. New York Times, February 3, 1995.

Forget the kiss! It comes late in the movie and the world keeps turning. The (Harrisburg, Pa.) *Patriot*, February 6, 1995.

Try if you must, but Fox's an institution you can't deny. USA Today, February 3, 1995.

THE QUESTION LEAD

As you can see, the variety is endless, but the rule is to select the best lead for the article. News reporters sometimes joke with one another that somewhere in the universe is a big book of leads made to order for the article that is underway at this moment.

Someone once suggested a Dial-A-Lead telephone service where frustrated writers could order a specialty lead using the keypad: Press one for a feature lead, press two for a summary lead, and press three for the question lead. I'm afraid such a device still doesn't exist, but the idea sounds good, doesn't it?

The question lead, also known as the interrogative lead, is one of the easiest leads to write. In this case, the writer just poses a question. The trick is to be sure to answer the question in the next paragraph or so. Never end the story unless some kind of answer is provided, or the reader may feel cheated. The *Williamsport Sun-Gazette* reported a story February 4, 1995 by asking,

"A 12-story mountain?"

Does that question make you want to read on? If not, the writer missed. (What's that number for Dial-A-Lead?)

The biggest disadvantage to the question lead is that writers must discipline themselves not to overuse this tool. I know a reporter who once became hooked on song titles and lyrics as a way to start all his news stories, even hard-news articles! The editors chuckled to themselves whenever they fielded one of these leads that started out cute the first 100 times but became trite after a while. The same can happen with the question lead. Use it sparingly, and it will brighten up the report.

MORE EXAMPLES OF QUESTION LEADS

Obama speaks out on marijuana. Why now? Christian Science Monitor, January 20, 2014.

The Texas Rangers in the pennant race? After Aug. 1? Believe it. USA Today, September 10, 1993.

The political upheaval of 1994? They saw it coming two years ahead of time. Williamsport Sun-Gazette, February 5, 1995.

What are kindergartners through third-graders learning in some of our public schools these days? Reader's Digest, February 1995.

Is O.J. Simpson's trial a high-tech lynching? USA Today, February 3, 1995.

Looking to buy something quickly and cheaply, but you don't know anyone who can get it for you wholesale? The (Harrisburg, Pa.) *Patriot,* February 6, 1995.

PUTTING THE CREATIVE LEAD TO WORK

Here are some facts for you to consider. Review them and try constructing one of the leads mentioned in this chapter.

FACT 1 The Office of Residence Life is proposing a charge to unlock dormitory room doors when students lock themselves out.

FACT 2 Each day the Office of Safety and Security must unlock as many as six doors for forgetful students.

FACT 3 Each year safety and security unlocks nearly 1,500 doors and spends nearly 260 hours responding to these calls.

FACT 4 The Resident Life Committee proposed the charge to help reduce the number of these kinds of nuisance calls and to encourage students to be more responsible.

FACT 5 The proposal calls for no fines for the first and second "lockout," where the safety and security office is called to respond to a locked dormitory door. Fines may be charged for the third and each succeeding lockout. The fines will increase as the number increases.

Armed with these facts, start with the stand-by lead, the summary lead. Answer the main questions of who, what, where, when, and later, how and why. Here's one attempt.

Students who lock themselves out of their dormitory rooms might soon have to pay a penalty as part of gaining access to their rooms.

The lead tells the reader all the information needed to decide if it's worth reading on, but the article warrants a creative touch.

Students who forget their room keys must remember to carry their wallets.

That lead, written by a student, is having some wordplay fun with the idea of forgetting and remembering. Working with duality often makes for a memorable lead. Here's another memorable lead from another student.

Use your keys or lose your money.

Here's a lead that retains this idea but presents it as an imperative lead.

The next time you lock your keys in your room, remember your wallet.

The idea can be reworked as a statement.

The Office of Resident Life is installing a price on lockouts.

This lead is another statement.

For Franklin College students, financial planning could soon include remembering their keys.

Here's the same opening using the question lead.

What's the price for forgetfulness?

That lead sounds reminiscent of the old "What price ignorance" slogan from broadcast TV. These next two leads are moralistic, yet they convey the same idea.

Should students have to pay for their forgetfulness?

Students getting punished for obviously unintended accidents?

THE LEAD AS A SPRINGBOARD

The emphasis of this chapter is getting started. Many times a well-crafted lead will suggest the remainder of the article. In other words, nail the lead and nail the story. In the following example, a new writer starts his article with a clever lead and develops it in the article.

Lockouts could be the key to more money for security.
The Office of Residence Life is proposing charging students for getting security to let them back into their rooms, which is a major problem, administrators say.

"This proposal is something I am in favor of," said Jeffrey Brown, director of the Safety and Security Office.
He said that security spends too much time on this problem. Security has already dealt with 1,034 lockouts in four months, which might pass the 1,587 of last year, 2015.

Tip: Apostrophes may be used to indicate a letter is missing, hence the phrase "rock 'n' roll." The "a" and "d" are missing, and the apostrophes are used to show the omitted letters.

Remember this rule when you are grappling with the use of "its" and "it's." *Its* is the possessive pronoun, but it doesn't need an apostrophe to indicate possession as in the case with the word "man" and his hat—"man's hat." On the other hand, *it's* uses the apostrophe to indicate a contraction for "it is."

Here is a sentence using both words. It's a dirty cat that scratches its fleas.

The apostrophe can solve other problems, too. Have you ever written "your" for "you're"?

PRACTICE EXERCISE USING THE CREATIVE LEAD

Use the following facts to construct an eight-paragraph news brief. A summary lead will be provided as part of the facts.

SUMMARY – Alternative media Paper Tiger urged college students and others to challenge mainstream mass media Thursday in the Madison Auditorium at the opening of a two-day Media and Technology Symposium at Abigail University.

FACTS 1-2 Paper Tiger is a group of volunteers in the New York City area who produce broadcasts that criti-

cize mainstream mass media for its support of the status
quo. The group hopes that the programs will provoke
audiences to fight back against mainstream mass media.

FACTS 3-4 Paper Tiger shows its programs on a public
access channel, a cable channel available free to anyone
who signs up to use it; however, only some cable companies around the country have public access channels.

FACTS 5-6 Michael Ryals and Shannon Bailey showed
videotapes of programs that they produced using a
low-budget production.

FACTS 7-8 The tapes criticized mainstream mass media
because they are too concerned with capitalism at the
exclusion of disadvantages of big business, including pollution and monopolies. The message also criticized the
mass media business and those who write the messages
and the content of the messages.

FACTS 9-10 "We are part of the struggle to get television into the hands of the people," said Bailey. "We critique the information industry," said Ryals.

SYNTHESIS OF THREE STUDENT STORIES

Paper Tiger showed its stripes Thursday at Abigail University.

The alternative media organization challenged the audience of 60 to question the creators and content of mass media. The program was part of a two-day Media and Technology
Symposium.

"We critique the information industry," said Michael Ryals,
one of the two Paper Tiger representatives who spoke.

Paper Tiger is the name of a group of volunteers in the New
York City area who write and produce TV programs that are
shown on a public access channel in Manhattan. The group

hopes that the programs will provoke audiences to fight back against mainstream mass media.

Public access channels are open to the public and furnished by some cable companies in the United States as part of their community service responsibility for operating a cable franchise.

Shannon Bailey, another Paper Tiger representative, joined Ryals in showing videotapes produced by their organization.

The tapes criticized mainstream mass media for their focus on the benefits of capitalism and neglect of the inequities associated with this economic system.

Ryals said Paper Tiger uses a low-budget program to comment on media monopolies and other issues.

"We are part of the struggle to get television into the hands of people," said Bailey.

Tip: Sometimes an article has so many facets that it is begging for additional treatment. What to do? Use the **sidebar**. Sidebars are often associated with the idea of a feature article, soft news. In this sense, the sidebar is used to humanize the story by providing information that the main story, the **mainbar**, can't include. For feature writers, the sidebar can provide more human interest material in the form of a long anecdote. It can be used to provide helpful information such as directions for travel, useful telephone numbers, and valuable websites. Sometimes the sidebar can provide analysis and other angles that would otherwise crowd the main article.

This chapter emphasized the news approach to help you sense the cadence of straight news. As you become familiar with the organization of ordinary news stories, you will be better prepared to develop your rhythm in a feature article. Examine the ideas below from editor Marvin Olasky on starting an article. Then read the feature article opening used by John F. Kelly in his article on restoring cars. What approach did he use? Could he have used another feature lead to open his article? If so, try your hand at composing one.

CRASH COURSE IN WRITING A LEAD

Take a page from Marvin Olasky. In his *Telling the Truth*,[13] Olasky, the crack editor, urges writers to use one of the feature leads in opening an article. What are they?

1. **Anecdotal lead.** Give a mini-story with a beginning, middle, and end. The ending is like a punch line.

2. **Descriptive lead.** Describe the scene using a wide-angle lens. End with a close-up.

3. **Situational lead**. Provide a look at this situation that sets up the rest of the information in the story. Discuss in narrative form the typical situation that exists. For instance, what series of events typically occurs during a police stakeout? Do the officers get coffee, record the weather, and count cars on a street, or what? A writer uses this type of lead to set up the situation to suggest that the events described represent a typical stakeout.

Olasky also suggests writers avoid summary, quotation leads, and the dreaded essay lead.

Next, insert the nut graf, the background paragraph that tells the significance of the story. The nut graf tells the reader the reason you are writing this piece. Typically, it provides the essential background and basics the article needs to make sense. Essential background usually includes the history of the issue in a sentence or two. After the nut graf, add quotations,

---

[13] Olasky, M. (1999). *Telling the truth*. Wheaton, IL: Crossways.

anecdotes and the other information you need to complete your feature article.

When John F. Kelly of the *Washington Post* examined a rural automobile refurbishing shop and told a story with the headline, "Where vintage cars go for salvation," he used an anecdotal lead.

WHITE POST, Va.—A year and a half ago, Julie Moore of Fremont, Calif., sent her beat-up 1962 Plymouth Valiant to this tiny Virginia town 60 miles west of Washington.[14]

Kelly went on to note that White Post Restorations removed each part from the car, restored the ones that were in poor condition, and transformed the Valiant like new. Kelly used a story of one customer's experience to illustrate the kind of restoration work this shop has been doing since 1940.

The **little story** suggests the **big story**. By personalizing the business of grease, pistons, and wheel covers, the writer helps the audience appreciate the novelty of a shop that has made its reputation on detailing the details.

To break through the clutter of boilerplate approaches, writers must reject the sterile writing of the stenographer in favor of experimentation. Good writers study language, read poetry, and gain a sense of playfulness with syntax. They want to be creative and think about ways to take an existing approach and bend it into a new form. They reach for imagery to make readers, listeners, and viewers see the emotion, the power of the moment. Good writers compress and use words with rhythm, but sparingly. The goal is to be clear, but with boldness, excitement, and style. When done well, the audience will see

---

[14] Kelly, J. F. (2003, Feb. 14). Where vintage cars go for salvation, At small shop in rural Virginia, restorers use brand-new old parts. *The Washington Post,* pp. B1, B6.

the world from the writer's pen. Ah, but the view. It will be so compelling that the reader will be unaware that words transported its mind from the cellar of the ordinary to the rooftop, where the air is clean and the view panoramic.

JOURNALING

A technique used by writers, particularly feature writers, is to include **personal impressions** in the prose. This technique should be used with care; otherwise, the remarks that you mean to be candid quips fall flat and sound amateurish. Nonetheless, good writers can follow the lead of Tom Wolfe's *The Electric Kool-Aid Acid Test*, Hunter S. Thompson's *Hell's Angels*, Norman Mailer's *Armies of the Night*, and others from the **Gonzo School,** where the writer deliberately inserts opinion into the article. This approach must be cleared in advance by an editor and should be used judiciously. Most readers aren't concerned with what the writer thinks unless the comments are dry, novel, cogent, and insightful. This style of writing, also known as the new journalism, became fashionable in the 1960s. "Earlier work by Lillian Ross and much earlier by George Orwell is clearly situated under the creative-nonfiction umbrella," wrote Lee Gutkind, professor of English at the University of Pittsburgh.[15] Gutkind commended creative writing and said, "Creative nonfiction, writing techniques like scene, dialogue, and description, while allowing the personal point of view and voice (reflection) rather than maintaining the sham of objectivity, is hardly a new idea." For new writers, however, the personal approach should be reserved for articles that require the treatment. Be judicious and discerning about the goal of your prose. Failing that course, check with your editor!

---

[15] Gutkind, L. (2003, November 14). Stewardship as survival; brilliant nonfiction. *The Chronicle of Higher Education*, p. B4.

To prepare for this kind of writing, keep a **journal**, a diary. A journal is the place for your personal reflections. Avoid reminding yourself of your meals and other routine activities. Instead, use your journal to capture that emotion that ebbs and flows with each sunset.

One writer captured this kind of introspection when he wrote, "I entered a period of listlessness, spurred neither by love of self nor love of God. During this journey through the desert, I drifted from one diversion to another, committing the worst deeds of my life along the way. Looking back, I think it would have taken just one Christian friend to have spared me all those barren years, a friend who could have explained to me that although religious feeling had gone, the reality had not; that the Christian life depends not on the Christian, but on Christ; and that our inability to lead a perfect life does not condemn us to lead a bad one. I started out well but had stumbled and fallen. I hadn't known that the point of the race was not to win, but to finish."[16]

Can you hear the emotion in those honest words? Those are the kind of deeply personal thoughts that can be recorded in a journal but hard to locate when pressed to write them on demand. The journal works much like a photograph album. It can be used to jumpstart a memory that links to other memories. The chaining may help you develop a series of thoughts that advance the article. Clearly, this technique works best for the personal narrative, but the Gonzo gang used it liberally to castigate a source for sloppy thinking, criticize someone mentioned in the article for a fashion faux pax, and, in general, tee off at someone else's expense. Clearly, this technique should be reserved for those rare times when your intellectual

---

[16] Hale, T. (1986). *Don't Let the Goats Eat the Loquat Trees.* Grand Rapids, MI: Zondervan.

antennae are wiggling beyond control and you feel compelled to weigh in.

Summary

Free writing is a technique that may help you probe the writing voice that you possess but can only be coaxed out on special occasions. It works best when writers allow themselves to relax and write without regard to punctuation and the mechanics of the word slave. It is not a failsafe method, but it sometimes provides inventive combinations of words, images, even leads. Feature writing is about the skillful use of **creative writing** that relies on **wordplay, imperatives, question leads,** and other openings that laugh out loud rather than sigh with relief.

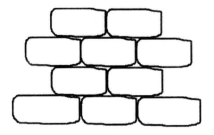

Building an article is a bit like building a wall.

Day 4

DEVELOPING THE ARTICLE AND MORE

CHAPTER AT-A-GLANCE

Q Selecting the right organization for your article

Q Inserting observation into your article

Q Understanding the story process

Writer William Least Heat-Moon tells a story in his *Blue Highways*[17] on the building of a wall. He joined a friend in New England and constructed a wall out of irregularly shaped rocks. Since the rocks were odd shapes, the men had to choose just the right one to put on top of another. The men began the

---

[17] Heat-Moon, W. L. (1999). *Blue Highways: A Journey into America*. New York: Little, Brown & Co.

project by surveying the inventory of rough fieldstones and selecting the best one to match the one before. In the end, the wall appears solid and Moon wonders if it could have been built any other way.

Moon suggests that the men **intuitively** knew what stone would be the best in the sequence. For writers, the sequence of information can't be based on a hunch; information must flow in a pattern that has some kind of order, even if it is transparent to the reader. The order may be chronological, but that is one of the weakest because the most important information may be halfway through the narrative or even at the end, and writers want the most crucial points to be read first. A better approach is to make a decision on the information based on the importance of the information.

RAW MATERIAL

Writers collect facts, often using interviews, and shape that raw information into an easy-to-understand report. They work hard to make their words flow so the audience can grasp the ideas quickly. The process includes selecting the best raw material available—the best quotations, the best anecdotes, the best observations—and arranging it in a story that makes sense and reads well.

Coherent reports begin with a lead that sums up the story, a second sentence that amplifies the first sentence with additional information, and successive sentences that follow logically one after the other.

Tip: When you know nothing of a subject on which you are about to write a feature article, read a children's book. Writers who pen long feature articles know the importance of speaking the argot of the experts. Before you talk to an expert on investing strategies for baby boomers, read a children's book on stocks, bonds, and OPM, a phrase some investors use to mean "other people's money." Children's books are designed to be easily understood while giving the reader access to the fundamentals. This idea works for the big-league writers, and it will work for you and me, too.

FACT ARRANGEMENT

One of the best ways to organize a news story is to systematically arrange the information with the most important information first. By arranging the facts from pertinent to less significant, your report helps the harried reader get the vital news first.

Imagine that you are a reporter assigned to find out about a couple who was about to be married on Valentine's Day on the 80th floor of the Empire State Building, a la a *Sleepless in Seattle* twist.

Here are the facts:

FACT 1 Rose Marie Higby and Alan J. Ross, both of Langhorne, Pa., signed up to be wed on the 80th floor of the Empire State Building.

FACT 2 Thirty-four couples also signed up for weddings on the 80th floor.

FACT 3 Right before Higby and Ross were wed, a gust of wind blew the couple's marriage certificate off the 80th floor.

FACT 4 The 34th Street Partnership is a merchants' group that sponsors the "marriage marathon" at the Empire State Building.

FACT 5 Dan Sieger, spokesman for the merchants' group, said, "They (the couple) had been dating for 17 years, and they finally made the move." He also said, "They were mortified at first" (when the certificate blew away). We happened to have a Xerox of it downstairs, and we were able to salvage the whole thing."

THE STRATEGY

The first task is to write a lead. Will you use a creative lead or a summary lead? Since the story is humorous with a happy ending, a creative lead is your best bet.

While it isn't given as one of the facts, the 1957 tear-jerker *An Affair to Remember* features a couple who pledge to meet on the 80th floor of the Empire State Building, if each decides the other is the one. This fact, part of the background that you might have to learn for yourself, might make a creative lead. If you wanted to refer to either *An Affair to Remember* or another movie, *Sleepless in Seattle*, you'd need to choose an element that relates to our Langhorne couple, too. In both movies, the lovers have plans for a meeting on the 80th floor, but somehow the plans are thwarted or confused, yet the conflict gets resolved. That bit of background, available by consulting a reference book on films or a telephone call to the reference librarian at the public library, might suggest:

The scene on the 80th floor of the Empire State Building had all the makings of a couple in love after the Sleepless in Seattle movie, plus added suspense when the marriage certificate they needed to be wed blew away.

Not to worry. This story ended happily, too, when a photocopy was used to complete the wedding ceremony today on Valentine's Day.

This creative lead, three sentences total, took longer than usual to get to the point of the story. Perhaps you can suggest a quicker approach, but be sure to get the place, the event, and the surprise wind in the opening to snag your reader's interest.

What do a couple in love, the Empire State Building, Valentine's Day and a sudden gust of wind have in common?

That's a question lead that gets all the elements in one sentence, but without a movie reference.

Here's one using the song title technique, which is to be used very sparingly.

Gone With the Wind? Right action, wrong movie.

The Associated Press led the story this way:

A couple who'd been together for 17 years planned to marry on Valentine's Day in the Empire State Building—only to have their marriage certificate blow out the 80th-floor window.

Again, a looooooooong lead. No matter. Now we can tell the story. The next task is to arrange the facts by selecting the most important information and arranging it in the right order.

The leads tell the reader that a couple was to be **wed,** but wind blew their marriage certificate away. The next pertinent bit of information is the **couple's identity**. Drop that fact into the story. Then offer a word of explanation in the form of a **quote**. This is similar to the paragraph below the story. Since we have a quotation from Sieger saying his group had a spare copy of the marriage certificate, the story could achieve a sense of completion by ending with that fact.

POSSIBLE VERSION OF THE STORY

The scene on the 80th floor of the Empire State Building had all the makings of a couple in love after the Sleepless in Seattle movie, plus added suspense when the marriage certificate they needed to be wed blew away.

Not to worry. This story ended happily, too, when a photocopy was used to complete the wedding ceremony today on Valentine's Day. **(FACT 1-2)**

"They (the couple) had been dating for 17 years, and they finally made the move," said Dan Sieger, spokesman for the 34th Street Partnership, a merchants' group that sponsors the "marriage marathon" at the Empire State Building. **(FACT 4-5)**

Right before Higby and Ross, of Langhorne, Pa., were to be wed, a gust of wind blew the couple's marriage certificate off the 80th floor. **(FACT 3)**

No problem. According to Sieger, "We happened to have a Xerox of it downstairs and we were able to salvage the whole thing." **(FACT 5)**

What version works for you? Think about the various approaches and decide on how you want your article to read. The first step is to think about the content and the appropriate approach. Now you are ready to engage the writer's imagination to devote your special gifts to capture this narrative with insight and panache.

QUOTATION AS AN ORGANIZING DEVICE

In developing an article, a writer must examine the facts to determine the proper order of the information for the maximum clarity and the most economical use of language. As stated earlier, the Valentine's Day story is an example of an article that presents the facts in order of most important information. One way to make this decision easier is to select **two quotations**. This idea works best when the two quotations are from the same person. Use the **first quotation** in **paragraph three** and the other quotation as the **last paragraph**.

SOME CONSIDERATIONS WITH THE QUOTATIONS

Quotations should be used for information that adds to the article; they shouldn't be used for facts and figures that can be better stated by the writer.

For instance, a quotation that says, "The party will begin at 5 p.m." is weak. You can state that kind of information, so why waste a valuable quotation on it. Save the quotations for the explanations, the answer to the "why" question.

Think of quotations as the sweet spot of the tennis racquet. It's in the center, where the strings are most taut and where the netting gives the ball the most power. Place the quotations in sweet spots in your article to give them the most power. Select phrases from your subject that are picturesque and well said. When a college dean of students once was interviewed by a leading newspaper on his opinion of a beleaguered college president, the dean said, "I would give him a D, not exactly a failure, but far from a success." The quotation works because it is clear, but it draws on the culture of education, the all-important grade.

Often the reporter can condense a statement from a source, the person who is providing information. In these cases, the reporter can paraphrase the quotation. Paraphrasing means putting the quotation in your own words. It works because writers often can recast a turgid statement into a concise sentence. One magazine writer, speaking on the use of quotations, made this clumsy statement: "The only thing that I'd say for the use of quotations is that effective reporting is, part of it, at least, is to know what you're looking for before the interview." Yet, the idea is a good one: Writers must consider the article angle before starting the interview, but that journalist's quotation is gaseous.

Now look at this quote. "Go where the reporting leads you," said Jeffery L. Sheler, former editor with *U.S. News and World Report*. "It's more than having a story in mind and going out quote-shopping."

Great quotation.

It plays on the metaphor that writing an article is like a trip to the grocery store, during which you pick up a little dairy, a little poultry, and quart of ice cream. The act of gathering the information, commonly called **reporting**, is the combination of good planning and quick wits, not just two parts quotation, one part anecdote, and a splash of humor.

In an article about nutrition labeling in a company cafeteria, the director of the cafeteria made the following question-and-answer response: "Can we do this? Yes. We will, with the help of staff, design, and post signs, write signs, and make the changes by the deadline, and we'll make them."

The quotation contains good information. As a quotation, however, it is too unwieldy. The syntax is strained, making the meaning difficult to understand. The writer can paraphrase the quotation in her own words:

> *By fall, signs labeling the nutritional content of food will be on display in the cafeteria, according to the director of dining services.*

In most cases, information must be attributed to give the reader some idea of the credibility of the source. In this case, the director of dining services is in the position to know about the labeling program. It's worth repeating that attribution is necessary. When it is missing, readers may wonder about the authority and source for information that stands alone. Avoid including attribution only in cases where the information doesn't invite contradictions.

EQUAL FACTS

In those rare cases when facts are of equal importance, the sequence is of no consequence. When writing an announcement of an event, for instance, the rooms where the function will be held may be considered to be equal in their relative importance. *Displays of old and rare newspapers will be shown Monday at 3 p.m. in the hospital lounge and at 8 p.m. in the Hicks Humanity Center.*

Notice in that sentence, however, that the earlier time was mentioned first, suggesting that even in cases of equal facts, a sense of order is useful.

Veteran news writing teacher George Hough represents the equal facts story this way:

FACT 1
FACT 2
FACT 3
FACT 4

Or

FACT 4
FACT 2
FACT 3
FACT 1

The **equal fact story** allows the writer to plunk the facts down in any order. Beware. This kind of story is best reserved for brief items of just a few sentences. While these items don't require much creativity, they should still follow the principles of good news writing—the concise use of a few well-chosen words. Strive for economy.

Suppose, for example, your organization asks you to write an announcement about a celebrity appearing for a fund-raiser. The most important information concerns the celebrity's name and when and where he will appear.

Here are the elements:
Celebrity: Film actor Richard Gere
When: May 13, 2014
Where: Talls Family Music Center
When: 2 to 4 p.m.

Other facts include that Gere will sign autographs, meet fans, and talk about his acting career. To help your readers recall Gere's claim to fame, you add that Gere made dozens of big-budget films, including *Franny*, 2014, *Henry and Me*, 2014, *Chicago*, 2002, and *Runaway Bride,* 1999, to name a few.

After the important information is inserted in the lead, these equal facts can be arranged randomly.

Here's one possibility:

Actor Richard Gere will appear June 13 from 2 to 4 p.m. at Talls Family Music Center, Center Square, as part of the promotion on the release of Franny, his latest project.

The sample brief above takes a straightforward approach to the story, but an enterprising reporter can have some fun with the material by using a feature lead. As you develop as a writer, evaluate the story elements and decide if a light touch or somber touch is required.

Here's a light touch.

The actor, known as much for philanthropy as oddball roles as a meddlesome do-gooder, will appear at Talls Family Music Center, Center Square from 2 to 4 p.m.

In this example, a reference to Gere's spiritual life is used to build a lead. Be advised, these kinds of leads can be considered too cute and readers (and editors) may be turned off, so use them with discretion.

Tips: Contractions are good!

He's still an actor. **Right.**

He is still an actor. Wrong. Wooden.

Often, the "be" and the "ing" form of the verb can be deleted in briefs.

He will speak. **Right.**

He will be speaking. Wrong.

The play will open tonight. **Right.**

The play will be opening tonight. Wrong.

The "be" can be used as the verb in the sentences where leanness is essential.

The meeting will be Monday at 4 p.m.

For briefs, the acronym SOP will help. In this case, it doesn't mean "standard operating procedure." The acronym SOP can help a writer remember the order of a brief by putting the name of the speaker (S) first, followed by the organization (O) involved, then the place (P). SOP also stands for standard operating procedure, and this mnemonic can be your SOP for this task.

Example: *Actor Richard Gere will speak to the Kiwanis Club at Talls Music Center Friday at 4 p.m.*

Use a.m. or p.m. for time.
Make up your own sentences using SOP.

I. _____

II. _____

III. _____

IV. _____

Choosing the right touch is part of the challenge in writing for mass media. Having some fun is appropriate for a feature article, but that kind of approach would be in poor taste for an article about crime, violence, and tragedy. Hard news is concerned with the hard parts of life. Counselor Scott Peck begins his bestselling book, *The Road Less Traveled*,[18] by telling his readers to learn that life is hard, and then they can respond well to the routine disappointments.

In news, however, hard refers to the more serious hardships of life, fires, car accidents, thefts, and any event that is timely, that must be published or broadcast immediately or it loses its value as information. All crime is considered to be hard news. Social occasions such as weddings are considered soft news. In many cases, soft news is read more readily than hard news, but

---

[18] Peck, S. M. (2003). *The Road Less Traveled*. New York: Simon & Schuster.

the function of the information often determines the approach the writer should take when constructing the article.

DETECTING THE HARD NEWS EDGE

Consider the story of a three-year-old child who called 911 to help authorities extract her mother from the trunk of a car. Is that hard news or soft news?

It sounds as if it could be a fun story about a woman who accidentally locked herself in her trunk and her daughter saves the day.

Would it make any difference if an armed robber locked the woman in her trunk?

Yes, that behavior is a crime, making the story hard news. The tricky part is that the happy ending with a surprise hero, a toddler, gives the story an added dimension. It sounds as if it could be a feature article, soft news. **Soft news** is considered to be less **time-sensitive** than hard news. Furthermore, the approach used for soft news often has a richer narrative quality and allows the writer to break free of the economy of language reserved for hard news. In writing the story as a blend of hard and soft news, the writer must strike the right quality, a matter known as tone. Tone refers to the way the words are understood. Is the piece jocular, deadly serious, light-hearted, or downright hokey?

In the rescue story, considered a standard in mass media writing, the Associated Press treated the report the way a master of ceremony might use in bestowing an award. Here's the beginning.

Mary Graves has always thought her 3-year-old daughter was something special.

The toddler proved it by talking to a 911 operator and leading
police to the car where an armed robber had locked her mother
in the trunk.
"She's just really bright. I don't know how to explain it," Graves
said Sunday night. "She has a photographic memory, and she's
learning three different languages. She's a special little girl."

The report goes on to tell the story of the robber who reportedly locked Graves in the trunk, but not before the mother pressed 911 and slipped her cellular telephone to the little
girl. The girl was left in the car and the robber left.

CHRONOLOGICAL DEVELOPMENT

Once the AP writer told the readers the end of the story, that
a toddler called authorities to help her mother escape from the
locked trunk of a car, she went back and filled in the crucial
details in chronological order.

Here's a way to practice this important writing technique.
Think about yesterday. What were some of the highlights? Tell
a story of one of those highlights, but instead of starting at the
beginning and spinning the account in 1,2,3 fashion, tell the
conclusion first, then go back and fill in the details.

Most of us are used to holding off on the dramatic conclusion, but in mass media writing, the audience usually wants
to know the outcome first. The following example is a long
anecdote that is notable for its lack of drama. However, it's
the pedestrian quality that provides a bit of charm found in
ordinary life.

Barbara Wojcik told me of her encounter at the swimming
pool. In the late 1990s, Taylor, a three-year-old, who had never
called 911 on a conventional telephone or a cellular one either,
spied a child in the baby pool. Toys surrounded the little girl

and Taylor decided this tyke was a good prospect for friend-ship. However, when she started over to the girl, the little toy czar barked, "These are my toys. Stay away. Go back to your mother!"

Taylor stopped in her tracks, put a finger to her cheek, and said, "Hmmmm. Let me think about this."

She really didn't know what to do next. Barbara sat about ten feet away and noticed Taylor mumbling to herself, and Bar-bara went over for a closer hear and discovered Taylor praying, "Jesus, help the little girl to be happy."

ANECDOTAL

As suggested in the previous example, an **anecdote** is a **brief story**, but a story nonetheless, told in chronological fashion. How could it be told with the ending first? Take a minute and think about the approach you would use in developing this ac-count, known as an anecdote or short story.

You need a way to sum up the story in a sentence. You ask yourself, "Is this hard news or soft news?" The subject isn't crime, it's politeness. It isn't tragedy, but it does have a sad note. In short, it's the kind of story that a proud mother might share with a friend, not the subject of an evening newscast; however, it still contains all the elements of a story that you can tell in mass media convention. This story has a clear end-ing, meaning that it must have a beginning, too. As you might recall from your literature days, short stories in fiction are de-fined as possessing a beginning, middle, and end.

The end of the intercession at the pool story is the prayer. As a writer, you could have asked, "But what happened next?" You could keep asking that question to peel the action back another layer, but let's stay with this version for the time being and work with the information we have.

The ending is a child praying. In searching for a feature opening, the writer wants a pithy statement that tells the conclusion, but hints that more is involved.

Here are three openings that could be followed up with the same narrative:

Word association

Children who pray may not walk on water, but they can sure rise above troubled currents.

That opening is OK, but it sounds a little moralistic. The tone should be light to avoid casting one child as the stark villain and the other as the angel. The idea is to use language associated with water to make the point. This idea is a good one, but remember not to take it too far or your reader will be turned off.

An unadorned statement

Three-year-old Taylor Smith found that an afternoon prayer by the neighborhood pool was just the right response when she met another child who didn't want to share.

This version is similar to the AP story on the toddler and the telephone call. It merely tells us the conclusion, and now we're ready to hear the details.

Wordplay

Some of us pay lip service to the idea of prayer in times of uncertainty. For three-year-old Taylor Smith, a prayer off the lips is as natural as the doggy paddle.

This lead is a combination of the two approaches. It uses some mild wordplay "pay lip service" and "prayer off the lips" to suggest a playful tone.

The lead tries to suggest the context by mentioning the doggy paddle, a type of stroke that is used in swimming. Most readers will understand this association, and the two sentences serve to set up the story. Enough details are missing to pique the reader's curiosity. Provoking the reader to continue is among the most challenging of techniques and the most satisfying of results when it works.

Now you can insert the details. Let's go with that last lead and add some details.

Some of us pay lip service to the idea of prayer in times of uncertainty. For three-year-old Taylor Smith, a prayer off the lips is as natural as the doggy paddle.

Taylor waded into the neighborhood pool the other day and spied a little girl about her age playing with toys. But when Taylor moved in closer for a chat, the little girl said, "These are my toys. Stay away. Go back to your mother!"

Dazed, Taylor's mother, Barbara, saw the encounter and walked over to Taylor and could hear her toddler mumbling.

"Jesus, help this little girl to be happy."

The waters might have been troubled, but Taylor wasn't. She retrieved a toy whale and cup from her bag and began splashing with her oldest friend, Mom.

COLOR

That anecdote has a few details not provided in the page before. As a writer, you might have to interview a source more than once to get the kind of detail called **color**. Sometimes the detail literally refers to the color of an object, the blue whale and red cup, for instance. In other cases, the **detail** refers to the person's facial expressions, the music playing in the background, the aroma of popcorn in the microwave, any sensation derived from your senses.

Among the best writers of color is Edna Buchanan of *Miami Herald* fame. In a feature article about Buchanan's work as a police reporter, Calvin Trillin of the *New Yorker* said he liked the color of her writing, particularly in an article about Gary Robinson, an ex-con.[19] Buchanan reported that Robinson bullied his way to the counter at a Church's Chicken restaurant only to be told that all the fried chicken had been sold and only nuggets were left. The man, drunk, slugged the woman at the counter and a fight ensued, leaving the ex-con shot dead by a security guard. Buchanan began her piece with, "Gary Robinson died hungry."

Buchanan has made a national reputation for writing about crime with the fascination of a person who wants to know what song played on the radio when the fight broke out, the kind of tablecloth that a widow used in the dining room, the year, make, and model of the luxury car where the gangster kept his golf clubs, and all the other details that vary from story to story. These details make for compelling reading regarding the genre, but the pro knows when the detail adds and when the detail is irrelevant. As a writer, you must use discernment to tell your audience the observations and sensations that add to the narrative. Add, don't detract.

The point for a short item such as the one about the little girl in the swimming pool is to keep it brief and snappy. By judiciously selecting the best words and reworking the prose to whittle it down to its leanest form, the item will read well. In this case, we added an extra dimension, a modest moral. In most cases, a moral is inappropriate, and readers will find

---

[19] Trillin, C. (1986, February 17). Profiles. Covering the cops. Reprinted from the *New Yorker* in a pamphlet, p. 1.

the lesson to be heavy-handed. However, if it works without calling undue attention to itself, then use it.

For those adventurous writers, try making a connection between a biblical account that mentions prayer and water. Can you think of any? Another angle is prayer and children. A writer could use a Bible concordance such as *Strong's Exhaustive Concordance of the Bible*[20] to find the precise biblical references to all these ideas. The word "children" takes up nearly five pages in that reference book. The potential danger of this approach is that a writer could lapse into a preachy tone and lose the sparkle.

The following short article uses the reportorial style of writing to tell the story of a public school and its practice of reading the Bible. Notice the use of numbers to add precision and the quotes to end the article. The last paragraph is an anecdote, a short story in the February 7, 1994 issue of *Christianity Today*.

BIBLE READING ENDS YEARS AFTER BAN

For nearly 40 years, students in Pennsylvania's Warrior Run School District began classes with Bible reading over the intercom system. In December, the practice stopped.

Since 1955, the 1,200-student district permitted public Bible reading and excused students who did not want to listen, even though the U.S Supreme Court ruled in 1963 such Bible reading was "indirect coercive pressure." The recitation continued unabated until teacher Jay Nixon condemned it recently and the Silver Spring, Maryland-based Americans United for Separation of Church and State warned school officials that "your continuance with this practice will open the school district to a lawsuit and resulting attorney's fees."

---

[20] Strong, J. (2001). *The New Strong's Exhaustive Concordance of the Bible*. Nashville: Nelson Reference.

Senior Janelle Smith read the last passage from Luke 1 in December. "It should have been 'Jesus wept,'" says school board president David Hunter.

He has received dozens of letters of support and is optimistic. "Now we have to see what's possible within the law."

WHEN YOU'RE STUCK

Sometimes a writer just can't seem to get started. The lead is elusive, and, worse, the writing seems lame, weak, and unimaginative. Here's a strategy used by Jeffery Sheler, the writer who is mentioned earlier in this chapter. When he is stuck for an opening, he **begins in the middle**, with the knowledge that he will return to the opening and hammer it out after he nails the middle. Once you begin writing feature articles on a regular basis, you, too, will develop some tricks that help you manage when you seem to be swimming in information. Sheler says that he can start in the middle because he has mastered the format of the typical article. Once you know the **formula**, you can deviate from it to write inventive feature articles that use refrains, regional dialects, literary devices, language that matches the topic, and more.

THE FORMULA

◊ The **lead**.
◊ A **quotation** from the primary source.
◊ A **background** paragraph called the **Nut Graf** or nut paragraph, which provides the essential background and often the reason you are writing the article. The idea is the important information can be said in a nutshell.
◊ The body of the article, which features **competing voices** that challenge each other.

◊ **Anecdotes** and **quotations** arranged in some kind of organization as outlined in this chapter.

◊ A **conclusion** that often echoes ideas mentioned in the opening. Frequently, feature writers conclude a work by using a quotation from the first speaker, the primary source.

When stuck, Sheler found that he could ease his way into his magazine article by jumping to the middle, just below the Nut Graf, and developing the article's tension. Editors such as Marvin Olasky say that many articles have a kind of rhyme scheme that reflects the tension inherent in describing the point-counterpoint of many features. The scheme may be on the order of **A, B, A, B, B, A.** Each letter represents a point of view or a quotation, and the writer can alternate from one view to the other using transitions such as, "Not all archeologists agree," or "The medical community is divided on the proper treatment." When you are hard-pressed to write, jump to this part of the article and work on it until the lead becomes apparent. Some writers even fashion the opening only after the rest of the article is complete. It's not a technique that will work for everyone, but it is a good one to keep in mind when you just can't get started.

Sheler often collects much of his interview by telephone, and he types his source's answers directly on the computer screen. This method can help a writer formulate an opening because the information is typed and easier to read than a notebook brimming with notes. To achieve this ease of reading, some writers type their notes. The **typed notes** make an **at-a-glance review** of notes very convenient. In addition, the theme of the article tends to emerge from the material when it can be examined easily. As you read your typed notes, highlight the rich quotations and underline the unusual anecdote.

Before long, the raw material of your article will stand out, and you, the architect, only need decide on the best way to design and construct the finished project. Get started. Write the draft, walk away from it, and then return for a second or third sweep. Soon, you will see the words take shape, and a crude word building will be revealed. In time, the building will become sturdy. Don't give up. Too many people, who want to "have written" but never write, give up before they start. The task seems too daunting. Forget yourself. Remember, it's not about you. It's about the article. Then write with the conviction that your efforts might not be immortal, but what effort made by us is? All of it will pass away, so do your best and be content knowing that you aren't the writer that you will be someday.

FEATURE STORIES AS SHORT STORIES

Writer Jon Franklin has a mysterious and thoughtful hypothesis. He says that feature writing for today is what **short stories** were to yesterday.[21] He calls it the **nonfiction short story**, but chides news reporters for focusing on the resolution, the end, without considering the complications. Journalists working in hard news, even feature writing, focus on the culminating event, the end of the drama, without exploring the events that led to the conclusion. To have a satisfying conclusion requires a thoughtful **beginning and middle**. As you develop your article, think about it as a part of the **human drama in which love, pain,** and death are part of life. Life is complicated and audiences want to witness the way a character resolves a problem. We all desire insight, coping skills, even easy lessons on the way life works.

Writers use devices to identify the action, often in pairs. Unemployment strikes a talented artist, Lisa, **first card**. Lisa overcomes and makes her reputation, **second card**. See the pair? Unemployment, a defeat. Finds art, a success. In the

---

21 Franklin, J. (1986). *Writing for Story*. New York: New American Library.

process of the **struggle**, the **conflict**, Lisa shows tenacity as she fights back. It refines her and builds her character, and others become inspired by her actions. The fight isn't without setbacks. Lisa tried and failed, tried again and learned from the mistakes. She learned about herself and about the world. As you write your feature article, remember to apply the narrative approach to tell us a story. You will feel more fulfilled, and your audience will be more gratified.

Tip: Avoid "due to," particularly when starting a sentence. It sounds stuffy. If you must start a sentence with this kind of reasoning, use "because."

Because of a death in the family, the shop will be closed for the next three days.

A better sentence, however, is:

The shop will be closed for the next three days following a death in the family.

Tip: Always use contractions of words suggesting negation. Use "don't" instead of "do not" and "can't" for "cannot." The reason: In mass media writing, the "not" may be omitted accidentally and the meaning would be distorted.

Don't be like the writer of a sex manual who told her readers the wrong facts about ovulation because she left the crucial "not" out of the sentence.

Developing the story, an example

Not long ago, a magazine asked me to write a feature article on U.S. Representative Randy Forbes, R-VA, who teaches an adult Sunday school class. The editor asked me to write a 1,000-word profile that examines this identity of an elected official's life—a congressman who regularly teaches Sunday school.

Time management as Swiss cheese

When writing any article, it is good to think of the overall task as a **series of tasks**. Some tasks require more effort than others and can be accomplished without heavy lifting. Think of the project as a wheel of cheese the size of a Volkswagen tire. You can begin nicking away at the job by **punching holes** in the cheese. Make Swiss cheese out of the wheel. By reducing the big task into discrete parts, you **manage your time**. Once you think about it, it is the most efficient use of your time because you end up breaking the task down one way or the other.

The holes represent the small tasks that you must accomplish to achieve your goal. Congressmen often are pressed from moment to moment, so I knew I had to apprise his staff that I wanted to observe a Sunday school class session and follow it up with an interview. In this case, I punched a hole in the entire project by making the mandatory calls to Forbes' district office and then his Washington, D.C., office. The calls took nearly a week because the congressman's communication person had to check with Forbes and others to make sure no other activity would overlap. To hedge my approach, I punched another hole into the project by calling Forbes at home to make sure he would be in town for the lesson. Writers can be a nuisance, but it's all part of the job to make sure the plan will work.

For the article, I knew I wanted anecdotes, so I contacted the class president and asked him to ruminate on humorous stories. Feature writers love those anecdotes that are too funny, almost unbelievable. I gave him a couple of days to mull it over, knowing that some of us can recite a funny story on the spot. It sometimes takes sleeping on it to produce a publishable quip. In this case, the anecdotes could be stronger.

Another source who I thought would be helpful was a state house representative who was a member of the class. I met with him and jotted down notes. He gave me his **business card,** and I quickly asked if I could get his **home telephone** number. I also asked him if I could double-check my information by calling him that day. By obtaining permission in advance, I bought myself **access** to the official after hours. During business hours, elected officials can be difficult to locate, so the home number and email address can be a real boon to the labor of gathering information and checking it for accuracy.

On the day of the class, I checked the batteries in my pocket **tape recorder**. I wanted the tool as a backup for getting information during that compressed time following class when the congressman would answer my profile questions. In addition, I took a **35mm camera** with film and a digital camera. For the **digital camera**, I recharged the batteries and took an ample supply of storage discs to make sure I'd get a good photograph. Next, I took a notebook and a couple of pens.

The congressman's office supplied background and a canned headshot, and I located a previously **published article** on the congressman. With this background in hand, I made my way to the class, getting there well before the class began. The night before, I called the class leader as a courtesy to let him know that I'd be at the class. I knew he wouldn't object; it's just a matter of courtesy. When I arrived at the class, I checked in and asked who would lead the class in announcements. Next,

I went to that person and told him that I'd like to take some photographs and asked if he would mind alerting the class. That leader took a light-hearted approach to the announcement and **put everyone at ease.**

Once the congressman began his lesson, the only real distraction was when I **stood on a chair** to get a better angle. Knowing how intrusive writers can be, I took the photographs of Forbes at the lectern and then retreated to the back of the horseshoe-shaped room to become a **fly on the wall.**

I listened to the presentation, did my follow-up interview, and later that day I typed up my notes that I retyped for myself to help me as I developed the article. Here's the article that the publication accepted, 388 words, from about three days of work.

CONGRESSMAN EXPRESSES FAITH ON THE JOB

CHESAPEAKE, Va.-Midway through the Sunday School class, U. S. Rep. Randy Forbes spread his arms wide and asked the class of nearly 50 adults: "Who here worries?" All but two hands went up.

"Come on. Put your hands up," urged the two-term congressman, a playful smile creeping across his face, and then he asked those who said they don't worry to give the remedy. The class spent the rest of the hour reviewing exhortations from the Sermon on the Mount as a strategy for beating the anxiety of finances, family, and a world fraught with peril.

Mr. Forbes is known at his Great Bridge Baptist Church in Southeastern Virginia first as a Sunday school teacher, he's been doing it for nearly 20 years, and then as an elected official. The class of 162 members can be too impersonal for some, leading to a modest but regular exodus of people who yearn for an ordinary teacher, yet the Republican congressman maintains a loyal following.

An attorney, Mr. Forbes gained election to the state house of representatives in 1989 and then to the state senate in 1997. A special election in 2001 put him in the House, and he was elected to a second term unopposed in 2002. He is one of four chief sponsors of HR 1897, the Unborn Victims of Violence Act of 2003. If enacted, this bill would make federal law the killing of a mother and her unborn child two deaths, not one. It is expected to come to a vote in the House sometime this summer.

For Ira M. Steingold, secretary of the Democratic committee in Suffolk, a part of the Forbes district, this law is a way for the GOP to expand its voter base: "It is a ruse to treat a fetus as a child." But Mr. Forbes seems to have a ruse-free voting record: it's 100% conservative, according to the American Conservative Union, which gave only 59 of the 435 members of Congress what it considers to be perfect scores.

Mr. Forbes received that rating on issues such as support for the partial birth abortion and tax exemption for religious organizations that participate in politics, as long as it's not their primary mission. Unsurprisingly, Americans for Democratic Action, the nation's oldest independent liberal political organization, gave Forbes a zero on his 2002 voting record.

EXERCISES

1) What kind of lead is used here?
2) Find an example of a transition. Does it work for you or not? Explain.

SUMMARY

Building the article is a bit like **fashioning a house**. It can be a summer residence with a bit of paint and thatch, or it can be the manor house with canopies and turrets. Writers learn to arrange facts in some kind of order, from most important to least important, with attention to logic or some other system. For instance, quotations can be used to provide necessary information while providing needed transitions. Other strategies for arranging the article include a **chronological development** or an **anecdotal pattern**. Throughout the development of an article, good writers explore the value of **observation**, known as **color**.

In a jam, when the natural organization for the piece just won't reveal itself, some writers have learned to resort to writing the end first, then the beginning, or they use a standard formula such as "lead, quotation, and then background." Be like Gumby, very flexible, as you prepare your first, then second draft of your opus. Rework it until you like what you read. Chances are that your editor will like it too.

Waiting for a call back from a source can leave a writer exhausted. Solution? Call a second or third time. Polite persistence will pay off.

Day 5

INTERVIEWS THAT WORK

CHAPTER AT-A-GLANCE

Preparing for interviews

Developing questions for interviews

Using silences and other techniques in the interview

Writers have two jobs. They gather raw information and then tell a story. Simple, right? It can be manageable, but all creative work takes effort. Writers have lots of ways to get information, including research and interviews. Research includes searching electronic databases, poring over documents, looking at public records, and so on. However, the better feature articles demand the voice of sources, **official sources** such as paid spokesmen and **unofficial sources** such as ordinary people. These voices will give the article a sense of verisimilitude. It will sound real because it is real. It's the difference from writing: "The mayor said voting is important" and telling someone, "His exact words were, 'Vote for me or expect a visit from the police.'"

DON'T IMPRESS YOUR NEW FRIEND

Interviews can be the most enjoyable part of the storytelling process. The writer will make a new friend, but it's important to realize that the goal is to gather information. The temptation is to impress the person with background about you, but that's not the point. The point is to collect information from the source. She's the main event, and you are the hired help with a unique role to get the story and get it right.

Some writers get lazy and use quotations from other writers. Even worse are writers who make up quotations from imaginary sources. The best writers arrange interviews and do their own questioning. The process can be fun, but only if the writer works hard to prepare well and handle herself with a sense of professionalism.

This chapter will provide a series of **steps** for making the most of the interview. It includes **preparing before the interview, strategies during the interview,** and **ideas on concluding the interview** and **following up**. In addition, this chapter will provide some ideas on conducting those interviews for which no planning is possible and some of the problems associated with sources who want to talk but ask you to shield them in your published work. As a convenience in this chapter, I usually call the **interviewer, the writer,** and the **interviewee, the source,** and **the project, the article.**

THE INTERVIEW GOAL

Among the most basic questions an interviewer must ask herself is the reason she chose the source. Is the article a **profile piece**, an article that highlights the subject's achievements and philosophy? Or will the interview be **in depth** and probe the source's life, philosophy, victories, and defeats? Or, is this interview part of a **series** of interviews that the writer is conducting to ventilate a topic? You decide and plan accordingly.

Think of an interview as a **directed conversation** with the writer in control. The writer will guide the source through a series of questions, some open-ended and some closed-ended. As the master of the "interview universe," you have the power to steer the conversation into the directions that are most relevant for the article that you envision. When your source gets off topic, say, "That's intriguing, and I'd like to pursue that topic in a few minutes. For now, "I'd like to know about ... " Make a note to yourself to ask about the stray topic and broach it at the end of the interview.

CONTROL WITHIN FLEXIBILITY

Be advised. At times, the source will interject a thought that you haven't considered, and you must be sensitive to the possibility of a new topic. One freelance writer tended to reject those little stories all of us tend to use when illustrating a point. The writer thought these anecdotes interrupted the flow of fact stacked upon fact. Years later, he learned the power and appeal of a little story and the role of a source in the collaborative effort to create an article of merit.

While it is good to think of your source as the key to the effort, don't allow her to bully you. Some sources feel entitled to **interview the interviewer**. They may demand to know your political identity, your marital status, or the size of your bowling shoe. Resist the urge to be combative; rather, tell the source enough information to get on with the business at hand. Should the source persist and demand to know personal information about you, gently suggest that her story is of more interest, and, if time permits, perhaps you can share some of your background.

This give-a-little to get-a-little approach is the basis of a conversation, and a writer must sense that good manners dictate that some exchange is necessary, but how much? As a religion editor, I often found sources questioning me about major and minor theological issues. Often, they were afraid that I might distort their views by virtue of my existing convictions. Try to put your source at ease by assuring her that your goal is to be accurate. Or, in very awkward moments, tell the source that you would love to share more personal information about yourself, but you can't because of doctor's orders. The statement makes no sense, but it has the power of authority, and it may throw the person off the scent. Be sure to ask your physician if you can use that line! You might be amazed how well this harmless rebuttal works. Say it whimsically with laughter in your eyes, and your source will get the hint that the story is about her, not you.

If all else fails, you can always answer a question by posing a question, "Why do you ask? Is that a problem? Are you concerned?" Again, remind your source that your goal is to write about her with gusto. Sometimes all a source wants is some reassurance. Give her as much reassurance as you can, but avoid deception. If your article is about the person's criminal past, be honest. Say, "I plan to ask you some tough questions, but I want to give you a chance to give your side."

Do your homework

To get to the meaty questions about philosophy, toil, hardship, and success, the routine questions must be satisfied. Questions about age, education, and work history can be avoided by doing **research before the interview**. The World Wide Web is one source of information about a person and the topic with which she is associated. Electronic databases such as **Lexis-Nexis** and others mentioned in Day 7, *Using the Internet*, will allow you to search newspapers and magazines for articles already published on the person and topic.

If that fails, contact the source and ask her to recommend articles that might have been published on her. Ask about articles on the topics that are associated with your source. Often the source can direct you to "the article" that you can use to develop your article. Failing that, obtain a copy of the person's resume or vita. Always **check** and **double-check** the information. Ask the source if anything has changed in the resume or if the previously published articles contained errors. I make it a habit of checking facts before the article goes to print. I've never had a source refuse a request to double-check my information.

Make a list

From your research, you can develop a series of questions. Your goal is to write an article that reveals the source in a fresh way, so think of questions that **build on what is already known**. It's a good practice to talk to the source's friends and co-workers as part of the interview preparation. Using the previously published articles, interviews with others, the vita, or resume, you can develop a series of questions that will help you in the interview. Have a direction to pursue, but be ready to change directions if the source offers new information that is compelling.

Some writers use three-by-five cards, like private investigator Kinsey Millhone in Sue Grafton's novels. The P.I. uses index cards to list her facts as she explores the case for suspects. You can use these cards to list your questions. Arrange them in order from easy to more difficult. It is good to memorize them, and be ready to jump ahead depending on the flow of the interview.

Above all, **listen well**. Listen for facts and listen for feeling. It's called **active listening**. A person who sighs as she tells you a fact may be saying she is sad, hurt, broken, or philosophical. Stop. Say, "You seem to be sad. Are you? Why?" This active listening technique works well, but it can slow down the rhythm of the interview if you are after just the facts, not the emotions. Use judgment. The technique works, but it is best to keep it in reserve for special occasions. Imagine the emotions that might erupt if you insist on identifying the effect on the source each time she speaks. Be careful, and don't use this advanced technique with people who are too young or too immature to know that they don't have to answer your questions. Sources are allowed to decline to comment.

One writer interviewed a poet about her literary work. The writer dutifully asked about the woman's career, including her first poem. In the process, the woman mentioned that she used her poetry as therapy for her cancer. The writer wrote down the remark and went on with her prepared questions. By not listening, the writer missed an opportunity to mine that intriguing area of cancer therapy, poetry! We must listen.

The beauty of the writing process is the challenge to think on the spot, to listen for that rare insight, to see the color that others walk by. It's the joy of writing. It's the gift of storytelling. To do it well, prepare hard with good questions, but listen well to hear the heartbeat of your source. At times, an interview will be a couple of questions that provide basic information; at other times, the interview will be an elaborate exchange where you might feel like a psychiatrist, parent, or confessor. Be responsible with this role. You are empowered to collect information for your audience. Don't waste anyone's time by probing into issues that are irrelevant, but be ready to ask the tough questions with all the skill you can possess.

FORMULATING QUESTIONS AND RECORDING ANSWERS

The better interviewers ask sources to provide an explanation. At times, the writer will ask routine information such as her work title, but the better questions, the ones that excite the source, **get at her opinions** and the rationale for them.

Your goal is to help the source relax and speak freely. It's a kind of dance, a kata, where the interviewer starts slow, gaining the confidence of the source, and then moves into more difficult questions. It requires taking notes, but the goal is to be unobtrusive about the note taking to keep the source relaxed. Pocket tape recorders are fine, but mechanical instruments can fail; notepads won't.

When using a **recording device**, allow the source to know that you are recording. You can reassure her by explaining that it will help with accuracy. It's better to keep the recorder out of sight once the source has agreed to the interview. When tapes are running, people tend to measure their words, and the rhythm of real speech is lost. If the source doesn't want the interview recorded, don't fight with her. Try to explain that the recording is meant to supplement your notes. If she still refuses, resort to the old-fashioned technique and write fast.

Most writers develop some kind of **note hand** where they get the subject and verb and some of the other main words. To get it right, take time immediately following the interview to insert all the words that you can in your notes; then type the notes. The writing of the story will go so much smoother this way. If possible, try crafting an article as soon after the interview as possible. Again, the article will go much better if it is written while the information is fresh.

New writers may not be aware of the **impressions** that can be banked following an interview. Your story will be better if you include more than the source's words. How did the source hold her head when she recounted the tragic fall off the ladder? Watch her hands. Listen for background noises, including traffic and music. When appropriate, ask the source to explain why she wagged her finger at you during her answer. How do these gestures link to the words? It is best for you to write down these gestures as the person is talking.

When you can't listen, write, watch, and think all at the same time; make sure you pause following the interview to fill in as much of the information as possible. One freelance writer admitted, "This is my weakest area. I'm so busy doing all the other things that I fail to listen sometimes and miss what's being said. I really have to concentrate. I rely on my tape recorder to bail me out."

You may not need it, but it gives you a sense of authorial power to know the carpet was a misty green color, that the cherry bookshelves have five shelves, and that the potpourri scent was apple spice. Irrelevant? Maybe. Only you, the writer, know how you will craft this article, and it is easier to have all the raw materials ready to go, rather than make a return visit just for one or two items.

COMPLICATED MATERIAL

Above all, make sure you understand the topic. That's rule one in interviewing, according to veteran newsman-turned-academic Merlin R. Mann. He says that if you don't understand, you can't explain it to the reader.

An environmental writer interviewed an entrepreneur about a maverick energy program that recycled previously recycled oil. Got that? She didn't. No one could understand the concept of recycling oil that was already recycled. Consequently, the article sagged miserably. Not to worry, the writer went on to become a lawyer and is quite happy not understanding re-recycled oil!

When someone explains a complicated process, you must go over the explanation until you **understand it**. Review your notes. Ask for definitions and metaphors that may make it easier for you to convey the information to your audience. Have the source draw you a picture, then think about using a picture with your article to aid in comprehension. Some educators say we think in pictures, so it only makes sense to reduce thorny explanations to a visual representation.

Writers use many approaches to get information and keep sources talking. When a writer doesn't understand, it is best to say so. Naturally, some sources will lose confidence in the writer who appears weak-minded. However, better writers know how to turn this weakness into a strength by playing dumb. Many times a source will go overboard trying to help the dim-witted writer. Like the character Peter Falk played in *Columbo* TV fame, by the enormity of his courtesy, the police detective eased his sources into talking freely just by asking the same question in a slightly different way, always with a smile and a nod.

When using this technique, try saying a few simple comments to keep the source going. A well placed, "No, really?" may help. Even a non-committal "Hmmmm" sometimes works. These comments work more like interview filler than questions, but the effect is the same. It propels the interview forward. Also called the non-question[22] question, this technique helps the interviewer sidestep those awful how-did-you-feel

---

[22] Tompkins, A. (2002, Fall). The art of the interview. *Poynter Report*. pp. 21-22.

questions. Instead of asking survivors about the death of family members in a house fire, the sensitive interviewer could ask what the person will miss most about his family and the happiest memory.

SILENCE

Another technique that will serve you well when the topic is simple or complex is the use of **silence**. Ask a question and be quiet. Mentally count to ten. The pause will seem very long and unnatural. Stare at your source and wait. Just wait. Is there anything harder for a writer? To yourself, count "One, two, three ... " Finally, your source will repeat herself, or, more likely, add information, information that you might have not received if you hadn't waited. This technique, like the active-listening technique, isn't to be used all the time. Use it judiciously with some thought.

If you ask a question for factual information, but the source is too sterile, try it. You might ask, "Why did you leave the job?" The source might say, "I got a better job," and you think to yourself, "There's more to this situation," and you begin counting to yourself. If she hasn't said anything else at thirty, you may have to pose the question again or move on. Remember, the interview is like a dance. You may be the lead, but your partner can limbo when you least expect it.

APPOINTMENTS

In the ideal, you prepare for the interview with research, interviews with secondary sources and some time to think about the questions you want to pose. Somewhere in this process, you will contact the source and **request an interview**. Sources agree to interviews for many reasons, some noble and some vain. Some sources are public-minded and want to educate others. Others see the interview as an opportunity to promote a cause. Still, others want to promote themselves.

In most cases, you will have to make an appointment and meet at the source's convenience. In some cases, the source is as anxious to talk to you as you are to interview her. Work it out but try to meet the source in her office, or better yet, her home. Why? You can learn about the source and the topic by observing her in her surroundings. Be sure to be a little early. If you're late, call and explain.

Dress for the interview. If the source is a banker, dress for the occasion. If the source is a landscaper, dress for the part. Arrive at the interview with enough time to look around the office, home, or meeting place. An office or home is better than a restaurant or other public place because of the personal touch. A person tends to extend her personality in the decoration of an office or home. **Observe** and **take notes** on the wall hangings, the awards, and the type of furniture, rug, and tools of the work, such as calculators, lighting, tables, and computers.

As you begin the interview, introduce yourself, state the purpose, take a deep breath, and relax. Begin the interview, but monitor yourself. Let the source speak. Avoid long preambles to questions. Just **ask the question**. Too often press conferences degenerate into monologues that put the klieg light on the interviewer. No good.

Avoid saying, "You were rather incensed when people protested at your film school's opening night because of the content of the movies. Even though you won't go into detail or tell us who was involved, could you tell us about what you plan to do?" Too complicated. The first part is an opinion; the next part is an interpretation that might be wrong. The final part of the question works. "What do you plan to do in light of the controversy?" Boom. The question explodes, and the source is free to answer it her way.

For the quick quotation or fact, the telephone is fine. For long-distance interviews, email is quite handy, but the interview in the subject's home or office is ideal. Face-to-face conversations allow for more rapport. You can see and hear the person interact with others, sense the pace of the workplace, and drink in the ambience of the décor. If the telephone is the only means to contact your source, you can still obtain that kind of valuable information. To duplicate this color-collection, the gathering of information from the scene, ask your source to describe what she sees, hears, smells, and so on. If you think it is necessary, you may contact the source's secretary to verify the information. Email also works well for this technique. The problem, of course, is that you can't verify the information, leaving you at the mercy of your source's ability to observe and report. Skype interviews also are popular, and an inexpensive add-on can help make a recording of the conversation. Call Recorder is one of the best software programs with Skype.

Whether by telephone, email, or in person, many interviews call for the quick response. You need information, like a piece in a mosaic. When rushed, skip discussions about the ivy in the potted plant and get to business, but make a game of taking a mental snapshot of the setting. It may pay article dividends later. Editor Lisa Farmer suggests that writers take a photograph of the scene to make sure the detail is accurate.

THE NOTEBOOK METHOD

Bob Dubill, famed editor of *USA Today*, tells the next generation of writers to keep a series of **notebooks**. One notebook is for the story that you are writing for deadline. The second notebook is a kind of Rolodex for telephone numbers, email addresses, and information on the source such as the circumstances on which you met. Keep this information to help you with future feature articles. The third notebook is for possible stories based on the leftovers from today's assignment. The observations from the office could be locked away in this notebook. These days, a smartphone can help you record all these ideas in a portable unit, but some of us do prefer the old paper-and-pen notebook. It is more tactile, and, in some cases, easier to use in retrieval. Low-tech has its benefits. No batteries. No on-off switches.

Tip: Dubill had other ideas you may want to consider. You might do only one interview a week, but you experience life every day and he suggests that all writers **keep a diary**. In it, writers can record the events and impressions that are memorable, but with a twist. Add a headline, a title, to the passage. It will make it easier for you to recall the time, and others will appreciate the summation. Among the benefits of the diary, Dubill says, is that it is a record of your unique life for your family to enjoy for generations to come.

DIFFICULT INTERVIEWS

As in the feature-oriented interview, the best approach is to find out about the person to be interviewed. Check with the editor in advance to discern the emphasis, the angle that will be used for the article. As a rule, regular contact with your editor will enhance your ability to sell the article. Practice this kind of interaction from the article suggestion to the article implementation in a joint effort that is commonly called collaborative editing.

In rare cases, you might receive an assignment where you have no time to prepare. A candidate comes to town, and you are assigned to meet her within a few minutes. In those cases, you have to be quick of wit. If possible, obtain a handout or press release in the moments before the interview begins. If no time permits, think about the five Ws and proceed accordingly. Ask the candidate what the most salient issues are facing the electorate. If it is an entertainer, ask her about the most pressing issues facing her or the act. If it is someone representing a cause célèbre, ask her to state the case and what she would like to see happen. If all else fails, say, "Why are you here?" and "What is the most important issue, idea, goal that you want our audience to know today?" That blanket question just about covers it all, don't you think?

In any interview, it is best to schedule an appointment with the source. However, many times secretaries and personal assistants screen contacts with sources, making it difficult for you to use the telephone to pose a question, let alone make an appointment. For this reason, it is important for writers to be as personable as possible, not duplicitous, just cordial in making requests. When the contact will be regular, it is worth your while to get to know these important gatekeepers. You might feel as if you are selling yourself or selling the interview. It's all part of writing. Explain the purpose and hope for the best. If the source persists in dismissing your overtures, you might have to consider the ambush interview. Watergate investigative reporters Bob Woodward and Carl Bernstein used **ambush interviews** for sources who refused to be interviewed. This approach is a last resort and to be attempted only with the approval of an editor.

In this interview, the writer meets the source when she is not expecting company. The writer may find the source on the way to work, taking a walk, or doing some shopping. As much as possible, be polite and explain that you have tried to schedule an interview without success. Be sure to identify yourself and quickly pose the question. Emphasize that you are trying to be accurate and you want her comments. If she refuses, explain that you plan to tell your audience that the source refused to comment. Say, "Unless you give a more complete answer, I'll have to use your no-comment." As stated earlier, no one has to talk to the press, and that number includes writers, authors, and freelancers. However, by telling the source of your intent to inform the audience that you attempted to get a remark, the source knows it might be in her best interest to say something of value. This approach can be heavy-handed, even mean-spirited. The goal is to get the information that is relevant for the article. That's all. If you are uneasy about the ambush interview, tell your editor, and she may have some ideas on how to proceed short of confronting a source without her foreknowledge.

As with any interview, save **embarrassing questions**, the bombshell question, for last. In the ambush interview, you might only get one question, the bombshell. However, a series of innocuous questions like the kind TV attorney Matlock uses before he levels his witness helps build to a point. A feature allows a writer to be more leisurely. Hard news sometimes requires tough questions. Regardless of the article, all writers must be ready to ask questions relevant to the assignment.

QUESTIONS AND APPROACH

Your preparation for an interview will lead you to a variety of questions. In some cases, you might want specific information. If you read that the person weeps after reading Benjamin Franklin's *The Way to Wealth*,[23] you may want to know what part in the 30 pages led to tears. That is a closed-ended question that typically elicits a short response. Open-ended

---

[23] Franklin, B. (1986). *The Way to Wealth*. Bedford, MA: Applewood Books.

questions are more fun and can be as simple as "Talk about blank," or can be more complicated such as "When you skydive through a cloud, what goes through your mind?" Mix them up. In an interview where you are fishing for information, but you don't know what you might catch, the open-ended questions work well. However, for a feature article about the weird trend where people allow themselves to be shot to produce a scar, you might want to know about fibroblasts, connective tissue cells, and their formation. See? Short answer responses are meant to give the audience specific, usually clinical information. Open-ended questions tend to get opinions, while closed-ended tend to get more factual responses, but the reverse can be true, too.

As the interview unfolds, make eye contact as much as possible and try to be unobtrusive about taking notes. Beginning writers will interrupt the source to make sure the quotation is correct. A better method is to take as good of notes as possible and telephone the source later to check the facts in a quotation. You don't have to read the quote word for word, but make sure you have the meaning correct. In keeping with the metaphor of an interview as a dance, consider the problems of the start-and-stop conversation. Like a dance, too much attention to words, like too much attention to the steps, will spoil the rhythm of the question-and-answer flow.

If possible, sit forward slightly in the chair. Avoid eating anything. And, that goes for chewing gum! Make the source your primary focus. Listen. Listen. Listen. As stated earlier in this chapter, listen to the words but listen with your eyes, too. How did the sentence sound? Happy? Sad? Occasionally, comment on the speaker's words with a statement such as, "That sounds as if it makes you very happy," or "You sound as if you regret that remark." Then stop. Let the source talk. She might change the subject or press on into more detail. People tend to talk more candidly when they receive encouragement such as head nods.

Some writers admit to feeling self-conscious during the interview. One writer confessed, "I'm often more aware of how I'm being perceived by the source and others on the scene, that I'm not doing what I need to do with much finesse." As a writer, work to blend into the background. In some ways, you are a talking prop who plays a supporting role to the star, the source. Remember that the interview is about the other person. When you concentrate on the job at hand, the tendency to be self-absorbed will fade.

When interest seems to lag, be ready to ask an **off-the-wall question** such as, "Did you ever call the White House," or "When's the last time you cried," or "What do you want your epitaph to read?'" Sometimes the best information from the interview comes out as you are about to leave. Be ready to change directions and do the interview that you had not planned. Stick with the questions that you formulated until better material comes along, then jettison the old questions and go freestyle.

As the interview winds up, be sure to ask the mop-up question. Say, "Is there anything I didn't ask that you'd like to tell me?" Another question along that line is: "What's the most important idea you shared with me today?" Sometimes sources miss the point entirely, and you can help them stay on track. Try, "I just have to ask you," and ask the question.

Odd occurrences happen during the **fare-thee-well stage** of the interview. Often, the source will say something brilliant. Be ready. Make your way to leave, but be alert to that last bit of information.

As you leave, be sure to **verify a contact number** and **electronic mail address**. Naturally, you should end on time. If you said the interview would conclude at 5 p.m., stop. However, if you are unsure of some of the information, ask if you can call back later and check the information. Verification might be the final part of the interview, but it is vital. Keep asking, "Is this correct?" Add, "Did I understand you correctly?" and "Did I hear you right?" Take time to think. Pause. Review in your mind the article that you envision. What did you leave out?

OFF THE RECORD AND BACKGROUND

As you talk to your source, she may become self-conscious and tell you, **"off the record,"** and plunge ahead with some kind of detail. Off the record is the idea that the information shared in an interview is not for publication. Work to keep your source on the record. While the information provided might help you understand a complicated situation, it will do no good in explaining it to your audience if you agree not to include the controversial information in the finished article. It's better to stop the source and question her on wanting to avoid using the information in an article. Often, the source wants to be polite and avoid unduly embarrassing a third party.

Most people rarely meet reporters, so you might have to explain to your source that she can't just say the magic words, "off the record," and continue talking with impunity. Once a reporter or writer identifies herself and tells a source that she is collecting information for an article, the source is on the record. To go off the record, the reporter or writer must agree to listen to the information with the understanding it will not be used in the article. How likely is that? When a source becomes uneasy and asks to talk off the record, stop her and say that it is confusing when sources go off the record. Explain that as a writer, you plan to interview others and someone will likely share the information that is questionable at that moment. By not agreeing to go off the record, the writer can say with honesty that no agreement was violated in obtaining information. However, if a reporter agrees to go off the record, she should negotiate. Be sure to ask when the source is back on the record.

Writers who go off the record usually make a point of putting their pens down or turning off the tape recorder. Should you continue to collect notes, be sure to make a mark in your copy indicating that those words should not be reported. See? It gets difficult to keep straight. Most writers use humor or some other disarming technique to keep the source on the record. Nonetheless, once a deal is struck, a writer must abide by it.

Background and **deep background** are other ways for a writer to use the information with the understanding it will not be linked to the source. Vague identification such as "a government source" can be used, but most editors will question the lack of specific identification. Too many inexperienced writers have avoided the hard work of getting a proper source, relying on other writers, or, in rare cases, their own imaginations to supply the missing information. It's dangerous because the information may be absolutely incorrect and it's wrong.

From time to time, a source will want to provide information and say it is not for attribution. At the very least, the source doesn't want her name used in the article or reference made to her in association with the information.

PRIVACY

A rule of thumb sometimes used is that the misconduct must demonstrably affect a public person's performance of his job before it should be reported. Publishing the name of a rape victim might well discourage other women from coming forward and pursuing sex crime cases in court. Newspapers and magazines continue to grapple with this issue and it is one of the more vexing dilemmas facing writers.

Protecting a person sounds noble, but too many writers are quick to allow a source to remain unidentified. The novice writer sometimes calls these sources anonymous, which is incorrect. If the person were anonymous, no one would know the person's identity. A better description is to say the person asked to be unidentified, presumably to protect herself from incrimination. The rule is to name all the people with whom you interact to allow your audience to know that a real person contributed to the article. Made-up stories happen, as witnessed by Janet Cooke's infamous "Jimmy's World" piece that won the 1981 Pulitzer Prize for feature writing, only it was fiction. In the article for the *Washington Post*, she created an eight-year-old boy named Jimmy, calling him a third-generation heroin addict.[5] The *Post* returned the Pulitzer and fired Cooke. She violated the idea of accuracy in her article, a non-negotiable principle.

SEVEN STEPS TO THE INTERVIEW

1) Prepare questions in advance.

2) Consider a mix of open-ended or general questions and close-ended or specific questions.

3) Avoid complicated questions.

4) Use silence.

5) Try to interview the person in person in her surroundings.

6) Listen for emotions.

7) Ask a clean-up or mop-up question such as, "Is there anything important about this subject that I haven't asked you about?"

EXERCISES

Identify the following questions as either open-ended (O) or closed-ended (C).

1) How old are you?
2) What was it like to jump off the house?
3) What do you want your tombstone to read?
4) What makes you cry?
5) When is the last time you cried?
6) Who is your hero?

Answers: 1. C 2. O 3. O 4. O 5. O. 6. O

Read the following article. Identify the quotations and write the questions that provoked those answers.

HOLY LAND TOURISM PLUNGES[24]

Visits to Israel fall 45 percent as violence escalates.

JERUSALEM—In the mid-1980s, visiting Israel around Easter Sunday was like shopping in a farmer's market at rush hour. "We'd wait three hours at some sites to get in," says Vincent Cioffi of Emmaus Tours in Margate, Florida.

In a typical year, Cioffi takes 2,000 people to the Holy Land. Recent months have been anything but typical. Only 41 people participated in Cioffi's $700 promotional package tour of Israel in January. Cioffi says that is roughly an 80 percent drop from the usual January business.

"I have no Easter tours," says Cioffi, a 20-year veteran of the tourism business. "This year is worse than last year."

Since the outbreak of violence in September 2000, more than 300 Israelis and more than 1,000 Palestinians have died in Israel, the West Bank, and Gaza. Tourism, one of Israel's largest industries, declined 45 percent last year compared to 2000.

---

[24] Smith, M. (2002, April 1). Holy Land tourism plunges, Visits to Israel fall 45 percent as violence escalates. *Christianity Today*. 46(4), 34.

Overall, the number of visitors to Israel has plunged from 2.2 million in 2000 to 1.2 million last year.

North American Christians, one of Israel's most important markets, appear to be in no hurry to return. About 485,000 Americans, most of them Christians, visited Israel in 2000. Only 253,000 made the trek in 2001. Educational Opportunities Tours of Lakeland, Florida, one of the largest Christian tour operations in the United States, transported about 5,000 people to the Holy Land in 2001. According to Susan Andrus, director of marketing, its best year was 1996, when it took 14,000 Americans to Israel.

Andrus believes it is still possible to travel safely in Israel. Speaking of her 3-year-old daughter, she said, "I would take her to the Holy Land in a heartbeat. I know it is safe, and it's important to support the Christian community there."

Some tourism officials blame the news media for the perception that travel to Israel is unsafe. But the U.S. State Department issued a travel warning in December. "Ongoing violence has caused numerous civilian deaths and injuries, including to some American tourists," the department warned. "The potential for further terrorist acts remains high. The situation in Gaza and the West Bank remains extremely volatile, with continuing confrontations and clashes."

This year, the Israeli Ministry of Tourism is sharpening its marketing efforts toward American Christians. "For many years, American Christians have been among our best friends and greatest supporters of the State of Israel and of tourism to Israel," said Mina Ganem of the Israeli Tourist Office. "We really appreciate it. We are calling upon all of those who have encouraged tourism in the past to work with us to bring as many American Christians to Israel as possible, despite the headlines."

The convention business has also slackened. The Evangelical Press Association agreed to hold its April 2002 convention in

Israel, but organizers switched the venue to Colorado Springs as violence escalated. Nevertheless, the International Christian Embassy Jerusalem, a Christian Zionist group, held its annual celebration of the Feast of Tabernacles in Jerusalem in October, attracting overseas Christians.

Following a time-tested strategy, Israeli tourism leaders are showcasing visits by high-profile Christians. "We believe that as this community sees Christian leaders they respect go and return with a good report, that will stimulate others to travel as well," says Butch Maltby, a Colorado Springs consultant who works with the Israelis.

"For example, author Kay Arthur faithfully brings hundreds of Christians to Israel each year," he said. "She has told us that many of the people on those tours have thanked her for the opportunity to travel and for her bravery to defy the majority."

Arthur's Precept Ministries is still inviting participants to an April tour of Jerusalem, Galilee, and surrounding areas. Others in the Middle East are turning to additional markets to boost tourism. Resourceful Arab Christians are looking beyond the United States in search of fellow believers willing to visit. Habib Khoury, co-owner of Shepherds Tours & Travel Co. Ltd., says he is working with a Christian group from Uganda for an Easter tour. A passionate Christian, Khoury urged more Christians to travel to the Middle East.

"Christians of the Holy Land can be Palestinians, and we are suffering the same as our Palestinian Muslim brothers," Khoury says. "Occupation does not differentiate between Christian and Muslim, and a pilgrimage to the Holy Land at this time is very important."

Summary

Conducting a successful interview requires a writer to think about the topic and prepare vigorously. Your role is to lead the conversation but allow enough flexibility to unearth those unpredictable responses that will make your prose sing. Writing questions in advance is a good strategy, so is being quiet and allowing silence to be part of the interview process. The joy of the interview is that you can't be sure what to expect, so be ready for a friendly response and be alert to a hostile response. Remember, your job is to get accurate information while showing respect for your source. Be wary of sources trying to tell you information that you can't use, but if you go off the record, you must respect the agreement even at your own peril.

Get the assignment before you write the article.

Day 6

SELL IT FIRST, SELL YOURSELF

CHAPTER AT-A-GLANCE

Finding the assignment

Attending writers' conferences

Participating in writers' groups

Veteran writer Norm Rohrer has a saying that should be the motto for writers: "Sell it first, then write it." This idea might sound odd, but it's the best strategy for success in penning a news article, feature story, inspiration piece, or any other work you hope to have published.

Publications have personalities, just like people. Your news story on a student who took a train, taxi, airplane, and boat to return to school during the worst blizzard in United States history might sound as if any publication would want it, but that may not be the case. A periodical published by the American Automobile Association might find the idea suitable for its purposes, but the Valley Entertainment Guide might have no use for this piece. So what's a gifted writer such as you supposed to do?

SELL IT FIRST, AND THEN WRITE IT.

Before conducting the interview, getting the quotations, and verifying the facts, experienced writers know to contact the editor of the publication for which they are interested in working and earning a freelancer's paycheck. Sometimes an article presents itself and a writer takes her chances that someone will want an interview with a luminary who is in town to give a speech, or a young woman who rescued a child from a fire, or a plethora of other ideas. Most likely, however, the periodical for which you want to write has a publishing schedule and topics of its own. For this reason, you must **think of a feature story idea** and **then approach the editor.** In the words of journalism professor William Ruehlmann, stalk the feature story by following the advice of philosopher Henry James: "Be one on whom nothing is lost."[25]

By reviewing the ideas in this book and reading the magazines you love (and forcing yourself to read those you dislike), you will develop a sense for the feature article. Soon your vision will radiate with unlimited possibilities and your idea notebook will burst with ideas. Resist the urge to write these articles without an assignment. Find the article a home, and then work with abandon. Here's a sales plan in 1-2-3 order.

---

[25] Ruehlmann, W. (1977). *Stalking the Feature Story.* New York: Random House, p. 28.

STEPS TO SELLING AN ARTICLE THE OLD-FASHIONED WAY

1) Write a short letter or email suggesting the idea and include the crucial information that you possess access to the valuable source. Access is crucial. Suggest a word length, deadline, and a working headline or title. This contact is known as a **query**. You can end your missive by requesting the publication's writer's guidelines, their letter to you on the publication's personality highlights.

2) Be sure to enclose a self-addressed, stamped envelope, commonly called the **SASE**, if you're using the old-fashioned approach. It's expensive to correspond with writers. This touch will alert the editor to your maturity as a writer, even if it's your first attempt.

3) Include a one-page **resume** highlighting your writing victories or other information that suggests you are a professional.

Often article ideas are posted on a Google doc for all the editorial staff to peruse. That's where your strong, colorful query letter will either impress the editors or leave them flat. Work hard to explain the reasons your piece is essential for that periodical's audience.

Or you can try the twenty-first-century approach and use some of the tools mentioned below.

You might be wondering where a writer gets the address of a publication or, equally important, the editor's name. Periodicals feature this information toward the front of the issue; however, most libraries possess the *Writer's Market*, a valuable reference book that lists the names of publications across the United States. In addition to the editor's name, the listing includes the magazine's address along with its editorial needs and other pertinent information. The *Writer's Market* is an excellent research tool, and you might want to request it as a Christmas present. Always use the most current edition because turnover is high in the publishing business.

For the inspirational market, Sally E. Stuart's *Christian Writers' Market Guide*, published by Harold Shaw, is considered the best source for contact information. Periodicals for writers are helpful, too, and many are online. Also see Day 7, "Using the Internet," for valuable sites for writers. Magazines such as *The Writer, Writer's Digest, The Christian Communicator, Editor & Publisher, Columbia Journalism Review*, and many others will help you keep abreast on who is doing what in publishing. Organizations from the National Association of Black Journalists to Religion Newswriters Association to Society of Professional Journalists are just a few writer organizations that can help you succeed in your feature-writing career. Consider joining some of these groups, which entitles you to receive a newsletter and gain access to member benefits such as exclusive job opportunities. Also, consider joining Profnet at http://www.prnewswire.com/profnet/ to establish yourself as a bona fide writer, and that organization will send your queries to valuable sources that you can use to develop a high-quality article.

When you locate a publication for which you'd like to write, pay careful attention to the guidelines and the contact information. More and more periodicals accept email queries, which streamlines the process and gives writers quicker feedback, but some still prefer snail mail. It is acceptable to call an editor after having sent your query and waited a couple of weeks after the publication's typical response time.

When you correspond, be sure to alert the editor of your ability to provide photographs and other art. Editors are always in need of illustrations and photographs to accompany articles. If you can take photographs or prepare computer images, include that information in your letter. Make sure your letter is word perfect with no typographical errors, known derisively as **typos**. Allow between four and six weeks for the editor to respond. These people are very busy, but they need content, and they need writers such as you to fill their pages or online holes day after day, week after week, and month after month.

That's fine, you might be thinking, but what about timely articles that have a short shelf life? In these cases, editors are glad to take a telephone call. A daily newspaper, for instance, wants the information now and will talk to writers about getting the story to them fast.[26] The same rule still applies: Sell it first, then write it. Obviously, a writer in search of a sale must have some information to share with the editor or the conversation will be short indeed, but avoid conducting a windy interview with a source before the sale is made. Get enough facts to make the call and sell the story.

While this process sounds as if only writing hacks deign to do it, it's not. Having made that point, let me urge you not to argue with an editor. They say no sometimes, often, in fact. Don't be discouraged. There are hundreds of publications and what one rejects this morning, another may thank heaven for this afternoon. When an editor does reject your idea, take a minute to determine if the idea is just not interesting. Once you have confirmed the legitimacy of your instincts, try again. As Churchill once said, Never give up. Never.

Keep in mind that most publications are planned in advance, so the prospect that your idea will fit exactly into the editor's plans is unlikely. For this reason, don't be unduly offended if one editor passes on your idea. If nothing else, you made a valuable contact for the future. Ask the editor to keep you in

---

[26] John McCandlish Phillips wrote for the *New York Times* from 1952 through 1973 and said that getting the story often included being at the right place. He attributed that good fortune to God honoring his work reporting in "Faith in the Daily News Chase," an Aug. 17, 2001 speech to the World Journalism Institute published by WJI in Asheville, N.C.

mind for assignments and contact another publication with the same idea. However, if the first editor raises a question that you couldn't answer, find that answer before moving on to your next target. That way you are prepared if the second or third editor raises the original point.

Keep your story **idea antennae** up at all times and your possibility well will never be dry. Larry Hicks won prizes as a columnist in York, PA, and he worried that he would run out of ideas when he began his columns in the early 1990s. Even today his files are backed up with ideas because he's always on the prowl for material. Seek and ye shall find, says the book of wisdom. Larry's story can be your story, too. Read newspapers, watch TV, talk to friends, and always keep some paper and a pen handy to jot down the next idea you can develop into a story for that next byline and paycheck.

Depending on the publication, cold calling, or initially calling an editor, may be an option, but be advised, don't expect a hero's welcome. The editor will be busy on some project when you telephone. This call means she will have to stop her progress and think about your idea. While it's her business to be on the lookout for new ideas, the interruption may not put the editor in the mental and psychological state that you want to get the best reception for your award-winning story. Use the U.S. Postal Service and you can excite the editor from the safety of your letter, or try a well-written email.

Build goodwill with the editor by proving that you studied her publication. Seasoned writers say to make sure and study it beforehand. Get a **sample copy**. Often it is free for the asking along with writer guidelines. Often, guidelines are available online. Monitor the topics and the advertising of the publication or the online service. Read between the lines to sense the bias and prejudice of the editor. It is best to create a grid and take notes on each article. How many sources are used? How many anecdotes are mentioned? Are articles top-heavy with statistics such as numbers, or is the magazine or online service built around long narratives with personal references? The grid will help you understand the slant used by the publication, but you'll have to do the interpretation, and your findings will be subjective. Nonetheless, this approach will help you gain an edge on sensing the content that is most likely to be used.

ROAD TRIPS

Among the best advice I ever received on selling articles is to **befriend editors**. Make a point of introducing yourself to editors when you are on the road, or when you attend a conference. Offer to take them to lunch. Explain your interests and offer to keep in touch with ideas. Enterprising writers make initial contact with editors by telephone or email and request a 10-minute session the next time they are in town. Most editors know the writer will be coming with an agenda. That's OK. Editors need writers as much as writers need editors.

You may want to try a **fact-finding, get-acquainted trip** to a number of publications. An inexpensive trip may be planned by restricting your meals to sandwiches in the cooler and overnight stays at inexpensive hotels. Websites such as priceline.com will allow a guest to submit a bid for a room. I have stayed at a four-star Washington-area Hilton for $60 per night using this kind of service. Youth hostels may provide another inexpensive solution.

When you arrive for your get-acquainted chat, keep to the time schedule. The editor can always extend it but be sensitive to her time. Editors are always facing a deadline. It's OK to leave a resume or one of your articles that you recently published. It's very likely that the editor will ask if you have any feature article ideas. Be ready with a list of five ideas that target her audience. Practice pitching the idea in one well-crafted sentence. Practice saying the line with grace and speed. Your new friend will be impressed. Monitor your time and then offer to take your leave. Ask permission to stay in touch. Assuming that you don't drag mud into the office and otherwise make a fool of yourself, the editor is very likely to encourage you to submit future ideas.

If all else fails, ask the editor if she can give you one piece of advice on succeeding in writing. This approach may sound demanding, even too self-serving. It isn't for everyone, but it may work for the new writer with lava coursing through her veins who is need of a place to erupt in print or online. Published authors sometimes quip, "Writing is easy; you just open a vein and bleed." For new writers, you can open a vein and let the fire saturate the paper. The words may be too hot to handle, but at least you got it out of your system! Getting to know editors on a personal level will help you use your eruptions for the byline and the paycheck.

SUBMITTING THE ARTICLE

Editors can be very forgiving to writers on the **format** of the submission, but why risk it? It's very likely that the periodical will want you to send the manuscript electronically, using a software program such as Microsoft Word, as a document with a name such as "tires.doc," or a similar form with your name in the title when writing about trends in tire swings. Double space your piece and use a 12-point size font in Times or something similar. National Public Radio in Washington, D.C., prefers Georgia font, which is an attractive font to consider using. Include your name, address, telephone number, email address on top, left side of the article. The top right-hand side of the document is a good place to include the rights you are selling, word length, a partial social security number, copyright symbol, year, and your name.

The right side of the top of your title page is the area where most writers tell the publication they are selling first rights, which means that the publication will be the first to use the piece. After it is published once, the writer can sell it again using one-time rights. In both cases, there is a one-time usage.

These days some publications are asking writers to sign a **work-for-hire contract**, which allows the publication to retain exclusive rights, including the right to publish the article on the Internet. This phrase means that the writer gives up copyright privileges. Most writers avoid those kinds of contracts when marketing their own freelance articles because the work cannot be resold (because the writer doesn't own it). With first rights and one-time rights, the writer is free to sell the article, once it is published, to another publication as long as the audiences don't overlap.

About halfway down the page, insert the suggested headline or title for your work and your byline. Allow some white space and begin your article. If you plan to submit it by paper, it's a good idea to format the manuscript to have a running head that includes a keyword from the headline or title and your name and page number. Some publications maintain a tradition of listing the number of total pages in the upper right-hand corner. For each successive page, the writer would list the order. So, "2/4" means "second of four pages." It's a technique that allows an editor to be sure that all the pages are intact. Another old convention is to add "30" to the end of the article to alert the editor that the article concluded. Tradition suggests that newspapers and press releases ended with the number "30" because Western Union adopted a number code around the Civil War era where "30" meant "no more—the end."

Your rights

A word about **copyright**. No one can copyright an idea, but your creative work can be copyrighted. Copyright protects a writer's right to copy the work, to use a portion of it elsewhere, and make money on it. New writers tend to worry needlessly about copyright. The work is copyrighted once it is published, but if you feel uneasy about someone purloining your unpublished intellectual property, write something such as "© 2016. Your name. All Rights Reserved," or just "copyright," and try to use the copyright symbol from your keyboard or handwrite it on the work. For $35, the U.S. Copyright Office will register unpublished works, which ensure you protection in the unlikely event of a copyright infringement suit. See "Online registration of a basic claim in an original work of authorship (electronic filing)" at http://www.copyright.gov/docs/fees.html.

Writers may sell many different rights. As stated earlier, when a writer sells a publication the right to be the first publication to use the material, those rights are called **First North American Serial Rights.** Once the publication in North America publishes your article, all the rights to it revert back to the writer. In general, First North American Serial Rights is sometimes called **First Rights**, but you could sell first rights for an electronic service. In addition, writers sell one-time rights, which isn't the same as **First North American Serial Rights. One-time rights** means a publication can print the article once. **Reprint Rights** means that your article has appeared somewhere else and now you are selling the right to reprint it. **First Electronic Rights or First World Electronic Rights** is the right to be the first to publish the piece to electronic media. Writers are cautious of selling this right because it is so broad.

A **work-made-for-hire** (WMFH) contract gives exclusive rights, including the copyright, to the publisher. Complete ownership of the work is transferred to the publisher, and if the publisher so chooses, the writer may not even be considered the author of the work anymore. A WMFH can't be resold by the writer because the writer no longer owns it and can't resell it. As stated earlier, many freelance writers are refusing to sign WMFH contracts because of this odious practice. For in-depth information on rights, visit www.writing-world.com. Moira Allen, the owner of this commercial site, publishes articles on rights and copyright information and other aspects of writing. The site includes excellent suggestions on what to charge for your work and other ideas.

TAXES AND EXPENSES

As a writer, your **expenses** can be taken off your taxes along with any other expenses associated with your work. Find a tax preparer who is familiar with the work of writers. He or she can show you how you can legitimately claim expenses, includ-ing travel to collect research for an assignment. The federal government allows a writer, or anyone who is self-employed, to deduct expenses. Desks, computers, paper, and other sup-plies may be deducted, but it is wise to work with a certified public accountant or licensed tax preparer. For instance, your computer must be dedicated to your work as a writer and may not be used for other purposes if you are seeking a deduction. Offices can be a problem unless this space is used strictly for writing. Computers, Internet connections, and software are legitimate expenses for the serious writer.

HABITS THAT LEAD TO SALES

Write every day whether you feel like it or not. Keep a jour-nal and that idea notebook. Write to editors and writers that you admire and share your ideas. Take them to lunch if you can. Attend their workshops and writer's seminars. Most importantly, be sure to read their publication. Nothing is as embarrassing as contacting an editor about a story idea that the publication ran just two issues before.

Enroll in a class at your nearby college and ask the academics about their contacts. Most of all, write. Write. Write. Write as if your legacy will be the influence of your articles and books.

Think of the influence that Oxford don C.S. Lewis continues to have today, years after his death in November 1963. His *Mere Christianity,*[27] that went into 50 editions, is as powerful as when it was first written in 1943. Imagine speaking to us beyond the grave through a book with great lines such as these: "I must keep alive in myself the desire for my true country, which I shall not find till after death: I must never let it get snowed under or turned aside: I must make it the main object of life to press on to that other country and to help others to do the same."

Right, he is.

MENTORS

Most artists go through a time of **apprenticeship**. It's no different for writers. Some hit their stride in a matter of months; for others, it may take up to five years of regular writing under the watchful eye of a good editor. For many of us, editors come and go, weakening our learning curve. One remedy is to seek **your own editor**, who will stay with you for a lifetime. Your goal is to find a trusted friend, a more mature writer, and ask her to peruse your copy from time to time. Reward her with lunches, books, or a magazine subscription. Let her know

---

[27] Lewis, C. S. (2001). *Mere Christianity.* New York: HarperCollins Publishers.

that her feedback, although jarring at times, will help you excel as a wordsmith. This person can serve as your mentor, and all us of need one.

The better writers will seek out a variety of **mentors** and create an informal group of voices. Perhaps it's best not to go to the same well over and over, and this circle of readers may serve as an intermediate step between writing of the article and the publication of it. Or, your mentor may help you by reading your published work and offering ideas on improving it. Keep a notebook on yourself and your craft. Study the original and the edited version. What is different? Sometimes, your mentor will suggest that you gather more information, talk to additional sources, or add direct observation into your article. At other times, the article might need a different organization pattern or the tone might be off. The target moves and you must be ready to move with it.

Remember the Woody Allen 1977 film, *Annie Hall,* about a nervous romance? It began as a murder mystery film, but in post-production, the relationship between the two characters emerged as central to the movie, and it was pared down and reedited as a romantic comedy.

Your writing can be like that. You collect the **raw material**, the quotations, the background, the facts and statistics, the anecdotes and color, and build a feature article on anti-terrorism strategies in public schools. However, your mentor might see the information differently and suggest that you refashion the piece to explore the increasing demands on schoolteachers to assume yet another role in our society. The best attitude for writing is to remain teachable. It's not about education or number of articles published; it's about the audience. What works? Once you've penned your work of art, you might not have the distance to see the article differently than the draft that you submitted. For this reason, consider showing your mentor your article.

In some cases, writers **share articles** with each other. Writers who share mutual respect for each other can weigh in knowing that the criticism will be received with gratitude, not surliness. All of us know the chagrin that accompanies an article weak in spots, or worse, that contains odd spelling and awkward grammar. It hurts to see this creative work castigated with the silent and eternal edits, hemorrhaging with red ink. Yet the hurt heals because each time you study a mistake, you learn. Each time you learn, you grow as a writer, and this maturity finds its way into another article, then another, and soon you will be sharing ideas with your fellow writers. Embrace the process. You may not want to celebrate, but see the experience as yet another opportunity to become the writer you are destined to be. Mentors can be the subterranean route to getting published. In a way, you are selling the article first to a mentor and then to an editor.

WRITING GROUPS

Many writers find that mentoring can go on in a series of directions simultaneously. Like the salons of yesteryear, writers can gather for a monthly meeting and explore the good, the bad, and the ugly of each other's work. The process worked for C.S. Lewis and his Inklings in Oxford, and it will work for you. Many universities sponsor **writing groups** and some have websites that promote meetings and special speakers. The best writers' groups make a commitment to each other to read a colleague's work in advance of a meeting. Members show up with the copy marked, ready to share constructive criticism with a fellow writer.

This technique, like mentoring, is a step within the sell-it-first model. Some writers skip it altogether. Others feel drawn to kindred spirits and yearn for a time to commiserate and celebrate the often-turbulent life of a feature writer. Find what works best for you and repeat a line from the British Royal Navy's Lt. Horatio Hornblower of the C. S. Forester novels. Hornblower charged his crew, "Put your back into it!"

WRITERS' CONFERENCES

Writers' conferences are one of the best ways to **interact with writers and editors**. These venues allow writers of varying ability to interact with newbies and veteran writers. In a weekend, aspiring writers will learn about contracts, publication rights, publicity, rejection, and other topics encountered in the craft. The Internet lists conferences and a quick search using the keywords "writers' conferences" will provide a number of hits. The cost can be as little as $75 for a daylong event to nearly $300 for a five-day meeting. The classes are valuable; the interaction is priceless.

Here's the story of one writer's experience at a conference. Karen Langley of Zion, IL sent me this anecdote of her success following a writer's conference.

I heard you speak at the 2001 American Christian Writers' Conference in Ft. Wayne. I was a shy college sophomore, it was the first writers' conference I'd ever attended, and I felt a bit out of my league as one of only a few under-30 attendees. I looked back through my conference notes, and I see that you talked about "Writing for the Secular Press." Honestly, I don't remember much about that, but I do remember thinking your suggestions for how to approach newspaper editors seemed pretty bold, too bold for my timid personality, but how cool if it could be that easy to get published!

That summer, my family took our annual vacation trip to Ocean City, N.J. I'd thought before about writing an article about our family reunion, a 27-year traditional "Pizza Blast" at a boardwalk pizza parlor. I remembered your suggestions and figured I had nothing to lose. So one afternoon before heading to the beach, I rode a bike to the newspaper office. I asked the receptionist if the editor was in; she went down the hall and brought him out front; I told him my idea; he said he was interested. He gave me a deadline, a word count, and his phone number and said to call and let him know what time he could send out a photographer. So I interviewed my relatives and the pizza place owners, and wrote the story. A photographer came out and shot our family after the Pizza Blast (all 37 of us!), and I turned in my story along with a few pictures I'd taken (one of which appears with the story). I got a byline and my family has a nice memento of our reunion!

My article appeared in September 2001 in The Sure Guide. *Since then I've published about a dozen articles in national teen magazines, another dozen or so on the web [sic] and a few devotionals. So, the idea works!*

MAKING FRIENDS AT CONFERENCES

When I spoke at my first writers' conference, I met Cecil Murphey, a best-selling author who exudes warmth. He and I hit it off, and he remains a friend and confidante. These friendships are important to writers, who need ideas on moving their intent to write into action.

In the West is Glorieta Christian Writers' Conference, usually held in October near Albuquerque, NM. In the East is Sandy Cove Christian Communicators, scheduled in October near Baltimore, MD. The Mid-Atlantic Christian Writers' Conference often is held in late May. Classes are held at the headquarters in Asheville, NC, and points north and south. Workshops are where writers and journalists abound, and you can find one near your home by checking the Internet and using the search term "writers' conference."

INTERNSHIPS

College students nationwide have discovered that **internships** are as important as classroom training. More than half of all students who graduate took advantage of an internship while in college.[28] It works. It may amount to free labor, something most of us can't afford, but it is worth considering. Many of us offered our talents for free while we earned some bylines. The goal is to build a portfolio today. Don't wait. When your church or organization says it needs a feature article on the new president of the committee, a humorous article on the group's pet issue, or a listing of coming events, volunteer, but insist on a byline. Parlay that byline into another byline. Keep a list of these successes with the most recent listed first. Before long, the volunteer work will yield to deadline work. When a publication is facing a deadline, the editor is more likely to ante up a paycheck to accompany the byline.

Whether volunteering or working as an intern, the ideal situation is to be paid; however, some writers have found that the free labor can lead to a paying job. The other benefit is that you get to test-drive your secret passion. Is it really for you? Writing isn't about a leisurely wait when the mood strikes. It is about collecting information, studying videotapes, or poking into statistical surveys. It means getting to the scene, talking to people, and reading documents. It's work, hard, fulfilling work that engages the mind and body like no other activity.

Internships can last a few weeks or a few months, part time or full time, and can be formal situations with training sessions and performance reviews. However, you might have as much success by creating your own opportunity and asking an organization if

---

[28] Altschuler, G. C. (2002, April 14). A tryout for the real world, Interning is good for the resume. Better yet, it may get you hired. *The Chronicle for Higher Education*. p. 20.

you can work for it in a guided project. You supply the creativity and labor, and the organization will provide the structure to nurse the project into a success.

For formal internships aimed at students, consider *The Internship Bible* by Princeton Review. Colleges and universities monitor internships for their students but don't generally allow outsiders to see the openings. Among the benefits of writers' groups and writers' conferences is the network potential that can short-circuit these otherwise published internship possibilities. By asking friends and associates for help, you gain a degree of intimacy, and possibly a better opportunity of breaking into the job. Once you land the internship, it's crucial that you do the job that the organization wants accomplished before you try more meaningful work. After the experience, it's good form to stay in touch with the organization. They know that you have ambition, and all they need is an excuse to give you a chance to exercise your gifts.

A COLUMNIST ON MAKING THE SALE

To sell an article, a writer needs some good fortune and hard work, but mostly **hard work**. For columnist Don Feder, it amounts to reading, researching, and re-reading.

Feder was a *Boston Herald* editorial writer and syndicated columnist from June 1983 until June 2002, when he took a sabbatical. Feder has been published in the *Wall Street Journal*, *National Review*, *Human Events, Reason,* and *Reader's Digest*. His books include *A Jewish Conservative Looks at Pagan America* (1993) and *Who's Afraid of the Religious Right* (1996). Among Feder's suggestions for making the sale with a good article are:

- ☐ Diction. Select the right word. This part of the process might be the technique that is most difficult to promising writers.
- ☐ Work. "Good columns are paid off in sweat equity," Feder said. "It takes a time investment."

- ☐ Humor. Feder urged the writers to use gentle humor, adding, "Nothing makes a louder sound than a joke that falls flat."

- ☐ Read. Read history, current affairs, economics, and material that is opposed to the conservative view. In addition, the columnist said some of the best writing and thinking can be found in speeches and poetry. He cited the Sermon on the Mount, Shakespeare's funeral oratory by Mark Anthony in *The Tragedy of Julius Caesar,* Lincoln's "Gettysburg Address," Martin Luther King's "I Have a Dream" speech, and Peggy Noonan's work for Ronald Reagan where the president said the ill-fated Challenger astronauts "touched the face of God."

- ☐ Read some more. Read anthologies by columnists such as Chicago's Mike Royko, who refused to write for a Rupert Murdoch newspaper for this reason: "No self-respecting fish would be wrapped in a Murdoch newspaper!" Murdoch, the British media baron, is CEO of News Corp.

- ☐ Variety. Write whimsical prose. Write angry prose, but be ready to learn. "Don't be a Johnny One-Note," Feder said. "Don't always be angry or readers will think you are a crank and you tend to metamorphose into the Incredible Hulk."

- ☐ Surprise. Surprise readers by providing something unexpected, such as a magazine piece that Feder penned that discussed J. R. R. Tolkien of *Lord of the Rings* fame and his influence on C. S. Lewis, the greatest Christian apologist of the last century. "Tolkien was instrumental in Lewis returning to faith," Feder said. When columnists fail to surprise readers, their writing gets wooden, predictable. "Move readers by avoiding the steady stream of clichés," he said. "Keep it fresh." Too many columnists refer to Bashar al-Assad as Hitler, abortion as the modern Holocaust, and so on.

☐ Personal. Among anyone's best prose are the personal narratives that describe the devastation of a drug addict, a homeless addict, or the quiet pain of a mother whose son overdosed. To get these portraits, Feder told the audience to visit a meeting of Addicts Anonymous to gain the vital research, scan newspapers, create files, study LexisNexis, and search for authorities who can speak with credibility on topics.

EXERCISES

1) Visit the library and read six magazines with which you are unfamiliar and take lots of notes on the content, even the way the periodical is laid out.

2) Create a grid and record the number of quotations, the number of anecdotes, and the number of sources used in each article and note the magazine's approach to statistics.

3) Write an analysis on the periodical based on your research. Explain the editorial slant to yourself. Be a student of your craft. What is working? What isn't working?

4) Check the Web for the writers' guidelines for each magazine.

5) Conceive of a feature article idea for this magazine. Write a 100-word query letter. Think trends. What is hot now? Better yet, what will the next trend be?

6) Then write the first page of a made-up article using the proper format.

7) Look up the copyright provisions on the Internet for the U.S. Copyright Office in Washington, D.C.

Summary

It is dangerous to write without an assignment, and this chapter provided ideas on **selling the article first** before it is written. Some writers use email addresses or the telephone or both to contact an editor; however, many writers still use the old-fashioned approach of a query letter to make contact. A number of reference books such as the *Writer's Market* provide contact information. For a more personal approach, consider meeting as many editors in person as possible using a **road trip**. Once you land an assignment, the next step is to follow the protocol for submitting the work to garner as much goodwill as possible. In some cases, editors will mentor new writers on an informal basis. If possible, work with a more seasoned writer to learn as much as possible using writers' groups and writers' conferences. Above all, go to a writer's conference. Christian writers' conferences are held around the nation, as are other writer conferences. Invest the money, make new friends, and watch your success blossom.

Day 7

USING THE INTERNET

CHAPTER AT-A-GLANCE

Understanding terms associated with the Internet

Appreciating the need to check for accuracy

Perusing the best sites for writers

With a computer and Internet service, any writer can get a sense of the big story as part of her feature story. The problem with the Internet isn't too little information; it is a matter of overkill and, worse, deception that can prove embarrassing for the downy types.

Michael Gorman captured the zeitgeist of the Internet in the following observation:

> *The 'Net is like a huge vandalized library. Someone has destroyed the catalog and removed the front matter, indexes, etc. from hundreds of thousands of books and torn and scattered what remains . . . 'Surfing' is the process of sifting through*

this disorganized mess in the hope of coming across some useful fragments of text and images that can be related to other fragments. The 'Net is even worse than a vandalized library because thousands of additional unorganized fragments are added daily by the myriad of cranks, sages, and persons with time on their hands who launch unfiltered messages into cyberspace.
From September 15, 1995 in "The Corruption of Cataloging," *Library Journal*, 120, page 34.

The goal of this chapter is to acquaint a person who has little understanding of the Web with getting her bearings. For writers who have some understanding of the Internet, the first part of the chapter may be skimmed. For you, the main event is the dozens and dozens of sure-fire websites that will make you a writer of power. You will find information that only the most prolific researchers had available just a few decades ago. The chapter ends with my picks for the top 10 websites for writers and journalists. Netward!

TERMS

People often speak of the Internet and the World Wide Web as if the two were one and the same, but one refers to the hardware that supports this system and the other refers to the computer rules that allow users to go from site to site. The **Internet**, usually capitalized, is the plumbing, the pipes, the faucets, and the valves. It is a network of networks. The network consists of computers, the physical structure, where stored information can be accessed. Typically, organizations have computers called servers to form a network. The networks are linked to one another to form the Internet, a kind of global water system, but instead of fluid traveling through the pipes, it is information.

If the Internet is the plumbing, then the **World Wide Web** is the science that the system uses to operate. It includes the computer language and computer rules, called protocols, that allow users to connect from one network to another, to move the water, the information, from a distant place to your personal faucet. The Web uses hypertext links to go from one network to another. Each network contains its own content, words, graphics, and pictures, often referred to as **jpgs**, pronounced "jay pegs," or TIFF files. Some sites include movies, audio files, and other information that users can download, replay, or search using commands such as "word search."

BROWSERS AND OPERATING SYSTEMS

To begin using the Internet to find information on the World Wide Web, computers must have a software package loaded in it called a **browser**. **Browsers** allow users to search and view a website; browsers also allow users to create a website.

The computer world is bifurcated into personal computers (PC) such as the IBM-brand computer and clones, and Macintosh computers. Each has a different operating system, which means some of the instructions vary from computer to computer. However, when a user is searching the Net, often called surfing, the websites do not appear radically different on either a Macintosh or a PC. Nonetheless, the book states Safari and Firefox are the most common browsers. Not sure this is currently accurate.

SEARCHING THE INTERNET

Looking for information on the Internet may be compared to trying to find information in the public library. Many people like poking around, randomly going from stack to stack, and selecting a volume as the mood strikes. Others want a more systematic approach. Perhaps the best way to begin is to log onto the Internet, and open the browser on your computer.

The information at the top of the screen that begins **http://** is the beginning of a Web address. When an address is underlined on a web page, that is an indication that it is "hot," and can be "clicked" to drive the user to that website. The http:// address is known as a **Uniform Resource Locator**, or **URL**. Often, a user can type in a topic and guess what the Web page theme will be. If a user wanted information on a college, she would type the college name along with what is called the site designation, **.edu**, which is short for education, and the college's website may appear, like so: pba.edu. When speaking of this designation, users say "dot edu," as in visit me on the Web at "pba dot edu," and listeners are supposed to interpret the "dot edu" as ".edu."

Users must use caution in guessing the names of URLs because innocent-sounding names can result in some chagrined faces if the page that opens turns out to be suspicious content. It happens. I often shudder when I see a black background opening on my computer screen for fear that the content is not family-friendly. In some cases, these websites load more than one page, so extracting yourself by closing each page, sometimes called a frame, becomes a time-consuming chore. Filters, some free, are available to block unwelcome content. Unwanted emails also can be blocked.

A more systematic approach is to use a **subject directory** such as the one on Yahoo.com. This page allows users to type in a topic in an open area called the search field and look for that subject. The user could select "autos," click "enter" or "go," and let the computer search the World Wide Web for web pages on automobiles. The computer is looking for pages that have imbedded words, called **metatags**, into their pages to help people with their searches. When you type "autos," the browser searches for that metatag.

Search engines combine subject directories for a high-speed approach. This type of search tool is called a metasearch engine. **Dogpile.com**, for example, allows users to search several subject directories just by typing in one topic in the search field. The web pages that the computer finds will include a domain name, and, often, a country code. The domain name that is most common on the Internet is **.com**, which means the organization that is supplying the information, the host, is selling something. Other names may include the following and more:

Domain names
.edu–education
.gov–government
.org–organization
.mil–military
.net–network

Country codes
.au–Australia
.ca–Canada
.es–Spain
.uk–United Kingdom
.us–United States

For instance, the web page for Taylor University in Indiana is **www.tayloru.edu**. The "edu" tells the user that the host institution is involved in education. However, an organization that services journalism education such as Association for Education in Journalism and Mass Communication has the name **aejmc** and the web address of **www.aejmc.org.** "Org" tells the user that the web page is hosted by an organization, but it also tells you that the site isn't commercial. (From hence forward, I'll drop the quotation marks around the site names to help you remember the name.) Knowing the suffix can help you decide the mission of the organization, but .com doesn't necessarily mean that the site won't be unduly forthcoming on the trade-offs of products or services that they are promoting.

TIP: When using email, you can sometimes guess at the contact person for public information if he or she works in government. Ken Wheeler, a public relations expert in Portsmouth, VA, has this suggestion. Reporters and writers use public relations contacts for much of the background that they use. These people go by many names: public relations counselor, media relations director or communications spokesman; in government, however, these people often are known as public information officers or PIOs. To contact a PIO using email, use PIO and the following address formula. Use pio@ci.name of city. Abbreviation state name.us. "Ci" stands for city. For a contact in Portsmouth, for instance, use pio@ci.portsmouth.va.us. For a county, use "co" and the name of the county, and the abbreviation for the state as in pio@co.spalding.ga.us. In this case, the "ga" stands for Georgia. Use the U.S. postal abbreviations for names of states. This formula doesn't always work, but it's a useful idea that you can try when you are in a jam.

EVALUATE

Understanding the components of the URL can help you evaluate the web pages you find. For example, government information from the United States is generally considered by librarians to be some of the most reliable information on the World Wide Web. When you encounter the site name **.gov** and it is associated with the United States, you can be confident the facts are correct. Having praised Caesar, it's now time to offer a warning. Government sites typically support the administration's agenda; therefore, a **.gov** site should be evaluated in terms of the prevailing administration's point of view.

Don't be discouraged. A writer may offer an informed conclusion when crafting commentary or news opinion. In most cases, however, the writer must use the reportorial approach to writing, meaning all the salient information must be attributed to a source. When reporting information from a government web page, the best writers will cite the page. This practice tells the reader, listener, or viewer where the information originated, and the attribution gets the writer off the hook. If a writer suspects that the facts are woefully sloppy or inaccurate, more research must be done to avoid perpetuating false information. Finally, it's important that the writer follow up a web page by contacting the source either by email, U.S. Postal Service, or telephone to confirm the information. Too many writers are relying on web reports without resorting to old-fashioned fact checking. Double-check. Triple-check. The reputation you save may be your own. Believe me. A reviewer of one of my books gave me a sound editorial thrashing for misspelling a name of an editor from the nineteenth century. (Big sigh. Alas, I deserved it.)

GENERAL INTERNET SEARCH TOOLS

Typically **search engines**, special sites that take a user to specific web sites, include **subject directories**. Browsers allow users to save favorite websites under a pull-down menu for "favorites" or "bookmarks." If you are like me, you tend to find a search engine that you enjoy and never bother to check the others. However, if you browse through the following list and save a number of these sites as favorites to which to return, you will have an edge over most writers. Why? Because writers are always in a hurry. They can't take time to do too much background work, which is too bad, because editors delight in the unexpected morsel of odd information. They relish it. Some get so giddy that they leave their seats, dance a little soft-shoe, and hum to themselves. They are delighted when you make them smile in appreciation for the work you did. You work hard, so the editor (and reader AND viewer) can savor an easy smile. See? Experiment with these websites as you write your article, and you will be more creative, write better prose, and sell more copy! Trust me.

Caution. Too many writers find a site, save it, and then find that their list of favorites is too long to be helpful. In this case, it may be worth your while to create a web page of your own with categories for websites. Most online services or personal weblogs or blogs can be used to park frequently used website and other information. In addition to building an online identity, your personal website page can be loaded with tools to help you build a page of online sites that will help you succeed as a writer. You can group sites according to topics such as news services, fast facts, resources, and so on. Short of your own website, consider subdividing lists within your favorites list. Some browsers allow you to subdivide your favorite websites into categories to achieve the same kind of system that allows you easy access to sites that you will want to peruse again and again.

Subject directories include those ready-to-go topics, which are **clickable**, meaning that the user can click on the word or phrase and be taken to a series of sites. In addition, the subject directory provides a quick list of websites on a subject that the search engine has already compiled. The topics include sports, for instance.

More and more often, however, frequent users of the Internet prefer to pick their own topic for a search using a search engine. The sites below are search engines that use a search field where the user can type in a specific topic such as "early American furniture" and click "enter" or "go," and get a list of websites that are associated with that topic. Be advised.

Overlap exists and the findings may not differ markedly from one page to another.

Excite–http://www.excite.com
Google–http://www.google.com
HotBot–http://www.hotbot.com
Infoseek–http://www.infoseek.com
Lycos–http://www.lycos.com
Yahoo–http://www.yahoo.com

Many writers often begin their work with a Google search, or use a meta-search engine such as dogpile.com, the search engine that was mentioned earlier in this chapter. Search engines are said to **crawl** specified databases to retrieve documents relevant to your search terms. Directories consist of links to documents arranged by subject. For instance, **beaucoup.com** includes a directory of topics on computers, software, employment, society, geography, references, and arts and entertainment. Under government, it lists links to the White House, the United Nations, the World Bank, and more. Other sites of directories include (and all are preceded by **www**):

LookSmart.com
Galaxy.com
Infomine.com
Webcrawler.com

Keep in mind that the designation, **.com**, means that the site is commercial. You should expect to see advertisements on the page or surprises called "pop-up advertisements" as you use the service.

Metasearch engines, also known as multi-threaded search engines, combine some of the search engines above for a comprehensive search. In addition to **dogpile.com**, other metasearch engines are (and, again, all are preceded by **www.**):

MetGopher.com
SavvySearch.com

A reference for new words is **wordspy.com**, a page that lists new phrases entering the language.

BUSINESS AND FINANCE

For business sites, consider and find links to human resources and personnel, e-commerce such as credit card processors, insurance, telecommunications, travel, and real estate. **Bpubs. com** is a thorough index with categories for information on entrepreneurs, intellectual property, marketing, and much more. Often these websites are lowercase letters while others are not. For financial sites, **WhisperNumber.com** includes a free service that allows the user to log into lists of financial earnings and other financial information. Other financial sites include:

dailystocks.com
financialFind.com
tradingDay.com

GOVERNMENT

For government documents, peruse **searchgov.com**, which allows users to search for documents on the federal, state, and local level and access reports from independent agencies.

For political information and links to other sites on public policy, try **politicalinformation.com**.

At **Fedstats.gov**, users can see an alphabetical list of topics, arranged like the list at the end of this book. From the home page, users can select topics from A to Z. For the letter "C," the site listed Cancer and had the following:

Atlas of Cancer Mortality in the United States
   Breast
   Cervical
   Lung
   Mortality maps
   Prostate
Charitable trusts

And many, many more.

LAW

Among the chief business of government are public policy and the formulation of legislation for the state. For the individual interested in the legal terrain, in general, there's **FindLaw. com**. It lists legal subjects, legal careers, experts and consultants, and more. Under legal subjects, it contains an alphabetical list. Among the topics are:

   Accidents and Injuries
   Criminal Law
   DUI
   Employee Rights
   Family Law
   Real Estate
   Small Business

Law.com features news, a lawyer locator, and links to resources such as the dealmaker that includes information on the latest and the biggest deals, and information on financial deal statistics such as arbitrage.

At **Lawcrawler.findlaw.com**, users can find information on law schools, case law, U.S. law, U.S. federal case law, U.S. state case law, and forms such as sample contracts.

For writers who want to brush up on copyright issues, consider **copylaw.com** as a source for information on the use of material in the public domain and the idea of fair use among other considerations important to anyone who is a freelance writer.

EXPERTS IN GENERAL

Among the growing number of web sites that feature experts is "ExpertClick," which is among the best. It says it is, "Connecting experts with the news media."

TRUST AND VERIFY

As stated earlier, credibility is crucial in delivering information, whether hard news or soft feature news. I once wrote a feature article on household hints. Among them was an idea that I read about for recycling coffee grounds by adding them to plant soil. I used that idea in my feature article and only later tried the practice with my own indoor plants. As the article went to press, here's what I learned: Coffee grounds may be great for some outdoor plants, but they can create mold in some indoor plants. At the very least, my article should have warned readers of this possibility. Readers trusted me, and I let them down. Rather than repeat an idea from a source, I could have checked it out by interviewing a landscaper, a florist, someone at a plant nursery, or by conducting more research to verify that the coffee ground disposal technique I recommended worked without complications.

Trust and verify, President Reagan once warned the United States as he described his policy of missile disarmament with foreign powers. Be sure to evaluate the information, he urged. Good writers must evaluate information, using the criteria of authority or credibility of author, accuracy of information, objectivity or point-of-view, currency of information, and coverage or relevance of information.

Librarian Karen Robinson agrees with Reagan's mantra and instructs researchers to apply that principle to print and electronic sources, including the website's visual perspective. Is the page easy to read? Are the links clearly visible? Do the images add to the content? Do they download within a reasonable amount of time? These are questions that help a good writer assess the overall value of the site.

FULL-TEXT ARTICLES AND E-BOOKS

The quality of websites runs the spectrum from first-rate to lousy. For writers, the best sites direct a writer to background she needs with convenience. For many writers, the best sites are those that allow a user to access full-text articles from journals, magazines, and newspapers. Here are a couple of sites that can provide full-text copy.

The Gutenberg Project may be found at **Gutenberg. org**. This site contains full-text of books known as electronic books or e-books. Authors include Shakespeare, Arthur Conan Doyle, the Tarzan books of Edgar Rice Burroughs, and Alice's *Adventures In Wonderland* as told by Lewis Carroll, to name a few. The site features books published before 1923, a benchmark year for some copyright laws. Some web services charge to download books; others do not. The Gutenberg Project is free.

Digital library links can also be found at **http://www.wdl.org.** This website can be a little busy, but it allows users to find full-text books. It led me to The English Server web site at **http://eserver.org**, where I clicked books and found a listing including G. K. Chesterton's novel, *The Innocence of Father Brown* at **http://eserver.org/fiction/innocence.** A fun site for quotations is **justquotes.com.**

BOOKS AND REFERENCES

At **Bartleby.com**, another website that offers full-text books, writers can learn about good writing style using William Strunk Jr.'s *Elements of Style* at **www.bartleby.com/141.** This book is considered required reading for all serious writers. You will learn that possessive in "Charles's voice" is preferred to the missing "s" in "Charles' voice," and learn grammar with little pain. This site includes many reference works. For an encyclopedia on literary figures, for example, consider: **www.bartleby.com/67.**

JOURNALISM WEBSITES

The websites of many institutions, such as Palm Beach Atlantic University, include citation and writing tools. To use it, go to pba.edu. Some are available to the public, but like most university libraries, often a login and password are needed. Check with the university in your area to see if you can purchase privileges to use the online function.

American Journalism Review NewsLink provides access to newspapers around the nation and an employment list at **www.fair.org. Fairness and Accuracy In Reporting** reviews the political slant of coverage. It is a national media watch group and tends to criticize mainstream mass media at **www.fair.org**.

Editor & Publisher magazine's website is considered one of the best sources for journalists on issues affecting the press. It is located at http://www.editorandpublisher.com. Among its many features is a listing of full-time employment opportunities across the nation.

Society of Professional Journalists is one of the oldest and most respected journalism organizations in the nation. Its site provides news links and news on issues of interest to writers at **www.spj.org**.

POLITICAL INFORMATION

For political information, try think tanks such as **The Heritage Foundation** at **www.heritage.org** for conservative views, or **The Brookings Institute** at **brookings.edu,** which features more unconventional views. **The Cato Institute** conducts public policy analysis and may be found at **www.cato.org**. For information on the financial aspects of politics, try the following site, **www.opensecrets.org.** **The Hoover Institute** examines freedom and other issues associated with democracy. It is located at **www.hoover. org**.

REPORTING

Journalist's Toolbox features links to maps, shareware, health and medical sites, government information, and many more helps for aspiring writers. See http://www. journaliststoolbox.org, a website by Society of Professional Journalists.

Writer Websites

Writers can help other writers, and writing groups can be a place where ambitious ink spots pool their knowledge, critique each other's work, and provide all-important encouragement through a writer's group on the Internet. Many writers maintain a web page as part of their overall identity, called "branding," and use their pages to post ideas for others to peruse. These web pages often have links to resources and include announcements about writers' groups, writers' conferences, and other helpful ideas. For instance, author James Watkins has an author's site at **www.jameswatkins.com.** To build traffic, Jim offers an exclusive list of references for anyone who receives his weekly columns via email. The exclusive reference page includes links to fellow ink writers. The sites often include ideas on getting published.

This site provides some practical ideas on breaking into print and suggests that writers browse a bookstore for ideas. Riddle also offers his own list of websites for freelance writers. The one that has provided him the most writing opportunities is **www.craigslist.org**. This site provides free classified advertisements. The area that is of interest to writers is labeled "writers and editors," or may be under arts, media, and design. In addition, opportunities for "education writers" may be listed under "education." The site is freshened up daily, and the classified advertisements are arranged by metropolitan area.

JournalismJobs.com is another site for journalists and freelance writers. This site features links to events, writing, reporting, and editing jobs for print, broadcast, and online. It includes articles and links to periodicals, including student newspapers. (Although the website is written with capital

"Js," it isn't necessary to capitalize the "j" to access the site, so **www.journalismjobs.com** will work fine.)

A similar site for freelance writers is **freelancewrite. about.com**, which has a fair amount of commercial content, but delivers nonetheless. It contains articles such as *How to Make Money as a Writer* and links to jobs, grant writing, even greeting card writing.

For publishing information, consider Sally E. Stuart's website at **www.stuartmarket.com** for lists of periodicals and book publishers. Each year Stuart publishes the **Christian Writer's Market Guide** through Shaw Books, and it is considered the best source for publishing in the inspiration press.

For background and information on film, including the names of characters and casts along with plot summaries, visit the Internet Movie Database at www.imbd.com.

SOURCES OF A GENERAL NATURE

Need an almanac, dictionary, encyclopedia, or an atlas? Try **infoplease.com**. This site provides reference helps, but it contains a few pop-up advertisements that can interfere with your search. For the dictionary reference, I typed in "vita" and the computer presented a number of phrases with that word, including cur•ric•u•lum vi•tae *Pronunciation:* (ku-rik'yu-lum vI'tE, vE'tI; *Lat.* kOOr-rik'oo-loom" wE'tI), —*pl. cur•ric•u•-la vitae Pronunciation:* (ku-rik'yu-lu vI'tE, vE'tI; *Lat.* kOOr-rik'oo-lä" wE'tI). [key]

> 1. *Also called vita, vitae. a brief biographical résumé of one's career and training, as prepared by a person applying for a job.*
> 2. *Latin. The course of one's life or career.*

Another valuable source for writers is a timeline that focuses on highlights from years past. For the year 1900, for instance, the U.S. population was 76 million people, Henri Matisse led the Fauvist movement in painting, and Austrian psychiatrist Sigmund Freud published *The Interpretation of Dreams*. The site includes detailed information under each topic, including a note that the term "Fauvism" is from French meaning wild beast, and this movement yielded to Cubism.

Bigchalk.com can be a worthy tool for writers. It is designed for children and youth, but it can help writers obtain full-text articles. Users must register, and a trial service is available. However, many public libraries use this site, making the cost of a full-text search of a database amount to the expense of a library card and a visit to your community's best place for research—the library. A trend these days is for young students to do research at a bookstore. If the bookstore managers only knew that those young people are doing their homework when they browse. Perhaps a business opportunity exists in that environment. For the rest of us, the library allows books and lots of electronic databases that will give you full-text articles.

Bartelby.com is the place for the hard-to-find quotation. Remember that great line, "I'm sorry to have written such a long letter, but I didn't have time to write a shorter one?" Who said it? George Bernard Shaw. This site may help with those kinds of connections, but it takes some time to search; nonetheless, it features an electronic version of *Bartlett's Quotations* and dozens of other reference books.

For reference information, try **www.refdesk.com** for fast, family-friendly information without advertisements. It has search areas for a dictionary, thesaurus, headlines, links to commentary by dozens of opinion writers, sports writers, and more, the word of the day, links to TV networks and the Daily Writer's Almanac, and a site that provides inspiration for new and veteran writers. It has a link to a free IRS tax preparation service, a white page telephone directory, and a reverse white page directory, where users can obtain telephone information from a street address.

As an experiment, I used **refdesk.com** to see what I could find for an explanation for A.D. and B.C. and found a good summary on A.D., Anno Domini, the year of our Lord, and the preferred use of B.C.E., Before the Common Era. B.C.E. is a usage that more accurately reflects the Western calendar with a sense of scholarship.

When interviewing an author of Christian books, try **Christianbook.com/html/authors/index.html/98320402.** This site provides an alphabetical listing of many authors and background on each.

For information on the top 150 best-selling books, try **www.usatoday.com/life/books/top-50.htm**. The list examines a book for this week's sales and last week's sales. Some titles include links to the books; most do not.

For a review of the trends in books for Christian audiences, try the entire online issue of *World* magazine at: **www.worldmag.com.**

For book reviews in general, the *New York Times* on the Web is a reliable source. It once required users to provide a login and password, but it appears to be a free service these days with pop-up advertisements.

For writers, one website that is sure to provide quality is the online site of the writer's magazine, *Publisher's Weekly*, at **www.publishersweekly.com.** This website covers the business side of publishing, an area that you might want to monitor to have that insider feeling. Other good writer sources include **www.writersdigest.com** and **www.writersmarket.com**, two sites that cater to the professional writer. Professional does not have to mean a writer who has published hundreds of articles. The articles are aimed at writers who are growing in their craft.

From time to time, a writer needs to know the day of the week from a distant year. **Perpetual Calendar** can help. This resource, as much of interest to academics as anyone, is at http://www.infoplease.com/calendar.php and allows users to select the year and determine the date. Want to know the day of the week for February 21 in the year 1955? Change the year to 1955 on this website, and you will find out that February 21, 1955, fell on a Monday.

Need to look up a name in a community newspaper? Try: **newspaperarchive.com**. It appears to have access to Midwestern newspapers primarily, but it can be a valuable source for a name search, particularly family history. For the more prominent person, try **www.s9.com/biography.** This site allows the user to locate a well-known person and obtain some modest background. A search of "Michael Smith" located the astronaut who died in the Challenger space tragedy.

A search engine that combines the commercial site of Amazon with a partner is **archive.org,** one of the Web's best kept secrets. Confused by all those worldwide agencies that find their way into news articles? Try the following website: **www.cia.gov.** From this page sponsored by the Central Intelligence Agency, you can access the **World Factbook**. When I reviewed an academic book on the press in Nicaragua, I brushed up on that country's history using a list from the World Factbook. The summary listed the country's geography, people, government, economy, communications, transportation, military, and transnational issues. The flag of the country also is included, with facts about elected officials.

From time to time, you will be required to know the value of money from country to country. The Universal Currency Converter provides accurate rates at a website: **www.xe.com/ucc.** I entered 10 for United States dollars and learned that in 2015, $10 was equal to 8.93 Euros and 6.48 British pounds. Naturally, these figures fluctuate constantly, all the more reason to save or **bookmark** the page to have ready access to conversion figures. It provides conversions for South Korean won, Sudanese dinars, Mexican pesos, Japanese yen and many other currencies.

As a writer, you are a curious person who initiates conversations with strangers, looks beneath tables, and takes notice of the books on a person's desk. (Ever look in someone's medicine cabinet?) In short, you're part of a peculiar people. At times, that curiosity can be satisfied when writing about technology and science using **www.howstuffworks.com.** This web page has animation on how an engine works and articles on how ATM machines operate, the background of aerosol cans, the delights of an electric dimmer switch, and more. The page may stimulate you as you think of ideas for articles.

Occasionally, you will need to find information on medical issues. The **www.webmd.com** website provides a search function for topics within the website, or the search can be sent to the web or another medical website. This medical site contains news articles on aging, diseases, and preventive medicine. Like all websites, it is not a substitute for interviewing an expert, but it may acquaint you with enough information to help you understand an issue as you collect information from a source. When using information from an Internet site, treat it as you would information from a publication. Cite the source and check it for accuracy. Never lift a quotation or a statistic from a website and drop it into your article without citing it. Why? Two reasons. One, courtesy. Someone did the work to put that information on the site, and she deserves recognition. Two, if the information is inaccurate, you are responsible for disseminating an error. That is the last action that you want to take as a writer. Be accurate. That's a noble calling, and you are worth the effort.

The website above is considered one of the best, but medical information, in particular, is problematic and should be verified over and over. One of the top medical frauds of the decade concerns AIDS. At **www.quackwatch.org**, users can read about the claims and use this information as they conduct interviews. According to this website, "Victims of incurable diseases are especially vulnerable to the promises of charlatans. AIDS is a prime example. Underground or 'guerrilla clinics' offering homemade treatments have sprung up in the United States, the Caribbean, and Europe." The site cautions readers to view cures with skepticism.

Not long ago, a magazine assigned me to write about a professional baseball player, easy enough. The hard part of doing an article on a public figure is characterizing the wealth associated with the person, an element that might or might not be important to your audience. In my case, I contacted the National Baseball League and asked what the average starting salary was for a first baseman. That worked. How about ordinary people such as bankers or somewhat unusual vocations such as acting? Try: **www.salary.com**. This site, which sells resume-writing services among other services, provides a guide on average salaries for a job in a specific geographical area. In addition, it offers advice, self-tests, and other helps on careers and earnings. The site could be helpful for you as you prepare for an interview or write an article on cost of living, unemployment, job creation, job losses, and so on.

SCAMS, URBAN LEGENDS, AND THE PARANORMAL

A website that helps you do background on scams is **www. scambusters.com.** The site monitors Internet hoaxes and urban legends and had the following report:

Urban Legend #3

*On Saturday, 24 January 1998, Naval Air Station, Joint Reserve
Base, New Orleans' Quarterdeck, received a telephone call from an
individual identifying himself as an AT&T Service Technician who
was running a test on our telephone lines. He stated that to complete
the test the QMOW should touch nine (9), zero (0), pound sign
(#) and hang up. Luckily, the QMOW was suspicious and refused.
Upon contacting the telephone company, we were informed that by
using 90#, you end up giving the individual that called you access
to your telephone line, and allow them to place a long-distance
telephone call, with the charge appearing on your telephone bill.
We were further informed that this scam has been originating from
many of the local jails/prisons. Please 'pass the word.'*

Scambusters.com reported, "Strangely enough this story
does have some truth to it. BUT it only works on telephones
where you have to dial 9 to get an outside line AND the system
allows you to make a long-distance call once you've gotten
that outside line." To use all the features of this site, a login and
password are required.

For similar information on those slightly eerie bits of urban
drama, you might want to experiment with **www.snopes.
com**. Snopes.com covers entertainment, among other issues,
and recently reported the following song trivia as true.

Amazing Grace
*Having survived a horrific storm, a slave trader promptly gave
up his livelihood, became a Christian, and penned the hymn
Amazing Grace in thanksgiving.*

The order of events may be off, but the gist of that Snopes.
com report is true; however, the following is false, although the website reported it as true. In 2015, the website

reported Bob Dylan didn't steal the song *Blowin' in the Wind* from a New Jersey high school student.

According to Scott Marshall, the rumor is untrue. Marshall wrote *Restless Pilgrim: The Spiritual Journey of Bob Dylan* with Marcia Ford, published by Relevant Media in Lake Mary, FL, in 2002. Marshall said, "For the record, Dylan, as a 20-year-old in the early days of 1962, penned *Blowin' in the Wind* himself." According to Marshall, Dylan said, "It was just another song I wrote and got thrown into all the songs I was doing at the time. I wrote it in a cafe across the street from the Gaslight [Cafe in Greenwich Village]. Although I thought it was special, I didn't know to what degree, I wrote it for the moment, ya' know. I remember running into Peter of Peter, Paul, and Mary on the street, after they had recorded it. 'Man,' he said, 'you're going to make $5,000.' And I said 'What? Five thousand dollars?' Five thousand dollars, it seemed like a million at the time. He said, 'It's amazing, man. You've really hit it big.' Of course, I'd been playing the song for a while anyway and people had always responded to it in a positive way to say the least. Money was never a motivation to write anything. I never wrote anything with 'this-is-gonna-be-a-hit or this-isn't-type of attitude.' I'm not that smart anyway."[29]

Again, this kind of information must be checked and re-checked, but snopes.com can be one of the sites that you use on your quest for accuracy.

In the ruthless pursuit of accuracy, sites such as **www. csicop.org** can help with scientific explanations of the paranormal. The site is hosted by the Committee on the Scientific Investigation of the Claims of the Paranormal.

---

[29] From Cameron Crowe, who interviewed Dylan about the individual songs that appeared on *Biograph*, a 5-record compilation (now 3 CDs) filled with Dylan originals. Crowe's work appeared in the 1985 liner notes to *Blowin' in the Wind*, New York: CBS.

U.S. CENSUS INFORMATION

As stated earlier, the government provides some of the best information. The U.S. Department of Commerce provides census figures at **www.census.gov.** This website is rich for mining feature stories. I chose a link for "Quickfacts" but an "Interactive Map" was available too. I quickly learned that North Carolina's population is about 9.8 million people based on a 2013 estimate. I learned that in 122,200-resident Harnett County where I once lived, it takes on average 28 minutes for commuters to get to work, and the per capita income was $20,039, compared to state average of about $25,285.

INVESTIGATIONS

Reporters and writers do the job of so many other like-minded people. We do sleuthing using many of the techniques of law enforcement, even private investigators. For the would-be P.I.s is the website **Virtualgumshoe.com.** This site has a fun feel, but it links to some powerful searches with the added bonus that the hot buttons on the left remain while you use the main window for a search. For instance, from the categories on the left side of the homepage is **FAQ,** or frequently asked questions. Under this page is a link to U.S. Vital Records, where a user can search birth, death, marriages, and other records. The topics include adoption resources, archives, area codes, and zip codes, associations, and attorneys. And, that's just the As. The page has links to missing persons, sex offenders, gangs, cults, fraternities and sororities, and more.

Two sites that are sometimes frightening for revelations of personal information are **www.anywho.com** and **switchboard.com.** Both allow users to obtain maps, telephone numbers, and other information using a reverse directory. When the street name is known or some other information, a writer can sometimes find the crucial telephone number that she needs. To contact a neighbor of a source for a slightly different viewpoint on the topic in a news story, for instance, the reverse telephone directory is handy.

PUBLIC OPINION POLLS

Among the best sources for reliable polling information is **www.pollingreport.com.** It provides up-to-date information on the State of the Union in the United States, elections, and trends.

Another source for public opinion polls is from a troika of information heavyweights —TODAY/CNN/Gallup Poll. It is: **www.usatoday.com/news/poll001.htm.**

A polling mine on spiritual concerns is sponsored by Barna Research Online and may be found at **www.barna.org**. It lists topics on beliefs, the Bible, church attendance, money, religious differences, family, and others. This site reflects George Barna's interest in religion, and the public opinion surveys often examine some aspect of Christianity.

ELECTRONIC DATABASES

Electronic databases often are subscription based, and too expensive for the ordinary person. Nonetheless, many public libraries and university libraries allow guests to access this information.

Factiva is a Dow Jones electronic database and users must pay to access it. Some college and university libraries have this service, **global.factiva.com**, and may allow guests to use it to search full-text articles in magazines and newspapers. An even better full-text electronic database is **LexisNexis**, but it is very expensive. For most of us, it is only available at good college libraries at **web.lexis-nexis.com**. It features "Comprehensive resources for business, news, politics and government, medical information, legal information, case law, U.S. and state codes, biographical information, and accounting and tax information."

ASSOCIATIONS

Associations such as groups dedicated to horseback riding to disability issues, and just about any pet cause of any kind abound in the United States. For example, enter the name "Mark Twain," and you will find a site for the Mark Twain Boyhood Home Association in Hannibal, MO; Mark Twain House in Hartford, CT; the Mark Twain Democratic Club in Whittier, CA; an appreciation society in New York City; and two Mark Twain Foundations.

In addition to ordinary brick-and-mortar offices, these lobbying organizations have web pages and live to interact with reporters and writers. Gale Group publishes a reference available at most public libraries, *Encyclopedia of Associations, An Association of Unlimited References.*[30] However, many libraries also have the online version known as **Associations Unlimited.** This electronic database allows users to conduct a custom search on a keyword that they pick. It can lead you to groups that advocate positions on topics for which you are writing. This publication remains a favorite of journalists because it points writers to sources that are well informed and articulate about a topic. Often these sources will send you press packets of background, photographic slides, fact sheets, maps, graphics, and other useful information in their attempt to get their side of the issue publicized. All of Gale's publications are one of the writing industry's best-kept secrets, and now you know!

---

[30] Hedbland, A. (2003). *Encyclopedia of Associations, an association of unlimited references.* New York: Gale Publishing.

The online version has a number of ways to access information. For instance, by typing the word "bells" into the association name blank, the directory provided the names of organizations that deal with bells. One organization is known as AIDS Memorial Bells and included an address in Largo, FL. However, Bells of the Lakes listed a U.S. postal address and email address along with the number of members, the president's name, the amount of dues, its budget, and this description: "Music and education through the media of hand bells."

Gale Group also produces these reference works:

Biography and Genealogy Master Index
Contemporary Authors
Gale Database of Publications and Broadcast Media.

MY TOP 10

At this point, you are thinking, "Ah, too many websites exist out there!" To narrow it down a bit, here are my personal top 10 favorites, in no particular order. We've tried to give you top-quality web sites in this chapter. Be advised. Websites come and go. It's called link rot. For now, the following were helpful in 2014.

1) **Theskimm.com** is an email newsletter of the top stories sent to you daily.
2) **Associations Unlimited** for names of lobbying groups or advocacy groups in this subscription-only electronic database. It's available at universities and colleges and some public libraries.
3) **Barna.org** for public opinion polling information on spiritual issues.
4) **Bartelby.com** for quotation help.
5) **Thestudentnewsdaily.com** provides current events and a weekly example of media bias.

6) **LexisNexis** for full-text articles in this subscription-only electronic database. It's available at college libraries at **web.lexis-nexis.com/universe**.

7) **Refdesk.com** for reference help.

8) **Pbs.org/mediashift/** for news about multimedia reporting.

9) **Scambusters.com** for fun content on urban legends.

10) **Virtualgumshoe.com** for searches of public records.

Bonus: For coverage of millennials, use Mic.com, which says "Mic's approach to news is as unique as our generation. We're founded on a simple idea: Young people deserve a news destination that offers quality coverage tailored to them. Our generation will define the future. We are hungry for news that keeps us informed and helps us make sense of the world."

SUMMARY

Freelance writing coach Norm Rohrer used to urge his followers on with the command, "Onward." The word is packed with power and optimism. It suggests energy unleashed. That is the idea of "Netward." You now have the web sites to access the best information, but you'll have to do the work. And you'll have to do the other important tasks of interviewing sources and observing for graphic details that can transform limp prose into bold writing. From today forward, use the Internet every time you write an article. Set a goal of finding one drab bit of information that makes you smile. If it makes you say, "Wow," "No kidding," or "Man," then probability is in your favor that others will say the same. Netward!

Repetition and the odd angle are among the considerations in composing your photograph.

Bonus
Extra Day

EIGHT HABITS OF HIGHLY EFFECTIVE PHOTOGRAPHERS

CHAPTER AT-A-GLANCE

- Enhancing your freelance income with photography
- Mastering the habits of good composition
- Thinking visually as you write

Writers tend to be poets at heart. They feel deeply, and use words to circle a thought, then creep up on it and sometimes actually capture it. The best writers speak for all of us, and say what we feel and think, but in powerful, memorable ways. Taking a photograph is to seize the mood, an idea, a feeling, an issue, all of which are involved in producing a winning feature, but as a visual representation. For the freelance writer and journalist, producing a quality image may mean doubling your paycheck. When done well, the photograph tells a story. It's a visual narrative that uses facial expressions, light, actions, and more to provoke a mood, a feeling that moves an audience to identify, to question, to pause, to feel at peace.

These days, publications and online services are as concerned with the art elements as they are the article, and you might be able to double your money by submitting a photograph that assists you in telling the story. Editors need graphic art, line art, infographics, tables of statistics, maps, and, most of all, pictures that can accompany the words of your article.

This chapter will explore a step-by-step approach to taking good quality photographs. By applying the eight timeless principles suggested in this chapter, you will be equipped to see the photograph that is required for the article and bring it to market. These ideas will work whether you are using a **disposable camera**, a **35mm camera**, which uses film and a developing process, or a **digital camera**, which uses a storage disc, or even a smartphone. Each camera has its trade-off, but the digital approach allows you to ship your art from your computer to an editor's computer without delay using the Internet. Whatever format you use, the goal is to tell a gripping story with words and pictures to move your audience, to help people see the wonder of life in all its tragedy and joy. The primary goal is to consider composition principles to improve the art you submit with your article.

HABIT 1 OF HIGHLY EFFECTIVE PHOTOGRAPHERS: MOVE IN.

The theme of this chapter is **composition**, the way the parts of the picture are arranged. For most photographers, getting close to the subject can enhance composition, your first step in becoming a highly effective photographer. For our purposes, most of your photographs will be of people, and your editor will want to see the person's face—not her back, but her face. Think head and shoulders for a photograph of a single subject. For now, concentrate on taking the photograph about four to five feet from your subject. That task alone will keep you busy. Call it the **triple F rule**, the four-to-five-feet rule.

Black Star picture agency began in the 1930s taking photographs of the world's hot spots. A 1997 review of their work from more than six decades in Hendrik Neubauer's *Black Star: 60 Years in Photojournalism* (Koln: Konemann), shows hundreds of graphic still photographs—and all are of people engaged in dramatic moments. Audiences want to see the **person's face**. A close-up of a hand or jewelry can work, but most publications want to see your subject's face. You will become a highly effective photographer with the practice of photographing a solid close-up shot of the person's face. As you gain confidence, ask your subject to avoid posing, and let him or her talk or show some kind of facial reaction. Let the subject react to your question and wait, pause just a beat or two, and allow the subject to laugh, look puzzled, express sadness, and so on.

Most of all, however, get the person's face, either as a three-quarter profile or by allowing the person to face the camera head-on. Take a photograph of the person looking at the camera; next take a photograph of the person facing forward, but not looking at the camera. Depending on the goal of the article, the eyes-forward or eyes-away look will take the day. In most cases, the portrait approach of the subject caught in a casual moment is the pose your audience will appreciate most.

When using digital or disposable cameras, be aware of getting too close. Four feet is about as close as a photographer can get with those cameras. In summary, practice the triple F rule for the shot that is most likely to be used with your article.

Habit 2 of highly effective photographers: Monitor the background and the foreground.

Highly effective photographers look at all parts of the photograph and see life through a rectangle, a **frame**. Better photographers see the clutter in a photograph, particularly the background, and next, the foreground. You now know to get close to your subject; next, monitor the background behind the subject's head. Beware of the painting on the wall, the stray light from another light source, or the busy traffic of the nearby street. The best background is a blank wall or a solid color background. Make your subject the **focal point** of the photograph.

Another issue associated with backgrounds and foregrounds is the idea of framing. Windows and doorways can be used to frame your subject, meaning the shape of the opening works like a picture frame to draw the viewer's eye to the focal point. Look for these **natural frames** as you take your photograph. A limb on a tree works to frame the top of your photograph when you are working outside.

Tip: When shooting outdoors, try to keep your subject in the shade and use the flash to provide what is known as **spot flash** to flatter your subject. Avoid taking shots when the sun is at its zenith to avoid harsh shadows. For the best light, consider shooting a color photograph at sunrise or sunset when the amber rays of the sun cast the warmest light. Be advised, however, this light fades within a few minutes.

Getting close to your subject might not be difficult, but finding an uncluttered background might take some work. Get in the habit of moving around to eliminate distractions. Try getting higher than the subject's head by standing on a sturdy piece of furniture and looking down on the subject. By contrast, try kneeling and looking up toward your subject. Select the angle that works best. As a last resort, have your subject move. With some creativity, however, the photographer can get close and avoid a busy background by adjusting the angle, the direction of the camera shot.

Keep in mind that the camera vision is different from your vision. The human eye can zero in on an object and ignore the objects that are unimportant. A camera sees all the objects the same, forcing the photographer to visually point the audience in the right direction. The most obvious way to direct your audience's attention to the subject matter is by reducing the number of elements in the photograph, thereby making the subject matter clear to us.

Once you begin getting close to the subject and looking at the background, you can begin to experiment with more dramatic approaches. At first, concentrate on the triple B rule: Background, background, background. Using the triple F and triple B rule will give the FB, **foolproof beauty**.

HABIT 3 OF HIGHLY EFFECTIVE PHOTOGRAPHERS: LOOK AT SHAPES AND LINES.

The doorway works as a picture frame in a photograph, but it also can be thought of as a **shape**, a rectangle. It is one of the many shapes found in man-made environments, or in nature. A student's desk may be square; a book, a rectangle; a clock, a circle; and a lampshade, a triangle. Natural and man-made objects can be reduced to shapes and boards, bricks and shadows can be thought of as lines. As you compose your photograph, consider the shapes and lines to arrange them in a pattern. Remember, as a photographer, you must move around to compose the picture inside the frame. Look for lines that lead the viewer's eye to your subject. **Leading lines** are one of the best composition principles of good photographers.

HABIT 4 OF HIGHLY EFFECTIVE PHOTOGRAPHERS: LOOK FOR THE Z PATTERN, OR THE S PATTERN.

Among the most pleasing patterns to the human eye is the shape of an "**S**," and the shape of a "**Z**." In each case, the line curves from either left to right or right to left. In the rectangle represented by the frame in a camera, the S or Z is a way to allow the eye to move from top to bottom in the frame. The mind sees the line and intuitively traces it throughout the photograph.

Winding country roads work as S patterns. Mountain ranges work as Z patterns. A series of clouds can create an S or Z pattern; even the gangway on a ferryboat can make the pattern. The playground equipment may imitate an S or Z. A rope, a walkway, or a driveway can do the same. Fabric, jewelry, and other objects also may be arranged in an S or

Z pattern. Force yourself to look for these patterns, and you will create a photograph that others will enjoy and be drawn to your words.

HABIT 5 OF HIGHLY EFFECTIVE PHOTOGRAPHERS: LOOK FOR CONTRASTS: WINNER-LOSER, BIG-SMALL, LIGHT-DARK.

Contrasts often help tell a story. Imagine a photograph of an athlete who is jubilant in victory with her hands stretched over her head, but beside her is her defeated opponent, shoulders slumped, holding back the tears. That's a contrast.

HABIT 6 OF HIGHLY EFFECTIVE PHOTOGRAPHERS: USE THE RULE OF THIRDS.

The viewing area in the viewing frame of a camera can be reduced to a kind of tic-tac-toe board with lines dividing the area of the frame into three equal parts, both horizontally and vertically.

According to the rule of thirds, the subject of the photograph works best by placing him or her where the lines intersect. The rule says that a major element placed at one of their junctions will create the more dynamic picture. Usually, you will have to impose the imaginary lines on the viewing area and move yourself around to put your subject either to the top left, bottom left, top right, or bottom right. However, sometimes the lines occur in nature, and you can use them to guide your composition. For instance, horizons could be on one of the horizontal lines just above or below the center of the frame.

Practice putting the subject of the shot in one of the corners of a kind of tic-tac-toe pattern to create a pleasing composition.

Avoid placing the subject in the center of the frame. In photography, the sweet spot tends to be **off-center**, not the bull's-eye. Place the subject where the imaginary lines of the thirds intersect, and your art will begin to have a professional feel about it, and your editor will remember you fondly.

HABIT 7 OF HIGHLY EFFECTIVE PHOTOGRAPHERS: LOOK FOR REPEATED PATTERNS

Anyone who decorates knows the benefit of repeating a pattern in the rug, sofa, and other areas in a living area. The use of a similar-colored wood or a stand of various sizes of candles creates a cozy feel to a room. As you dress, you think colors and fabrics. Corduroy goes well with cotton but might appear odd next to a satin sports coat. Khakis and leather might match, but black trousers with a dark navy, nearly black turtleneck might not look good together.

The best composition uses **repeated patterns** for a well-balanced feel. The patterns can be dramatic, such as a checkered pattern on a floor, on a pillow, and in your subject's shirt; however, the better patterns are subtler and have the power of a whisper over a shout.

HABIT 8 OF HIGHLY EFFECTIVE PHOTOGRAPHERS: SATURATE THE SCENE WITH A VARIETY OF SHOTS.

In **saturation photography**, a highly effective photographer takes a series of photographs from long range, middle range, and close up. Habit 1 of highly effective photographers taught you to move in; now you might want to consider two other angles. The idea is that your editor might want to show a panoramic view, a long shot. To play it safe, it's good form to take a long shot.

The long shot provides lots of visual detail, but notice how small the subject might appear. That's the trade-off in these kinds of photographs. In general, it's a good practice to keep your subject's head about the size of a quarter.

In the long-range photograph and the medium-range photograph, the photographer dropped to one knee to shoot the subject's face straight on. Most people shoot photographs from eye level. For a novel effect, consider getting very low or very high. Lie down and shoot a photograph from the worm's eye view; then take the same photograph from the bird's eye view. The results will surprise you, and, more importantly, your editor.

By submitting a series that includes the long shot, medium shot, and close-up shot, your editor will have a choice in layout. This choice will provide a variety of design solutions to play the article. The saturation approach can only improve the chances of your work getting published.

You now know the eight habits of highly effective photographers. These ideas can be summed up with the three **C**'s:

1) Choose a strong focal point.
2) Close in on your subject.
3) Capture the moment.

SUMMARY

You're ready. You know about good composition and the eight habits of highly effective photographers. You've read the eight chapters on beginning your article and developing it. It's time to set a goal. You are on your way to a byline and paycheck. You are a writer. Discipline yourself today to do some writing and leave the world better for your efforts. Onward!

Bonus Material

The following are columns and essays by seasoned writers who have compressed a lifetime of meaningful experience with prose in an accessible way to help you excel as a wordsmith.

Building relationships of worth as a journalist

By Stephanie Bennett

What's the difference between becoming an excellent journalist and one who is mired in mediocrity? Clearly, the answer to that question is multi-dimensional, but when it comes to good reporting, there's no substitute for finding solid sources that are cooperative and reliable. Once found, you're only halfway there. It isn't always easy to land an interview or get a quote on the record. To increase your chances of success, it's important to cultivate strong relationships with your sources, and that starts . . . in your head.

First, remember that your source is a person, not just a quote. That doesn't mean you get emotionally involved with her, but it does mean she deserves to be treated with respect. So, word one resonates with Aretha Franklin: *R.E.S.P.E.C.T.* It's a good starting place.

When you respect someone, you do not stalk, bulldoze, or strong-arm her. You simply give an opportunity to answer a few questions and you make her as comfortable as possible.

Next, the importance of establishing simple rapport must not be underestimated. Rapport is what communication researchers refer to simply as the "likeability factor." It is extremely important if a journalist wants to "get a story" and get it right. Countless interpersonal cues take place in an interview, some of which fall into the nonverbal realm. In many cases, nonverbal communication represents as much as 93 percent of the exchange. What does this mean to you?

Many sources will simply refuse to speak with a journalist who appears gruff and grimacing. Smile! No need exists to become a jolly comedy act, but a simple smile is welcoming and will help a source feel safe. As important as facial expression is to establish positive affinity, it is even more essential to maintain proper eye contact. (No staring, please.) Whether intentional or not, we send a message with every movement. When we refuse to look at someone in the eyes, we send a strong message of avoidance. Physical proximity is part of this dynamic as well. Stand close enough so that your source can see you are a human being, but not so close that you invade her personal space.

This point leads to the third and final way to build relationship with your source, and that is establishing trust. Our fast-paced world of mobile communication may make quick quotes possible, but rapid-fire responses and missing nonverbal communication cues can create havoc when it comes to building trust. Thankfully, people are becoming a bit more careful about what they write or say—at least the savvy ones are.

Twitter, Instagram and SnapChat have accelerated the scandal factor, and with the emergence of viral videos that plow through the entire media landscape, sources may be more skeptical. This observation may be particularly evident if a past quote was poorly edited or misinterpreted. When this happens, your source might hedge, equivocate, or try to avoid you altogether. The key to cooperation is drilling down to the interpersonal level. Make a personal visit; give her a call; reach out in ways that do not breach her private space, but also let her know you're not a hack.

Respect, rapport, and trust; these three are like jewels in a crown. Once they are yours, the important job of the journalist takes on a whole new luster.

Word gets around.

Stephanie Bennett, Ph.D. is a professor of Communication and Media Ecology at Palm Beach Atlantic University in West Palm Beach, FL. She is the author of several books, most recently a futuristic novel about technology and human relationship called "Breaking the Silence."

FROM SKEPTICISM TO SYMPATHETIC OBJECTIVITY

By Tony Carnes

In the nineteenth century, news producers infused emotions and opinions into news stories through new innovations like tabloid, opinion, and entertainment journalism. By the end of the nineteenth century, emotional hyperbole in reporting was so overboard that a reaction against it started to set into the newsroom.

In January 1897, the *New York Press* delivered its epithet "yellow journalism" against the lurid, often propagandistic practices of certain news organs, and a month later the *New York Times* placed its lofty seven words, "All the News That's Fit to Print" on the upper left corner of its front page.

The era of surplus subjectivity was then supplanted by a revolution in favor of objectivity and restrained emotions in news reports. Both the tone and look of news reports became overly sober. Emotion was boxed into ads, and public relations became the scientific production of emotions.

A method of journalism developed so that reporters would start with skepticism in order to arrive at an objective picture, then add sympathy toward the end of the reporting process. Over time, the reporter's skepticism can harden into cynicism about her informants and, at worst, about life itself. The exciting age of big-city journalism in the first half of the twentieth century idealized the hard-bitten, cynical reporter.

However, the public too was developing a cynicism about journalists. The public came to believe that the journalist tactically fakes sympathy at the beginning of the interviews in order to advance her reporting. So, it would appear that an important source of the distrust between the journalists and their public lies in the philosophy and training of modern journalism.

Yet, in 1897, another model of journalism situated itself between the yellow journalism and the industrial model. Its run lasted just a couple of years, but the digital age has made its revival essential.

In reaction to then-current models of journalism, Lincoln Steffens, Jacob Riis's friend who later became famous for his exposes of big business wrongdoing and the miseries of the underclass, tried out a new form of journalism at the *New York Commercial Advertiser*. He decried "the rise of impersonal, advertising-based 'commercial journalism.'" Steffens believed that both the sensationalist and sober daily news media were missing most of the human life of New York City. He proposed to hire a new type of reporter and send them into the streets to catch life as it was actually lived.

Steffens sent his reporters out with a love for all of New York City, not just that part beloved by the elite newspapermen in Manhattan. He wrote, "[My] ambition was to have it reported so that New Yorkers might see, not merely read of it, as it was: rich and poor, wicked and good, ugly but beautiful, growing, great." Like the web magazine *A Journey Through American Religions* this city editor placed a premium on covering the newcomers to the city and his reporters walking the streets. As a disciple of Jacob Riis, he himself had already published many articles on New York's Jewish ghetto and the life of immigrants in the city.

His aim was to write newspaper stories "so humanly that the reader will see himself in the other fellow's place." Steffens wanted his reporters to have an empathetic understanding of even the baddest actors in the city. He sent Abraham Cahan, who would become the legendary editor of *The Jewish Forward*, to write about a man who killed his wife in "a rather bloody, hacked-up crime." In *The Year that Defined American Journalism,* Joseph Campbell observes that Steffens "encouraged Cahan to go beyond relating the crime's sordid details and find out why a man who had 'loved someone once well enough to marry her' came to hate her so intensely that he cut her to pieces. 'If you can find out just what happened between that wedding and this murder,' Steffens told Cahan, 'you will have a novel for yourself and a short story for me.'"

Steffens grew tired of the experiment, and it ended after a few years. However, some of the lessons of finding "the charm and beauty and significance of commonplace men and women" should teach us how to do journalism.

At *A Journey through NYC Religions* we have a different approach, which is built into our organization. Our idea of sympathy is that we have a "fellow feeling" with our respondents. This solidarity is extended to "fellow understanding." We empathize with them to the extent that we can think and feel like them. This reproduction of the other person in ourselves is not complete but is enough for empathetic understanding. Of course, the reproduction is constantly revised in light of comments and actions of the original, the person being understood!

Objectivity

Reporting should always pass through a zone of objectivity. This is a zone where one tries that super-hard task of seeing a third party oneself, seeking to best understand the people being interviewed. Fortunately, in this city of outsiders it should be easier to latch onto an outsider's perspective. We try to accelerate this process by building an objectivity into our reporting process.

One way *A Journey* does this in our reporting on religions in New York City is through the use of four sensitizing questions that we always use during our interviews. We ask, what is unique and different about your religious organization? I.e. what is special, how would you convince us to check you out? What kind of impact is your synagogue, mosque, temple, or church having on your neighborhood or your network of people? And can you give an example of this impact from the last couple of weeks? If you were mayor of NYC, how would you change the city?

You can see right away that we start with sympathy by asking how the religious group is special. However, we also give a chance for the religious person to prove the fulfillment of her hopes. This step toward objectivity comes with the participation of the respondent. It is a joint project.

We assume that if a person says that she has a big impact on youth but can't give an example of that impact, then either the person isn't involved with that aspect of the religious organization or the religious organization's hopes for impact haven't happened yet. The questions act as a sounding board by which the respondents can hear themselves talk. Often, we get explanations of problems encountered and future plans. We get to know the history of the group and its deepest hopes and fears for the future. Of course, the person might have forgotten their successes. In some cases, we have interviewed people who had such a reluctance to brag that they would discount their own successes as "not much."

Then, we ask in a questionnaire for a congregational leader to list his three biggest programs and to check off a list of programs to indicate what the congregation does. If we don't see "youth" listed as one of the three biggest programs or checked off as one of the programs of the congregation, then these discrepancies raise further questions. In such a way, we act like good psychologists who use probing questions to bring recognition about what the truth of the situation is.

Skepticism
Skepticism and its journalistic embodiment in investigative journalism are essential options for the reporter. In the first place, the reporter needs to reflect skeptically on his own "sympathy"—is it just a pose to manipulate interviewees or is it real? It is so easy to fool oneself about one's own virtue.

Second, a reporter needs to be tough-minded in asking questions about the details of someone's assertions. The reporter needs specific, concrete details to properly inform the reader and to write rich, interesting stories. Bloviation should be avoided at all costs. Then, the reporter needs the details so that claims can be checked. The audience wants to be able to trust the report that it is reading.

Before he wrote novels like *1984* and *Animal Farm*, George Orwell worked as a very fine reporter. His strength as a reporter was that he was rooted in his own empathy and fairness to the people about whom he reported. In his diaries of the World War II years, Orwell wrote of his deep skepticism of the official accounts about how the war was going. At the same time, he acknowledged the difficulties that the British government was having in balancing out different priorities of truthfulness and averting panic. His empathy with the British officials in no way cut off his skepticism.

Fast Company's Jeff Chu tweeted a neat summary of sympathetic objectivity: "Get more bang for your buck with empathy first. Open ears and heart make for better interviews. Skepticism later, if needed."

Tony Carnes wrote for Christianity Today, then developed the award-winning web magazine, A Journey through NYC Religions, on which some of this material is based.

SNAPCHAT IS ONE OF THE BEST TOOLS FOR NEW WRITERS

By Kay L. Colley

A photo messaging mobile application that allows users to send messages to a controlled list of recipients, Snapchat seems like a good tool for news-producing organizations to use, at first glance.

Individual posts, otherwise known as "snaps," can be put together in "stories" so that viewers can see a complete thought or story for 24 hours. In today's visual society, the focus of Snapchat, the photos, gives viewers what they are looking for: quick, bite-sized bits of information that are visually oriented.

For these reasons, Snapchat seems a natural for journalists who plan to cover an event, especially an event that is visually oriented and personal. This approach is just how some legacy and online media outlets have been using Snapchat. The *Washington Post* used Snapchat to live-Snapchat the Super Bowl's ads in January 2014.

Casey Neistat of online media outlet *Vice News* reported on the events in Ferguson, Mo., using Snapchat. His 24-hour coverage is still available on YouTube, although Snapchat claims that "snaps" and "stories" are deleted after a certain time period. But there are other ways that some media have experimented with the use of Snapchat:

- Now This News and Mashable, both online news organizations, have used Snapchat to tell original stories focused on the platform, such as day-in-the-life stories and stories with a visual focus.
- *Bloomberg Businessweek* offers previews of its weekly issues through Snapchat.
- National Public Radio sends snaps with staffers reading a fact of the day.
- NRK P3, a Norwegian radio station aimed at a younger audience, produces newscasts using Snapchat.

Much like experiments with other social media outlets that are now common, such as Facebook and Twitter, these experiments have yielded a variety of results for media outlets. With the goal of reaching a younger audience for a news brand, Snapchat could be the answer. However, after the first glance, news organizations discovered some things about Snapchat that make it daunting.

1. Your account is difficult to find on Snapchat. The search function in Snapchat is less than rigorous, making it difficult to find news organizations or individual reporters for those news organizations, unless you know them. You cannot browse content nor can you re-Snap content. The inability to find users is one of the biggest drawbacks to using Snapchat for a brand and leads to challenge number 2.

2. Gaining more followers can be a challenge because marketing a Snapchat account is hard. Snapchat is a young person's social media tool. The predominant demographic of Snapchat users (80 percent of whom live in the United States) is between 13 and 23 years of age, a market that legacy media have found dropping out at increasingly larger rates than any other age demographic. While legacy media want to re-engage this demographic, marketing to them in traditional ways will not work. Younger audiences are more mobile-oriented and more likely to view traditional marketing techniques as cheesy or dated. So how do you market a Snapchat account to younger viewers, especially when those viewers aren't viewing your social media or website?

3. Snapchat has just recently begun accepting advertisements, but the ability of news-producing organizations to recoup the investment on editorial content in Snapchat coverage is a challenge they will face—nothing new for many legacy media outlets that are still puzzled with how to make money on mobile and social media.

4. Snapchat offers limited text posting capability, so a picture is truly worth a thousand words. With a maximum of approximately 30 characters per post, Snapchat trumps Twitter in its value of terse prose. This function truly focuses on the bite-sized aspect of "snaps."

5. The transient nature of "snaps" has led to workarounds and additional apps that make the use of Snapchat a challenge for news-producing organizations that want to keep content available for review. While Snapchat says it does away with "snaps," more of a capital investment on the part of news organizations can make the content available online, but does this defeat the initial purpose of Snapchat and what its users expect?

Snapchat is yet another tool that individual journalists and news organizations can use to reach their audiences, particularly their younger audience members, since Snapchat is dominated by the youngest demographic of any social media platform. While content focuses on bite-sized, visually oriented posts, nothing new in social media, its focus on the personal aspect of messages gives media organizations a way to really target audiences and elicit specific user-generated content.

While Snapchat might not be the best social media platform for every news organization or every story, it can help extend legacy media's reach into a younger demographic. That alone could be worth the added investment.

Kay L. Colley, Ph.D., associate professor, is chair of the Communications Department and Student Media Director at Texas Wesleyan University.

THE HUMBLE ART OF THE AWESOME INTERVIEW

By Paul D. Glader

John McCandlish Phillips was an award-winning journalist for the *New York Times* for 21 years (1952–1973), *whose* most famous story exposed the hidden background of an American Nazi and Ku Klux Klan leader, a story that inspired the 2001 film *The Believer*. Phillips passed away in April of 2013, but his journalistic legacy lives on through the McCandlish Phillips Journalism Institute at The King's College in New York City and the NYC Semester in Journalism program, which welcomes college students to spend a semester learning and interning in New York.

In addition to being a crack newsman on deadline, Phillips was known for the lyrical quality in his writing, an eye for offbeat feature stories, and his keen observations in writing profiles about people. His journalistic abilities and his appreciation for humanity led some of the top writers and editors at the *Times* such as Arthur Gelb, A.M. Rosenthal, and Gay Talese to tout Phillips as the best writer at the *Times*. The fact that Phillips was a Pentecostal Christian who kept a Bible on his desk seemed to only make him a more valued eccentric and member of the family-run newspaper.

Phillips quit the *Times* after 21 years and focused on planting churches and encouraging people in New York City. He remained passionate about good journalism and encouraged young people from faith backgrounds to pursue journalism as an important calling. He also encouraged them to follow the highest standards of journalistic ethics and practice. In a wide-ranging speech he gave to students at the World Journalism Institute in the mid-2000s, Phillips explained some of his secrets on successful journalistic interviews. He argued that good interviews start with the right humility and perspective from the journalist. Here are 7 tips in his words:

1) Interviewing is an art.

The reporter's job is not to show off her skills as a reporter or to challenge a source. The reporter's job is to get as much information as possible. "If your subject feels that he or she is with a friend, rather than an enemy, or at least with someone who is unthreatening, she or he will more likely open up and let it come tumbling out."

2) A key focus for journalists is *attitude*.

He suggested reporters resist the arrogance that comes from thinking they have an elevated access from their access to important people. "You've got a role but the subject has the goods." Better than assuming omniscience is adopting humility. Keep in mind that the subject "may have gems that you can't mine, but she can yield—if you give room for that to happen."

3) Reporters have a function, but that doesn't give them importance

In some cases, some interviewers tend to "treat the subject roughly—because doing so fits the sense of the interviewer's self-importance."

4) Use a conversational tone as a default

Questions that are hostile in tone are rarely effective. It's better to assume a conversational tone. "I aimed in every situation to make the subject just as comfortable as possible, to get her or him talking freely and unguardedly." Phillips suggests journalists ask tough questions in a "quiet, ordinary manner."

5) Plan. But leave room for randomness and improvisation

Phillips suggested leaving half the time of an interview for unplanned questions. Reporters who insist on sticking to a rigid list of questions and answers are assuming omniscience. They're assuming they know everything worth asking about. Instead, they should realize there's more to the story discoverable by giving the subject room to move. "Some kind of material is just not going to come out by your line of questions, but if you get the subject to talk freely, you might be quite surprised and delighted at what comes out." He adds that, "the best anecdotes come out this way."

6) Achieve absolute accuracy in your note-taking

Reporters should create a system for accurately recording the interview. Specifically, Phillips suggested creating a shorthand system for note taking. Words in quotes must be words the source actually spoke. Indirect quotations are paraphrases of what the source said, but not direct quotes. Don't hesitate to stop a source and have her repeat a line or statement so you can write it down word for word. A reporter's job—correctly focused—is first of all to inform the reader accurately and do so interestingly. "The feeling of breadth and depth in any story comes from gathering more than you need and having more than you tell." He tells young reporters: "Gather massively and write selectively."

7) Don't grant "off-the-record" status flippantly

Phillips advised reporters to avoid the "off the record" trap by only allowing the information *after* a source says, "this is off the record," to be so. "What people state is off the record is very often self-serving, designed to instill a certain attitude or outlook or even bias in a reporter."

Paul Glader is associate professor and director of the McCandlish Phillips Journalism Institute at The King's College in New York City. He was a staff writer at the Wall Street Journal *for a decade and writes for the* New York Times, The New Yorker, Forbes.com, *and Bloomberg Businessweek.*

Copyright: McCandlish Phillips Journalism Institute 2014. Used with permission.

CAN I GET AN (EYE)WITNESS? RELIGION REPORTING VS. RELIGIOUS NEWS

By Kyle Huckins

Reporting on religion is an important beat, as nearly three-quarters of American adults attend church every month, according to a Pew Forum poll. That's a far greater percentage than engages in almost any other segment of life in these United States.

However, only one in five respondents to another survey by the group said journalists are friendly toward religion, with nearly twice that percentage stating that news people have an unfriendly relationship with faith.

As a veteran religion reporter and news pundit on the subject, I see two forces at work here: One, the faithful don't necessarily understand the distinction between religion reporting and religious news, and two, news reporters and editors aren't the most knowledgeable regarding beliefs of the faithful.

Religion news is unbiased journalism about the events, people, places, and ideas that make up spirituality. Most writers in the news profession aspire to this. They do not evaluate claims that this doctrine is correct or that God is doing a particular work, but report positions of religious leaders and followers and allow the audience to make up its collective mind on the subject.

Some possible stories along these lines would be Sunni vs. Shiite teachings about the Prophet Muhammad, the re-dedication of the now-Catholic Crystal Cathedral, and black church officials' thoughts on the American racial divide on law enforcement. Religious news takes a proactive stance that a particular set of faith claims is true and seeks to advance that belief.

Those who write inspirational articles are an extension of the church. Authors may put in passages from spiritual texts to support their views and instruct the audience.

Other examples of these news items include favorable accounts of conversions and interpretations of world events as foretold in Holy Writ.

Only a third of professional journalists say religion is very important to their lives, a significantly smaller proportion than in the population at large. About the same percentage, 34 percent, have no religious affiliation, much greater than the USA in general.

While an atheist or agnostic can cover faith-related events, practices, and people, the nonbeliever's lack of firm belief in a spiritual world may lead to marginalizing the religious adherent's tenets. The many examples of inaccurate reporting on Islam's principles, stereotyping of evangelical Christians, and the campaigns for gay rights and pro-choice laws on abortion would appear to bear out such an assertion.

If you're researching a story from the religion beat, do your homework well. Read both what those in the belief system involved say about the issue as well as that coming from objective reports or studies. Understand the origins, history, and tenets of the group so you can ask good questions and grasp the answers.

When writing up what you found, attribute all opinion to others and refrain from putting your stamp of approval on it or deriding what someone asserts. Your job is to get the facts and let the audience figure out who's got the truth.

If you're putting together a piece for a religious news outlet, you're still a journalist, and even inconvenient truths shouldn't be avoided. Remember, no less than Jesus himself said, *You shall know the truth, and the truth shall make you free* (John 8:32).

At the same time, you can outwardly work to advance a particular belief system because of the group members' clear identification of their outlet as religiously affiliated. You're not sneaking in your position since it's on the cover or front page for everyone to see.

Remember, however, that when you cite unscriptural or other outside sources in support of your piece and team, that with scripture, you likely will reach beyond your audience base and may bring in new fans.

Whether you do religion journalism or religious news, do your unquestioned best, as unto the Lord as prescribed in Colossians 3:23. That will get you plaudits here and above.

An Azusa Pacific University journalism professor and ordained elder in the Church of God in Christ, Kyle Huckins, Ph.D., is the author of Getting From Here to Eternity: A Spirit-filled View of the News, *a collection of more than 100 of his columns on faith honored by both the Religion Newswriters Association and Indiana Society of Professional Journalists.*

IDEAS, IMAGES, AND IMMEDIACY ARE THREE BIGGIES, BUT THERE ARE ISSUES #TWEETAWAY

By Deborah W. Huff

Twitter presents a new dynamic to the task of reporting, and one that holds great potential. Three key things that Twitter affords the reporter are ideas, images, and immediacy.

Because story ideas are the lifeblood of a journalist, Twitter is simply a new place to find them. Whether gathering information on breaking news such as a six-car pile-up or a weather-related catastrophe, Twitter can be in places where a reporter is not. People on the scene can be sending tweets within seconds of an occurrence and better yet, photo images can be attached. When a man survived an 11-story fall from a building, CBS Evening News used a Twitter photo of the car with a collapsed roof to help tell the story. Pew Research from March 2014 finds that 50 percent of those who get their news on social media tend to engage with the delivery of news by posting, reposting, discussing, or sharing videos or photographs of the event. A reporter or editor can take advantage of that, adding depth to the reporting of that event.

A former editor for the Charleston *Post and Courier* found Twitter to be full of feature ideas as well as news. One of his favorites included developing a story about a handicapped woman who was training for a marathon with a course that included running across the 2.7-mile span of the Arthur Ravenel

Jr. Bridge—a long bridge with a steady incline that allows ocean-going ships to pass below. He saw a Twitter post about how she was training and followed up by contacting her and getting a full-page story with photos.

In addition to ideas and images, immediacy provides a layer to modern reporting that previous generations only dreamt about. Immediacy allows the reporter to tell the story before the press runs or even before airtime. The topic for these tweets can be anything from highlights of the event to personal musings about what just happened. Some of these observations will make it into the story and others may just add to the texture of the story.

This immediacy also gives the reporter an ability to get feedback from his or her followers and can help push readers to the Web, the printed page, or the station.

ISSUES

Twitter text can be rife with errors. From simple typos to errors in fact, reporters have to do their job and double-check all content. Yet, sometimes in the middle of a breaking story, reporters have to share what information they have with their audience. If the information has not been confirmed, reporters need to let their audience know and make every effort to update or correct the information as soon as possible.

Additionally, crossover exists between news to opinion editorial, and reporters must keep the two separate. After the school shooting in Newton, CT, Pew Research from March of 2014 reported that two-thirds of the tweets turned to criticizing gun control laws and supporting stricter gun controls. While reporters can use that type of information in building a story related to audience reaction, they cannot use it as content for a news story on the event itself.

Another concern on the list of issues is being aware of the public relations social media machine. An article on WSJ.com highlights the practice of buying Twitter accounts for the purpose of pushing publicity and influencing trending topics. Reporters looking to find story ideas need to be aware of this PR tool and realize that it might provide a few nuggets of news, but most of them are simply publicity.

Like most new technology, there is a learning curve. Some Twitter mistakes are easy to get over and others provide lifelong lessons. A sports reporter for a college paper was reporting on his team facing the Bryant College Bears. His first exposure to covering an event and tweeting at the same time was exciting for him. As the game progressed well for his team, the faster the tweets flew.

His two dozen tweets had been followed by several hundred readers. At the end of the game he submitted his story for publication, and it was all about the drumming the Bears took. The article printed and not until it was in newsstands did anyone mention that the mascot name was really the Bulldogs and not the Bears. For the next week, the reporter received notice of his mistake from friend and foe alike. In the excitement of doing the tweeting, the reporter said he had confused the legendary Paul "Bear" Bryant with the Bryant College Bulldogs—a mistake he said he would not have made had it not been for trying to do something different. He has not made that mistake since.

STAY CURRENT AND TWEET AWAY

As fast as Twitter has made an impact, Instagram is following right behind with what promises to be a better way of communicating to and with audiences. Poytner.org and Pew Research Journalism Project provide the latest information on the use of modern technology and its impact on reporting and reporters.

Deborah W. Huff is a professor in the Department of Digital Media and Communication Arts at Liberty University.

JOB NUMBER ONE: GET IT RIGHT!

By Michael A. Longinow

You're wrong—until you're right. That has to be the mind-set when doing reporting on sensitive stories such as alleged rape, misuse of public money, or abuse of power by elected officials or people enforcing the law. Reporters have to come at their work this way, and their editors do, too. It was true generations ago when people actually believed the press. Today, it's all the more necessary.

Allegations are easy to find. In fact, accusers will find you when you're doing your job as a journalist. They have a conclusion. They're sure of it. And they want you to work backward from it to tell their story. But when you give in, bad things happen. It's what led to the December 2014 implosion of the *Rolling Stone* blockbuster story on alleged rape culture at the University of Virginia.

In that case, a source told a reporter for *Rolling Stone* she'd been gang-raped at a fraternity party, but asked the reporter not to talk to her accusers. The reporter agreed—and didn't get corroboration from other sources. The upshot was an apology by the magazine and an internal investigation of its vetting practices on big stories with help from the Columbia School of Journalism. The *Washington Post* reported April 5, 2014, "The Co- lumbia report provides powerful evidence that *Rolling Stone* was negligent in its investigation . . ."

Check it out. Why do we so easily forget this admonition we heard from the crusty prof in our reporting class? In the newsroom, we're in a hurry and we go with our gut. We like the reporter. She's done good work in the past. It's all good, right? It shouldn't be all good until it's all good—with a fact check (maybe by several people) that demands proof. Hard facts.

It's time journalism educators borrowed a page from their counterparts in the English Department. Remember that argumentative research paper you had to write when you were 19? Argue both sides with equal intensity, supporting each with convincing evidence from respected and established researchers. In the end, you have to come to a conclusion—you make an argument for one side—but it comes from showing that while both sides have strengths (and flaws), one side's evidence is stronger and the other's flaws are more serious. And at the graduate school level, your paper is more likely to get accepted for publication if it contains several paragraphs showing how the very strong research you have is actually somewhat inconclusive. There's a lot more to be looked at, though the conclusion reached is worth considering.

It's a principle used in law schools to prepare for courtroom debate. If you don't know the plausibility of other perspectives, you're setting yourself up for problems. Because it could be you're wrong; you don't really know your own story until you've argued its faults and flaws.

If professional reporters are impatient, we shouldn't be surprised at the lack of intellectual stamina our students show. We tell them to find three sources for a basic story, and twice or three times that for an in-depth investigative piece. They want to know why. "Everybody knows this guy did it," they tell us. Or worse, "Why would you doubt this student's story? She's a marginalized person in this community. You're majority culture and you don't get it." Okay. So she's marginalized. And yes, I'm mainstream culture. But we do our students a disservice—and, by extension, the profession we want our best students to enter—if don't push our students to get the story right and corroborate it. Call it mean, call it picky, but it's what we're called to do. And the next generation of American journalism sits before us in those desks.

Michael A. Longinow, Ph.D., is a professor in the Department of Journalism and Integrated Media at Biola University in Southern California.

Blogging: The Word became flesh

By Wally Metts

"The Word became flesh" is an apt metaphor for what we do as bloggers, or even as writers more generally. We start with an idea. In the beginning was or is, a word.

And then, "the Word became flesh." This refers to the incarnation, of course. But any idea must be fleshed out, in a sense.

Writing is like that. We start with an idea. It "becomes flesh" as we express it, and then there is some effect. So this is what we will talk about today—the idea, the expression, and the effect. All communication concerns itself with this.

The idea

Matthew Arnold once said, "Have something to say and say it as clearly as possible."

This something to say is the basis for all great blogs. Or books. In the end, people don't come to our blog for its functionality, plug-in, or design. They might not come back if these things are not done well. But they come for information, entertainment, and understanding.

Each post or article, then, requires a strong idea. But so does the blog or website itself. Mine is a Christian cultural critique, helping me and my readers make sense of a fuzzy world by being "biblically faithful and culturally thoughtful."

But what's yours? Put it on your about page or in your tagline. And then keep on doing it. For years, your teachers said you needed a thesis. You still do, each time you write, even if you don't put it at the end of the first paragraph. But your blog needs a thesis, too. The idea of your blog is a social contract, an agreement about what I will find there. I come back because you deliver it over and over again.

This contract is also part of any individual post or article. Within three or four sentences, I should know where it is going. Good writing is almost always about making and keeping a promise.

The writer has to know what that promise is. He or she needs to think about it more, plan for it by filing away links or resources (I use Delicious for this).

Every blog needs an editorial calendar or some sort of plan that keeps it focused. And every blog and every post needs an idea that holds it together.

The expression

The expression of that idea should be credible, concrete, and concise.

Being credible has to do with your sources, knowledge, and understanding, of course. This would be true even if you were trying to be funny. I was "freshly pressed" once, trying to be funny about marketing to Boomers.

But there were references to several companies and techniques. Writing humor is difficult and challenging. You actually have to know what you are talking about before you can make fun of it.

More often, however, we are not writing humor but providing information. What we want is to be a trusted adviser. We want people to come to our blog because they want to know about technology, or food, or fashion. And over time we want them to trust us enough to come back.

This trust has been part of our understanding of rhetoric from before Aristotle. Credibility involves creating this trust, through both our reasoning and our identification with our readers.

What you don't want is generalizations, red herrings, slippery slopes, and bandwagons. What you do want is experience, success, reputation, endorsement, and longevity. Getting what you want requires consistency, planning, and research.

But you need more than credibility; you need clear, concrete writing. This is what your teachers meant when they asked you to explain or give more detail. It involves turning boats into battleships, moving from the abstract to the specific.

Better examples help. But the clearest path to concrete writing is stronger verbs and stronger nouns.

Sometimes it helps to turn adjectives into nouns. There is no need for an educational system when what we are really talking about is an education. You've been using flowery adjectives since junior high, when what you needed were better nouns. The adjective is the enemy of the noun in the end, diluting it through overuse.

Nouns can also be turned into verbs. You can have a decision. Or you can decide.

Deciding is better since it forces you to name the person who did it. Nominalizations like this are often linked to a wordy style. And to find them and fix them is to do what your teacher told you to do but you never understood how—avoid the passive voice.

I would add that good writing is often sensory as well. More concrete nouns and active verbs. We write easily about things we see and hear, but once we introduce texture, even smell or taste, our writing is more vivid and memorable.

Don't tell me you like to be at Grandma's house. Make me smell the bacon. Because there is no place for more limp, passive prose on the Internet. Enough of that. There is a place for clear, crisp, concise writing.

Unfortunately, most of us still live under the tyranny of the 500-word essay, padding your prose to get to the required length when all you had to do was have more or better content. Instead, you learned to write fat.

Stop it. You rarely need to say really. Or rarely, for that matter. (Adverbs are as bad as adjectives.)

It's redundant to say something is full and complete. Or that you have future plans. A tragedy, by definition, is terrible.

Almost anything an educated American writes can be reduced by a third without missing anything at all.

The effect

These disciplines of purpose and practice provide a more powerful effect.

When the Word became flesh, the effect was grace and truth. And I think this motivated the first blogger ever, Martin Luther, the German reformer. Right on the cusp of a new technology he posted his 95 theses (you only need one), and its effect was multiplied by the printing press, just as ours is by WordPress and similar tools.

I'm sure he would be blogging today.

But across the top of the paper he posted on the door of the Wittenberg Chapel, he wrote "Out of a love for the truth, and a desire to bring it to light . . ."

That would not be a bad goal for any blogger today. But regardless of your purpose, Luther shows us that our motives matter. And always have.

The creation story tells us that Adam and Eve were naked and not ashamed. I think there is something about that which suggests a marriage, a conversation, a forum, or even a blog can be a safe place, where people can be honest and not afraid.

A good blog is a place readers come because they know what to expect, a place where their needs are respected and their comments are welcome. This is a place where the idea, the expression, and the effect come together so you can create conversations that matter about things you care about.

Wally Metts, Ph.D., is director of graduate studies in communication at Spring Arbor University. He lives on a Christmas tree farm and his grandchildren call him Santa. He blogs at thedaysman.com.

Ten things editors hate about you

By Dean Nelson

Actually, they don't hate *you*, per se, but they hate these things that rookie writers do. And the less discerning editors can't separate your work from you, so some of them might hate you after all—if you do these things.

These are common mistakes rookie writers make.

Rookie Writers ...

1) Try to preach. "I am going to write something that will show people why racism is bad." Or "I am going to write about why we should all love America. Or God." They do all the work for the reader. "So, dear reader, the point of my story is ..." Garrison Keillor said, "I would rather read two sharp and snappy pages about geese than fifty fat and flabby pages about God or the American people." So don't preach.

2) Lack focus and try to accomplish too much. Narrow it down. E.B. White said, "Don't write about man. Write about a man." So don't try to accomplish too much.

3) Haven't studied the web site or publication for which they are writing. When they don't know the site, they end up writing about topics that don't apply, or that have already been written about, or that contradict the site in general, or aren't

in that site's style or tone. Don't ignore your first audience—your editor.

4) Miss deadlines or word counts. They can be really good writers, but if they miss these obvious requirements, a person with lesser skills will get the assignments. One of my professors at the University of Missouri was under contract to write six stories of whatever topic, length, and deadline for *Sports Illustrated* each year. You're not that guy. Editors will go with people they can depend on. Don't ignore the rules.

5) Don't check spelling or grammar. This is like going to a formal event with your pants unzipped. It really does matter. Many editors love the language, and when they see writers repeatedly messing it up, they get more and more angry, to a point where they'll just stop reading. Know your AP Stylebook. Know the difference between compose and comprise, fewer and less, among and between, averse and adverse, astronomy and astrology, cosmology and cosmetology, virile and viral. The only difference between marital and martial is where you put the "i." Spelling and grammar mistakes create too much work for editors. They're busy. Again, they'll go with a lesser writer who causes them less grief. Don't ignore the rules.

6) Don't verify information. Rookies accept hearsay and rumors and don't check them out. Don't perpetuate rumors, myths, dominant narratives, and assumptions. *Rolling Stone* magazine, are you listening?

7) Don't write regularly. This must be part of every writer's diet. It's almost impossible to sit down and knock something out that's really well done if you only do it once a month. Can you just decide, "This morning I'm going to run a triathlon"? I didn't think so. Or, "Tonight I'm singing in an opera"? It's all about practice. The great violinist Jascha Heifetz said, "If I don't practice one day, I know it; two days, the critics know it; three days, the public knows it." Don't avoid practice.

8) Spend too much time on first drafts. This is a HUGE problem with college students. They inch along, word by word, phrase by phrase until it's perfect, then finally finish, and assume it's great. Absolutely not true. Spew it out. This goes against your nature, some of you OCD anal retentives, but this is the best way. Once you get it all out there, THEN you can look for the nugget, the part that's worth writing about. There is a good chance that you had no idea what this piece was RE-ALLY about until you backed the truck up and emptied it all out there. Don't spend too much time on first drafts.

9) Don't revise. Writing is rewriting. I know that sounds like a cliché, but it's true. It takes several passes and some time away from it to reflect on it. The people who crank something out, assume they've carved out a pearl, and send it in, are in for a big surprise. Blog posts might be a little different in this regard, but even then, most bloggers would feel a lot better about what they posted if they had reflected a little and revised a lot before they hit "Publish." Mary Karr's book *Lit* was 300 pages long. But she wrote 2,000 pages. Wallace Stegner said, "Hard writing makes for easy reading." Don't turn in your first draft.

10) Sacrifice clarity for what they think is "artistic." Cutting out the adjectives was good enough for Hemingway, and it's good enough for you. The reason Mary Oliver's poetry is so beautiful is that it's so simple. Same with Billy Collins. You don't have to sound smart. You have to tell the truth. And you can do that when you stop trying to impress people. When my son was in high school, he asked me to read a paper he had written. I crossed out all of the unnecessary stuff and said he didn't need it. He protested: "Teachers love this kind of crap," he said. He was probably right. But you're not in English class anymore. Same thing with being cute. This prose isn't your diary. You're not 12. You're trying to be a professional, writing

for a professional audience. Act like it. Don't focus too much on the art of what you're trying to say.

Special bonus for committed readers!

11) Don't offer anything new or fresh to the discussion. Good writers complicate your thinking. Don't insult your reader by oversimplifying.

12) Try to ride a particular market. "What is selling?" Stories about vampires and Amish? What about an Amish vampire? Write what's interesting to you, what you would have liked to have found. Asking "Will it sell?" is a question for later. "Is it any good? And did I tell the truth?" should be your earlier questions.

13) Think they know what the story is about before starting the research. When you start full of your own certainty, you'll miss something important, and run the risk of perpetuating propaganda. Let the research/sources lead you to what the story is about. Be nimble and agile in what you think the real story is.

14) Wait until they feel like it before they start writing. One of the myths about writing or any other creative enterprise is that we should wait until we are inspired, and then BOOM! the magic gets turned on like a faucet. A lot of a writer's energy is spent in head games. Am I good enough? Am I an imposter? Do I have anything to say? Just get started. Jack London said, "You can't wait for inspiration. You have to go after it with a club." And how about a final word from Stephen King? "Amateurs sit and wait for inspiration, the rest of us just get up and go to work." So get to work whether you feel like it or not.

Dean Nelson, Ph.D., is the founder and director of the journalism program at Point Loma Nazarene University in San Diego. He has written for the New York Times, *the* Boston Globe,

Christianity Today, Sojourners, Relevant, Christian Century, Risen, *and dozens of other publications and websites. He is a frequent contributor to Donald Miller's Storyline blog and is a Senior Fellow in Journalism with the Council for Christian Colleges and Universities. He also directs the annual Writer's Symposium by the Sea. His most recent books are* **Quantum Leap: How John Polkinghorne Found God in Science and Religion** *and* **God Hides in Plain Sight: How to See the Sacred in a Chaotic World.**

JOURNALIST OF TOMORROW MUST RETAIN BEDROCK PRINCIPLES OF THE PAST

By Michael Patrick

When *Rolling Stone* magazine published graphic details of an alleged brutal gang rape of an 18-year-old freshman at a fraternity party at the University of Virginia in November 2014, the reporter appeared guided by a larger narrative of unreported sexual assaults on campuses nationwide. What quickly emerged in this incident was that many of the details in *Rolling Stone*'s account were never confirmed and soon proved false.

Rolling Stone's story, "A Rape on Campus: A Brutal Assault and Struggle for Justice at UVA," does not stand alone in journalistic failures by major news media outlets. For example, many critical details that shaped early news reporting on the shooting death of an unarmed black man by a white police officer in Ferguson, MO later proved false and misleading. Rioting ensued, and the results of that early false reporting reverberated nationwide.

To paraphrase author Samuel Johnson's observation that truth is the first casualty of war, one might reasonably argue today that truth is too often the first casualty in breaking news coverage. In the 24-hour news cycle, major media organizations no longer serve as gatekeepers that control the news. Thousands of people instantly capture and relay their versions of the news via social media. While some of these accounts are helpful to offering a complete picture, more often than not, these accounts are incomplete, deeply flawed, or untrue.

Such false reporting can damage efforts to deal with sensitive issues such as violence against women on college campuses and troubled relations between police and the African-American communities. The corrosive results of inadequate reporting are becoming more visible with the advent of a democratized news environment.

Unfortunately, rocky financial conditions in the news business, combined with competitive pressures from unconfirmed web reporting via Twitter and pseudo-news outlets, has eroded journalistic efforts to get the story right before getting it first. Such failures are reflected partly in studies that show that the credibility of journalists and the trustworthiness of their work have hit record lows. For example, a Pew Center study shows that less than 3 in 10 Americans say journalism contributes a lot to society. At the same time, Pew Center studies reveal a sharp rise in the numbers of people who rely primarily on social media and new media sources to inform them about the world.

The journalist as curator

News organizations no longer serve as gatekeepers that can control the news flow. Today's professional journalists are called to curate the news; that is, to selectively engage a non-stop news environment in a manner that takes extra care to sort facts from fiction. Curating news coverage means that journalists must resist the temptation to report everything they hear instantly. Today's professionals must act responsibly to investigate and provide an authentic, reliable, and complete picture of unfolding events, to cross-check the related facts, and place coverage within a meaningful context for their communities.

If news media outlets are to distinguish themselves and re-build public trust, then they must reassert those enduring ethical practices to *get the story right before getting it first.* Here are five keys to shore up journalistic practices and help ensure that you're reporting an accurate and reliable story:

1. Be wary of the dominant narrative. Reporters are tempted to place their stories as examples within powerful political, cultural, or social narratives, whether or not the facts fit a popular storyline. Explosive issues such as existing racial tensions involving African-Americans and the police can easily overwhelm the material facts of a particular case, as happened in Ferguson, MO. Early reporting that is dangerously wrong can result in terrible consequences. In cases where street protests erupt, the media's presence alone can magnify the violence and lead to imaginative witnesses whose claims are never corroborated but are reported as truthful. Reporters must cover the story, but remain wary of feeding a frenzy with shallow reporting.

2. Weigh unsubstantiated accounts carefully. Reporting every claim as if it were valid or true should not be confused with creating balance in a story. Reporters should collect multiple views and accounts, but the purpose of gathering those perspectives is to substantiate claims and discover a more complete and accurate picture. Simply passing along unsubstantiated accounts can flood the environment with falsehoods. Results of reporting every sensational claim on the street have a corrosive effect that prevents the public from ever piecing together trustworthy accounts for themselves.

3. Interview all of the stakeholders and ask the hard questions. In more than a hundred pages of emails with University of Virginia officials, *Rolling Stone*'s reporter and assistant editor did not explicitly ask for comments on the particular sexual assault in question. *Rolling Stone* also failed to interview any of the accused perpetrators or fact-check other critical details in its story. Under deadline pressure, reporters are tempted to shape their story from the people who are initially willing to talk. Those accounts are often riddled with misapprehensions, hidden agendas, and misleading or false information.

4. Vet your sources. Simply attributing a single source to your story's account is insufficient. Cross-check your sources by comparing the accounts of other people with firsthand knowledge, verifiable documents, and demonstrably reliable secondary sources. What do other sources say about your key sources and their reliability? What other agendas or "spin" might be in play in the story they tell? Someone may be well meaning in their accounts, but mistaken. The goal in curating a story isn't to simply get a lot of sources on the record, but to assemble reliable facts in a trustworthy context that contributes to the emerging story.

5. Tell the story you know, not the story you think you know. Too often, reporters build their stories on an account that someone gives them early in the process; then the reporter tries to fit the facts into that storyline. Contrarily, when reporters remain open-minded and build their story from confirmed facts and corroboration, a different picture frequently emerges. That takes time and investigation. In a 24-hour news cycle, the pressure is high to go with the story that you think you know, rather than what you have confirmed. The results of following the early story spin are often misleading or untrue.

In the midst of the turbulence and pressures of a changing news marketplace, the enduring principles and ethics of professional journalistic practice still apply. When you take care to get the story right, you might not be the first to report the story, but you can be the first to report a trustworthy account.

Michael Patrick, Ph.D., is a writer, speaker, consultant, professional-in-residence, and former university dean. His journalistic career spans more than 30 years in the news media and public affairs, including posts with news organizations such as CBN News and CNN International. He writes about the intersections of media and journalism, organizational leadership, higher education, Christian faith, politics, and aesthetics.

Five tips that every PR professional wished journalists knew

By Mia Moody-Ramirez

It is no secret that the relationships between PR professionals and journalists are reciprocal. Journalists rely on PR professionals for information and PR professionals rely on journalists for media coverage.

For this mutual relationship to succeed, PR professionals and journalists must work together. Here are five tips to help facilitate healthy connections.

1. Not all PR professionals are "Spin Doctors."

Simply put, PR practitioners wish journalists knew that the ethical standards, knowledge, training, and skills between both professionals are now quite similar, said Cassy Burleson, Ph.D., a professor in the Baylor Department of Journalism, PR & New Media.

In other words, not all PR professionals are "spin doctors." Once commonly perceived as placing a spin on news or disseminating propaganda, today's PR professionals have raised industry standards.

PR has clear ethical standards, and practitioners generally have a wider range of skills across multiple platforms, Burleson adds. Leading the charge is the Public Relations Society of America (PRSA), which helped raise the bar with its Code of Ethics. The organization provides traditional and up-to-date information on ethics for the PR industry.

2. Ethical considerations for PR and News

Like PR practitioners, journalists face difficult ethical issues they must solve by following the industry code of ethics. Journalists serve the important role of interpreting events and facts for the public. The SPJ Code of Ethics states, "ethical journalism strives to ensure the free exchange of information that is accurate, fair and thorough. An ethical journalist acts with integrity."

Marlene Neill, Ph.D., an assistant in the Baylor Department of Journalism, PR & New Media, states that it is important for journalists to know that the best public relations practitioners adhere to industry codes of ethics.

"Having worked both in broadcast news and public relations, I think ethics is one of the most important considerations for journalists," Neill stated. "Just as there are so-called 'bad apples' in public relations, there are 'bad apples' in the media. I think it is important for both sides not to stereotype based on the worst offenders in our industries but to respect and appreciate how our professions can complement each other."

Burleson adds that a wider audience across social media and shrinking personnel in traditional newsrooms has increased the need for transparency.

Social media, for example, produces a wider range of critics who can then communicate directly with one another, she said. "It's one thing to advocate. It's another to lie. Part of the practitioner's job is to convince those in control that telling, then dealing with the truth, is the best long-term alternative."

Burleson adds that practitioners who burn those sitting at the news desks are quickly ignored because media are under more public scrutiny, and in a litigious society, mistakes can cost more than credibility.

3. Transparency is a necessity

Transparency is a necessity in the news industry. While all journalists should strive to be objective, those who are not should be transparent and state their platform.

Neill adds that public relations practitioners can aid in the process of transparency by encouraging openness in communication. For instance, the media play a valuable role in crisis communication by distributing information the public needs to know.

"However, journalists must keep in mind that public relations practitioners have loyalties and obligations to their employers and have to respect privacy and confidentiality," she said. "Balancing those obligations with the public's interest is important."

4. The PR industry is evolving

Journalists may not always need to contact a "public relations" office to gather information. According to Michael L. Turney, Ph.D., Northern Kentucky University professor emeritus, "public relations" is still one of the most popular terms for the field; however, industry names have changed in the last few decades (http://www.nku.edu/~turney/pr-class/readings/plan_kfd.html).

One trend is to merge PR departments with other departments and to rename them. Common names include:

- community affairs
- community relations
- consumer affairs
- corporate communications
- customer relations

- integrated public relations
- investor relations
- marketing public relations
- media relations
- promotions
- public affairs
- public information

Along with the changes to PR departments, names for PR professionals have evolved. Some of the more common names are:

- communication specialist
- community outreach specialist
- information officer
- integrated-marketing specialist
- PR manager
- press agent
- public affairs representative
- publicist
- social media manager

5. Building a good rapport

Forming a good relationship with PR professionals is essential to facilitate the flow of information. From a journalist's perspective, PR professionals must understand the immediacy of the 24-hour real-time news cycle, said Rick Bradfield, news director at KWTX, Waco's CBS television affiliate. "We need more prompt responses."

From a PR professional's standpoint, journalists must be willing to publish information in a timely manner. This give-and-take dynamic between journalists and PR professionals creates a love-hate relationship. The good news is both parties need one another, so relationship building is mutually important.

An associate professor, Mia Moody-Ramirez, Ph.D., is the American Studies Program Director and Graduate Program Director at Baylor University.

KEEP READERS COMING BACK WITH FRESH CONTENT

By Shannon M. Ryals

The Internet remains a vandalized library, which means writers must work harder than ever to connect with audiences searching for relevant information.

Readers can overcome their tendency to search without a system when writers do the hard work for them. Here are five ideas that will help writers design website content that will keep readers returning.

1. Keep the web page focused. A web page is a road map for readers to slide effortlessly deeper into additional pages.

2. Simple. Web page designer Edward A. Johnson tells his disciples: Simplicity is the essence of good design. Less is more. Keep the text font to two styles and avoid elaborate fonts. Include a dominant piece of art but don't overdo it with too many visual components.

3. Avoid clutter. Too much content can be overwhelming to a reader. Think generous white space.

4. Include a teaser sentence on every page. For instance, every page should include the contact information, including a telephone number and email address or a link to glide to a page for more information.

5. Freshen the content frequently. Google and other search engines use strategies that look for updated content. New content daily may be too much, but strive to have fresh content at least once a week.

Readers need a reason to return to your website. Reward them by always thinking of ways to make navigating your content easy. Be sure to promote your website using social media to point readers to your work.

Shannon M. Ryals is founder of Watauga Marketing Communications, Kingsport, TN.

"Six Secrets to Faux Pas-Free Writing"

By Taylor RaeAnne Smith

When I tell people that I live in Paris, France, they have a tendency to think "baguettes," and "Eiffel tower," as opposed to copy-editing English advertisements in a crowded metro, or hours spent transcribing interviews for your professor (Luckily, I love all of these things.) As a graduate student at the Sorbonne and a former intern in the press office at the French Embassy in Washington, D.C., I've been fortunate enough to dabble in the realm of both journalistic and academic writing. Since living in Paris, I've also had the opportunity to consult and copy-edit for French publications, especially those aimed at expats. Along the way, I've picked up a few tips to avoid any feature writing *faux pas*. Here are six secrets to writing your best piece ever.

1. Never submit anything without a cursory Google search.

Not long ago, I was giving an end-of-term presentation for one of my courses on the varieties of French spoken throughout Haiti. I was presenting an academic article, and I had spent weeks critiquing its strong and weak points, as well as adding my own observations. I felt really prepared, but as I launched into my presentation, my professor quickly stopped me—to my shock and horror, the "he" to whom I kept referring (the author of the paper) was in fact a "she," and a close colleague of my professor. A simple five-second investigation with the help of any search engine would have clarified this! The same principle goes for understanding all the terms you use in your writing, as well as any historical events you're referring to. A five-minute fact-checking session could just earn you a byline and avoid a massive gaffe.

If you have access to university databases, consider checking LexisNexis, Mass Media and Communication Complete, and Academic Search Premier for background.

2. Understand the difference between their, they're, and there.

Small grammatical errors such as this make your writing look careless and unprofessional, but luckily, the difference between them isn't hard to master, especially when the examples involve crêpes.

Their = possessive
Is that *their* stack of crêpes?
They're = contraction of "they are"
They're really enjoying those delicious crêpes.
There = demonstrates a location, not "here"
The crêpes *there* are the best I've ever tried!

3. The same thing goes for its and it's.
Its = shows possession
A crêpe is known for *its* thin texture.
It's = contraction of "it is"
I don't know what your secret ingredient is, but *it's* delicious!

4. Reading about something on Wikipedia does not count as formal research.

Don't get me wrong, Wikipedia is, at times, a great tool, and can be a good jumping-off point when researching a new topic, but it alone cannot replace scholarly articles and books. Use the footnotes and works cited on a Wikipedia page to guide you in the direction you need to be going. Remember, not everything you read on the Internet is true. (Didn't Abraham Lincoln say that?) If you're a student, I can't emphasize enough the importance of using the databases at your disposal. If you're lucky enough to have access to resources like JStor, use them. Subscribe to any publications that interest you and read everything you can. When you graduate, you'll realize how expensive a subscription to a scholarly publication is.

5. Try unconventional editing techniques.

When proofreading becomes cumbersome, try walking away from your work and doing an activity you enjoy. Put on some music and dance, run, make a collage, whatever works for you. Then when you come back, start reading your writing from the end, line by line, looking for mistakes and enhancing clarity. Reading in this way can shake up your brain and help you see things you might have missed before.

6. Invest in an Associated Press style guide (and then, read it).

When I started my internship at the French embassy, we were all motivated and experienced writers. The one key that helped me to become the publication's managing editor during my time there was that I was familiar with AP style. It's a great idea to have a guide with the most useful things tabbed for reference (state abbreviations, punctuation); it will save you time and help your writing appear extra polished.

Taylor RaeAnne Smith is studying linguistics at the Sorbonne in Paris. You can read her work at Baguettes and Bad French, http://www. http://taylorinfrance2.blogspot.com.

These are my thoughts: Here's why you shouldn't steal them

By Amanda Sturgill

Sometimes in student writing, you can find words and ideas that aren't the students' own. This isn't really a surprise. You can find plenty of examples of plagiarism in the professional world, and even some of those students' teachers have been accused of misappropriating the words of others.

I think there are two kinds of mistakes that lead to plagiarism—omission and commission (ideas I am borrowing from both legal argument and religious studies). In this case, **omission is when you just aren't careful** to keep records of where your ideas come from. When you put the ideas together in a piece, you don't remember where you got that idea so you never give the credit. **Commission is when you deliberately don't provide credit**, often to make it seem like you have done more work than you have. Many times, search result listings will show these acts of commission. Just search for "How do I (insert task here)" and often the results will show exactly the same text appearing on multiple pages. Here's the thing.

Copying the ideas of others is bad for three reasons. It can often be illegal. Even if you don't get caught right away, it remains illegal into the future, so it is always a threat to your credibility.

It makes you look stupid and unethical. When someone is looking to hire you in the future, you can be sure they will do a thorough examination of your work that is available to the public. If you are creating things to prove expertise in a field so you can work in it, your future coworkers are already experts and know where ideas come from. If you copy, that's an easy reason to reject you.

It misses an opportunity to win support. As Dale Carnegie points out, people like others who find them interesting. Flatter people with good ideas by citing them, and they will like you more, which can be a real asset in life.

Amanda Sturgill, Ph.D., is associate professor of communications at Elon University, Elon, NC Her blog is https://drsturgill.wordpress.com or catch her on Twitter: @drsturg

ABOUT THE AUTHOR

A professor of journalism at Palm
Beach Atlantic University, West Palm
Beach, FL, Michael Ray Smith teaches online ideas and communication to
university audiences and professional writers. In 2013, he was elected
to lead an interest group known for
teaching and issues of interest to small
programs for the Association in Education in Journalism and Mass Communication, an international group of
educators.

In an independent search, journalismdegrees.org recognized Smith as one of the "Top 50 journalism professors for
2012." The list was created using independent research with
the sole purpose of being a resource.

Also in 2012, Campbell University in North Carolina selected him from 216 professors for its first university-wide
teaching excellence award. In 2001–2002, he was recognized
as professor of the year.

In 2011, World Journalism Institute, Manhattan, named him
the John McCandlish Phillips Scholar. Philips was the internationally known reporter for the *New York Times* in the 1960s,
known for his reporting acumen and his rich faith.

Smith earned a Ph.D. from Regent University and taught at state and private universities, at graduate and undergraduate schools.

An award-winning journalist and photographer, he has been quoted in the *New York Times*, the *Boston Globe*, the *Chicago Tribune*, the *Philadelphia Inquirer, USA Today*, the *Arizona Republic*, the *Christian Science Monitor*, the *Louisville Courier-Journal, Editor & Publisher, Christianity Today, Writer's Digest* and other periodicals. He has been a guest on radio and TV, including French *TV 24*, a Paris-based television broadcast, and online sites such as Ourblook.com.

He speaks at writers' conferences and draws on his 10 years of experience working in the newsroom and more than two decades working in the classroom. He worked with the Association for Education in Journalism and Mass Communication on issues of equity and disability along with media and religion.

In 2008 Shippensburg University in Pennsylvania, his master's graduate school, honored him as a Distinguished Alumnus of the Year, the highest award presented by the university. That same year, Prince George's Community College in suburban Washington, D.C., recognized him as one of its top 50 graduates. He and his wife, Barbara, live and work in West Palm Beach, FL. They have two daughters who work in mass media here and abroad.

ACKNOWLEDGMENTS

Thank you to all my writer friends, ones who have poured out their prose for years and those who are just beginning the editorial journey. I'm grateful to webmaster and brother Stanley Smith and cheerleaders such as Ronald W. Smith, Ceedie Rae Smith, William O. Smith and Barbara Jean Smith, along with Taylor RaeAnne Smith, Shannon and Michael Ryals, and muses Madison Ryals, Abigail Ryals, Hannah Deadman, David Williams, James Hall, Dana Stancavage, Katie Forsythe, Peter Amirata, Taylor Branham, Jasmine McCranely, Ryan Teason, Amanda Higgins, Celeste Brown, Jackie Streng, Greg Halmos, Ryan Arnst, Ashley Suter, Lee Pitts, Donald Antlsperger, John Vernon Lawing, Les Sillars, Marvin Olasky, Lamar Keener, Dennis Bounds, William Brown, Benson Fraser, Jack Keeler, Michael Graves, Dennis Fulk, Edward A. Johnson, Pete Kenny, Adam English, Charlotte Paolini, Tim Metz, Wally Metts, Edward Fubara, Ran Whitley, Sam Engel, James Watkins, Stanley McQuade, Dennis Hensley, Cecil Murphey, Michael Longinow, Bob Cisneros, Brian Cannon, Bruce Eversen, Eddie Jones, Hannah Deadman, Lisa Herndon, Katie Forsythe, Robert Fortner, Brad Nason, the late Arne H. Fjeldstad, Tim Morgan, Manny Garcia, Bill Newcott, Russ Pulliam, Tony Carnes, Melissa Lilley, Sara Acosta, Michelle Medlock Adams, Andy Specht, Lisa Farmer, Tyler Douglas, Trevor Normile, Kim Collins, Paul Glater, George Archibald, J. Douglas Tarpley, Bob Case, Melinda Jackson, Ann Kuy, Paul "Alf" Pratte, Stephen Shulman, Tiffany Hudson, Wee Wan, Meredith Brunson,

Nathan Brunson, Jamie Chong, Astrid Rivera, Gretchen Ross, Kelly McGovern, Atsuko Tateishi, Sharon Mumper, Beth Glover, Jullian Martin, Holly Brown, Tanaka Taro, Shelley Faircloth Hobbs, Tamara Welter, John Clark, Michael Chute, Stephanie Bennett, Don Piper, Antonio Zarro, Gene Fant, William Fleming, J. Duane Meeks, Terry White, Norm Mintle, Quentin Schultze, Roy Atwood, Polly Arnold Thatch, Ciara Wade, Jenelle Krnc Wermer, Stan Guthrie, Rich Olsen, Marlene Legaspi-Munar, John Sizemore, Steve DeVane, James Martin, Baxter Ennis, Todd Starnes, Will Hall, Vie Stallings Herlocker, Debra Stamp, Bennett Scarborough, Jim Walz, Keith Cannon, David Whiteman, Dave Keener, Amanda Sturgill, Kay Colley, Tim Clark, Andy Freeman, Jim Dahlman, Mark Merry, Mark Steckbeck, Haven Hottel, Billy Liggett, Cherry Crayton, Jonathan Bronsink, Deborah Jo Blue, Matthew Melton, Barry Jones, Paul Glader, Stephen Perry, Kimberly Snider, Terry Lindvall, Faithe Beam, Marc Newman, Frank Keegan, Paula Sassi, Terry Mattingly, Andrew Quicke, Deborah Strong, Mitch Land, Randall Johnson, Borree Kwok, Dan Maynard, Eva Marie Everson, Louis Park, Michael Simmons, Art Toalston, Keith Faulkner, Dwight Stephens, Dianna Shpritz, Natalee Ezell, Amanda Johnson, Melinda Jackson, Evelyn Cruz, Lorna O'Connell, Jack Ryfiak, Susan Lunetta, Israel Balderas, Astrid D. Rivera, Lisa Phillips, Robert H. Woods Jr., Mike Soderling, Shonda Savage, Brian Cross, Robert Fortner, Rebekah Lewis, David Knight, Wes Jamison, Alex M. Wainer Jr., and James Wendell Curtis, to name a few.

INDEX